W9-DDQ-169

FIGHTING FOX COMPANY

FIGHTING FOX
COMPANY

The Battling Flank
of the Band of Brothers

BILL BROWN & TERRY POYSER

CASEMATE

Philadelphia & Oxford

Published in the United States of America and Great Britain in 2013 by
CASEMATE PUBLISHERS
908 Darby Road, Havertown, PA 19083
and
10 Hythe Bridge Street, Oxford, OX1 2EW

ISBN 978-1-61200-212-5
Digital Edition: ISBN 978-1-61200-213-2

Cataloging-in-publication data is available from the Library of Congress and
the British Library.

10 9 8 7 6 5 4 3 2 1

Printed and bound in the United States of America.

For a complete list of Casemate titles please contact:

CASEMATE PUBLISHERS (US)
Telephone (610) 853-9131, Fax (610) 853-9146
E-mail: casemate@casematepublishing.com

CASEMATE PUBLISHERS (UK)
Telephone (01865) 241249, Fax (01865) 794449
E-mail: casemate-uk@casematepublishing.co.uk

All maps courtesy Steve Bacon, Reno Nevada.

*All photos are either property of the author, Terry Poyser, or contributed by the following indi-
viduals: Tom Mulvey/Bill Brown, Mario Patruno, Tom Alley, Art Peterson, Ramona Bettelyoun,
Bob Noody, David 'Bud' Edwards, Jack Emelander, Helen Buchter, Don Replogle, Marion
Grodowski, Brenda Thornburg, Nita Hicks, Flora Hogenmiller, Ken Hull Jr., Scott Hegland,
Merlin Shennum, Marian Provenzano, Raul Ochoa, Robert Bossey, Sue Hisamoto, Juliann
Thompson, Anthony Supco, Homer Smith Jr., Lorna Tuck-Colbert, Bob Janes, John Taylor, Bill
True, John Himelrick, Roy Zerbe, Cees Jansen, Nancy Shrout-Kaiser. Stick photos are courtesy
of the AAF.*

CONTENTS

PREFACE & ACKNOWLEDGMENTS

In 1979, Bill Brown began a search for the facts and circumstances of the life and death of family friend Pfc. Orel Lev, a member of the 506th Parachute Infantry Regiment of the 101st Airborne Division in World War II. Bill had visited with Ronald Lev, a high school friend, and the topic of Ron's younger brother, Orel, was discussed. Not much was known about Orel's death, and Bill felt there was more information that could be discovered if he could contact the right people.

What followed next was over twenty years of research, correspondence, and interviews with the members of Orel's Fox Company of the Second Battalion of the 506th—abbreviated as Fox 506th and F/506—as well as the Army Air Corps. Bill spent years detailing the jump manifests for the company in the Normandy drop and exhausted every avenue of research at his disposal, with the intention of publishing a book for members of the unit and their families.

In 2000, I contacted Bill for any information he may have on Kenneth Hull, a member of Fox Company who was killed in action alongside Orel Lev back in October of 1944. Hull was from my hometown of Napa, California, and I was curious about who he was and what his life had been like before his unfortunate death. Bill asked for my help in researching his book and to assist in tracking down Hull's family.

What followed next was an amazing tale in itself. I located Ken Hull's son in Napa, who knew little of his father or his death. Being a parachutist, I had joined the WWII Airborne Demonstration Team and capped my time in that organization with parachute jumps in Normandy and Holland on the sixtieth anniversaries of D-Day and Operation Market Garden. Hull's son was in attendance for my jump on his father's drop zone in Holland, sixty years to the day and hour when his father parachuted onto the battlefield.

I flew around the United States and interviewed every member of Fox 506th that I could locate, as well as the family members of those killed in action. I obtained the company's morning reports, after-action reports, individual deceased personnel files of those killed in action, map overlays, original maps, personal memoirs, historical questionnaires, plus over one thousand letters home and over five hundred photographs of members of the company from 1942 to 1946.

Bill and I have combined our efforts into this new book on Fox Company. Yet without the following people none of this would have been possible:

George Koskimaki of the 101st Airborne Division, George Goodridge (F/506), and the USAF Still Photos Lab. From the 439th Troop Carrier Group: Col. Charles Young, Lt. Adam Parsons, Lt. Wayne King, Lt. Martin Neill, and Lt. Ernest Turner. From the 440th Troop Carrier Group: Lt Russell Hennicke and Lt. Wilbur Leonard.

George Rosie (3/506), Charles Randall (B/506), Knut Ruadstein (C/506), Joe McMillian (D/506), Burton Christenson (E/506), Bill Guarnere (E/506), Carwood Lipton (E/506), Bob Rader (E/506), Harry Welsh (E/506), Richard Winters (E/506), Ed Pepping (E/506), and Lou Vecchi (H/506).

From Fox Company: Gaston Adams, Ray Aebischer, Tom Alley, Henry Beck, Eugene Brierre, Linus Brown, Matt Carlino, David Edwards, Herbert Eggie, Don Emelander, George Goodridge, Frank Griffin, Marion Grodowski, Leonard Hicks, John Himelrick, Joe Hogenmiller, Les Hegland, Kenith Hovorka, Charles Jacobs, Johnny Jackson, Robert Janes, Dick Knudsen, George Martin, Bill McNeese, James Mackey, Otto May, Tom Mulvey, Robert Noody, Vince Occipinti, Harry Ostrander, Mario "Gus" Patruno, Robert Perdue, Arthur Peterson, Paul Peterson, Huber Porter, Raul Ochoa, Walter Pusker, Loy Rasmussen, Herbert Rockwell, Don Replogle, Thomas Rhodes, Ralph Robbins, Russ Schwenk, Merlin Shennum, Ben Stapelfeld, Bob Stone, Alan Summers, Victor Tamkun, John

Taylor, Bill True, Bob Vogel, Harry Warnock, E. B. Wallace, George Yochum, and Roy Zerbe.

101st historian Mark Bando, Paul Adamic, Richard Wolf and the members of the WWII Airborne Demonstration Team. Jason Wolcott, Jerry Gomes, Dave Berry at Pathfinder Historical Consultants, Tom Potter, Dan Limb, Lori Berdak at Redbird Research, Paul Clifford, Brian Siddall, Rich Riley. Todd Schalberg, Mike Duggan, Bret Clark, Jim O'Connell, Jeff Bassett, Eric Jensen, Josh Caitham, Kevin Kelley, Mike Ferguson, Dave Santi, Nick Provenzano, Rick Wanzie, Jack Allen, and Gordon Moore.

Ginny Novak (Supco), Anthony Supco, Charles McDaniel (Green), Scott Hegland, Jack Emelander, Sarah Robertson, Michael Taylor, John Himelrick, Lane and Martha Johnson (Ochoa), Julie Thompson (MacDowell), Robert Bossey (Rhodes), Andrea Tamboer (Occhipinti), Brenda Thornburg (Morehead), Blaise and Patricia Colt, Bill Mulvey, Scott Knudsen, Debbie Schunk (Mackey), Marian Provenzano, Helen Buchter, Sue Hisamoto, Barbara Webster Embree, Ramona Bettelyoun, Dolores Hovorka, and Nita Hicks. U.S. Congressman Mike Thompson (representing California's Fifth District and a veteran of the 173rd Airborne Brigade) was also helpful.

"Team Holland": Cees Jansen, Peter Hendrikx, Tom Timmermans, Frank Van Lunteren, and Ben Overhand. "Team France" J.B.Valognes, Roger Delarocque, Alain Hasley, Denny Dennebouy, Jil and Dom Launay and Paul Woodadge at DDayhistorian.com. "Team Belgium" Joel Robert. "Team UK" Tony Fletcher and Jon Fletcher.

Fox Company 506th was a very unique and special group. Bill and I found its surviving members to be very open and candid about the events of 1942–1946. Without everyone's help and contribution, and without the support and understanding of our wives, Lynn Brown and Josefina Poyser, none of this would have been possible.

This is the story of Fighting Fox Company.

—TERRY POYSER

CHAPTER 1

TOCCOA

D rab Army trucks sat silent near the railroad tracks as a train
pulled into the station in the small town of Toccoa, Georgia, in
the summer of 1942. Volunteers for the newly formed 101st Airborne Division, dirty and tired from their travel, exited their train cars. As the trucks
coughed to life, they loaded up for the short ride to their new home, Camp
Toombs. Leonard Hicks, seeing a sign for the Toccoa Coffin Factory at the
train station, and the name Camp Toombs on arrival to his new home,
could not help but be more alert, and concerned. Fortunately for Hicks and
the other worried men, the name of the camp was changed to Toccoa a short
time later.

The men were taken to an area on the post with approximately a hundred tents, with eight assigned to each tent. This group was referred to as W
Company. Each tent had cots for the men and a single lightbulb suspended
from its canvas ceiling. The ground was muddy from a recent rain. As Roy
Zerbe recalled, "It was the muddiest, dirtiest place I ever saw. We had
wooden planks to walk on to try to stay out of the mud."

Wooden blocks had to be put under the cots as well, to keep them from
sinking into the red mud. The camp was bustling with activity, and building
was taking place almost every day for both new housing and training facil-
ities. Eventually the men moved from their muddy tents to hastily built barracks, and sixteen to twenty men were assigned from the tent city to one of
the new buildings. A mess hall situated at the end of the street could house
an entire company of 130-plus men, with benches aligned to feed ten men
at each table.

A group of men were soon assigned to F, or Fox, Company of the Second Battalion of the 506th Parachute Infantry Regiment. Once they were assembled, they were welcomed by their regimental commander, Col. Robert Sink. Sink told them that they would be the first parachute troops to be trained outside of Fort Benning, Georgia. They were told the training would not be easy, would be the toughest in the US Army, and would occur day and night. Sink told them they would be second to none, and the men soon learned to believe him.

Haircuts were soon given to the men of Fox. Men from all over the country, from all walks of life, soon looked the same, with shaved heads and uniforms without ranks or unit insignia. Physical examinations soon followed. Many were frightened they would not meet Colonel Sink's tough standards. One man from Fox was forced to pack his bags when he was found to be color-blind, but another snuck through with the same problem. Bill Tucker remembered their exam was not over until they had gone unclothed in front of Colonel Sink, who looked them over like a horse merchant.

The men ranged drastically in height and weight, with the average trooper being five feet, seven inches tall and weighing 155 pounds. Although the regulation cutoff was six feet, one Fox lieutenant was over that. Some men were as short as five feet, four inches.

Physical training (PT) began immediately on the men's arrival to the camp, and they never walked anywhere. "Double time," Army jargon for jogging, was soon their only method of movement, and they quickly became accustomed to briskly moving to every assignment. With the crack of dawn and the bugling of "Reveille" each morning came formation, "police" (cleanup) call, and then calisthenics. Clad in blue swim trunks, GI shoes, and sometimes without t-shirts, the men were run through their exercises by the well-conditioned Lt. Andrew Tuck. Bill True remembered the morning PT as vigorous to the point of exhaustion.

David "Bud" Edwards wrote home on September 8 about his initial experience at Toccoa:

We started our thirteen weeks of training yesterday and we really started out with a bang. We drilled all afternoon in the rain, and it really rained. We were soaked to the bone when we came in. This morning we had about a half hour of exercise and we had close order drill. After all this we are given lectures and other demonstrations. In the afternoon they taught us how to pitch tents.

After morning PT would be breakfast, and the company barracks would be readied for inspection. Then the company would fall in for either a run or the obstacle course. The most notable feature of Camp Toccoa's landscape was nearby Currahee Mountain. Currahee was an Indian word for "Stands Alone" and became the motto of the 506th.

According to Vince Occhipinti, each Monday, Wednesday, and Friday the men of Fox Company ran up and down Currahee Mountain, initially taking just over an hour to complete the course. Eventually the run was made in fifty minutes. Mario "Gus" Patruno remembered that after he got into peak physical condition, the mountain run "was a breeze for me. We would run three abreast up, and some guys could even run it backwards." Tom Alley recalled, "We would run the mountain after dinner as not only a challenge to ourselves, but to assure our place in the unit."

The company commander, Lt. Thomas Mulvey, warned his men that the run up the mountain would "separate the men from the boys," and he would wait at the top of the mountain to encourage his men on. "Boys" who fell out during the run or any other physical training were sent packing, while the "men" continued with their grueling schedule.

On each Tuesday, Thursday, and Saturday, the Fox Company physical training consisted of an obstacle course. It was run in groups of four or five that started at the top of a small hill. After a steep seventy-five-yard run down the hill, the participants would cross a fifty-foot ditch of water by swinging hand over hand on monkey bars. Rope-swinging over ditches and crawling through wooden tunnels followed over the next fifty yards. An eight-foot sloped log ladder was climbed up over a creek and then participants jumped from the ladder over the creek bed into a pit of shredded bark. There was an inclined pipe ladder to cross and wooden logs spanned a creek, with three or four logs for men to cross at a time. Finally, there was a sloped fifteen-foot log wall to clamber over. Some remember using ropes to assist in pulling themselves up and over, others only brute force.

After completing the course the men would run back to the top of the hill to where they'd started and wait, exhausted, for their next turn. "I liked running the obstacle course and was rather good at it," said Roy Zerbe. "I was one of the fastest in the company. Merlin Shennum was really good at it as well—seemed to always be having a good time while running it."

The PT staff at Toccoa was very creative, and other physical fitness tests awaited the troops beyond their mountain run and obstacle course. Fifty-yard duckwalks, hundred-yard sprints, standing broad jumps, pull-ups, and a knotted rope climb of twenty-five feet without the use of one's legs were practiced as well. Men were constantly made to do twenty-five to fifty push-ups for the slightest mistakes, infractions, and sometimes for no reason at all.

Log training was added to the physical curriculum as well. Men in groups of six or eight would pair off. They would pick up ten- to twelve-foot-long logs, similar to a telephone pole, then together would toss it in the air, catch it, lower it to the ground, and then start over. Vince Occhipinti remembered an added strain to the log exercises. Six men would get on the ground, and six others would lay a log across their chests. Then the six men on the ground would, in unison, lift the log straight up in the air above them with their arms extended. It took complete teamwork to accomplish without injury.

Outside of PT was the basic Army training, which usually happened before their ninety-minute lunch and later in the afternoons, right after mail call. Close order drill, such as being taught to stand at attention, at ease, and at parade rest, and marching with and without rifles were taught. No actual rifles were yet available, so the men trained with broom handles.

Barracks were regularly inspected, with the men tightening their bunk blankets so tight that quarters could be bounced off of them during the inspections. If one man in a barrack made a mistake during the inspection, the entire barrack's occupants were punished. The men quickly learned to help each other out to assure they all passed with perfection.

Lt. Carl MacDowell, the company's executive officer (second in command) taught the men general orders for guard duty and the regulations of military courtesy. Lt. Freeling Colt taught infantry tactics, and Lieutenant Tuck taught map reading, compass use, orienteering, and land navigation. Other classes included articles of war, military sanitation, first aid, sex hygiene, protection of military information, and organization of the Army. The classes were given both indoors and outside the barracks in a newly built amphitheater, and were often a relief from the long hours of difficult physical training.

One thing that came with the intense training and conditioning was superior physical fitness, and with that came an intense camaraderie and confidence. Len Hicks described it as an attitude that "nothing can stop us, to never give up and that you can do better than anyone." It was an attitude and bond that made the 506th one of the finest fighting regiments in the

US Army in WWII. The bonds made and spirit gained lasted a lifetime.

In addition to the military instruction, inspection, drill, and physical training, was parachute training. A mock C-47 transport aircraft's fuselage was built, and the men formed into groups of sixteen—a full planeload, or "stick"—for practice exiting the aircraft. Sitting on buckets inside the pseudo plane, the men were given their jump instructions while wearing their parachute harness equipment. The first orders were "Stand up!" and "Hook up!" The static line attached to their parachutes was hooked to an overhead cable that ran the length of the plane.

Next came equipment check. The jumpers looked over their gear to make sure everything was fastened correctly and secure. They then looked over the men in front and back of them, thus ensuring a complete safety inspection. "Sound off for equipment check!" followed, and the troopers counted off down from sixteen. "Sixteen OK!," "Fifteen OK!," and so on was shouted down the line. "Stand in the door!" came next, with the lead jumper placing his left foot in the lone door of the mock aircraft. "Go!" followed, and the men exited quickly by swinging their right legs out the door and turning left, with their backs to the left wing and to the nonexistent prop blast coming from it.

A stick could exit a plane in practice, and later during actual jumps, in seconds. As each man exited the mock plane, he shouted, "One one thousand! Two one thousand! Three one thousand!" to mark the time it took for him to fall away from the plane and have his parachute deploy.

After the mock plane exits, the men would move to nearby platforms, where they practiced jumping to the ground and tumbling forward or backward, to simulate their rough parachute landings. Also included in the training was a platform that had parachute harnesses hanging from overhead supports. The men buckled themselves into the harnesses and suspended themselves off the platform. This was also known as suspended agony due to the pain that was caused by their dead weight on their lower extremities while in the harness.

During this training the men were taught how to steer their parachutes by pulling on one or more of the four riser straps that went from the parachute harness to the suspension lines above. The steering allowed the men to turn their parachutes into the wind, stop oscillations, and assist in their landings. It seemed to be a simple exercise but later saved several of the men's lives during their first combat jump.

The next lesson in parachuting was jumping from thirty-five foot towers. This proved to be both a physical and mental challenge—at thirty-five feet their depth perception was severely impaired, and the height seemed greater than it actually was. The trainees would put on a parachute harness that had its overhead risers attached to a pulley on a cable that ran outside the tower and gradually ran down to the ground below. The jumper would stand in the tower, also made up like a mock aircraft, and jump out as was done from the previous grounded mock plane. He would then count to "three one thousand," be jolted in his harness as the risers became taut with the pulley and cable, and then ride the pulley down the cable to the ground and practice a parachute landing.

The parachute training was practiced daily in Toccoa. When the men eventually arrived at jump school at Fort Benning, the process of exiting, steering, and landing was second nature to them.

As explained by Bud Edwards in a letter home on September 21, the men were motivated by an exhibition put on by the camp staff:

> After lunch we fell out in coveralls and went up the mountain to a different spot than we usually go and were given a demonstration on how to jump out of an airplane. A plane came over about four times and each time they dropped out a colored chute with some kind of equipment. The plane then came over twice and dropped out seven men each time it came over. They dropped from about a thousand feet. It looked fun!

Each Friday night the men went on night maneuvers or on marches, and either could last four to seven hours. The marches would cover from ten to twenty miles along all the dirt trails and back roads that twisted through the mountains. The maneuvers would test their compass skills.

VINCE OCCHIPINTI • *They took us in trucks in units of about squad size about ten miles from camp. This was all mountainous country, and pretty soon you weren't sure where camp was. Now, you could walk back on the road you came in on. But this was a winding, mountainous road, and the distance was more like twenty miles back to camp along that route. Or you could cut cross-country by the compass route, which would be a lot quicker if you managed an accurate compass reading.*

The best thing about the Friday night activity was the return to camp, because the kitchen would be open. Fresh, warm sugar doughnuts and hot coffee awaited the troops as they filtered in from the maneuvers or marches. Those who got lost often did not return until daylight, and some would even have to be later located by searchers sent out in the morning to track the disoriented men down.

Bud Edwards explained a night march in a letter home:

Last Friday night we went on a hike with field equipment. The equipment consisted of a pup tent, blanket, towel, toilet articles, rifle belt, rifle, and canteen. This hike was supposed to be only fifteen miles long, but as it turned out we got lost a couple of times, and we marched twenty-six and a half miles. We left camp at 7:00 p.m. and got back to camp at about 2:00 a.m.

M1 rifles, still coated in Cosmoline (a heavy, dark protective grease), soon arrived to the excitement of the men. After assisting the troopers in cleaning up the .30-caliber rifles, Fox Company's first sergeant, Willie Morris, showed them how to break down the weapon, explaining what parts went where and what their function was.

Serial numbers of issued rifles had to be memorized, and drill now included the new rifles instead of broom handles. Bill True remembered Morris, a career soldier, explaining the proper terminology for their newly obtained rifles: "His first admonition was that the military correct term for the weapon was not a 'rifle' but a 'piece,' and you must never ever refer to it as a 'gun.' Your piece will be your best friend in the combat to come. Take care of it accordingly, and treat it like your first love."

Lieutenant Colt provided instruction on how to fire the shiny new rifles. With no ammunition, the men practiced "dry firing" their "piece" while Lieutenant Colt emphasized that they squeeze the trigger slowly and not jerk or quickly pull it back. This along with briefly holding one's breath just prior to firing off the rifle would ensure a steady aim on target.

Additional dry-fire training was given with other platoon weapons: the .30-caliber machine gun, the M2 60mm mortar, and the .45-caliber Thompson submachine gun, also known as the "tommy gun"—the weapon of 1930s Chicago gangster fame. Instruction was also given on the M1 carbine.

Saturdays had full barracks inspection, and with the new rifles the entire regiment would march on the athletic field for Colonel Sink's review, while recorded marching music played over loudspeakers. When the inspection and parade were over, the remainder of the weekend was usually free for the men of Fox Company to do as they pleased until Monday morning. Some went into town for meals or to look for girls, some took off to Atlanta, and others remained around camp writing letters home, running the mountain or obstacle courses, making purchases at the post exchange, or trying to catch up on some much deserved sleep.

Trucks took the coverall-clad men of Fox Company to Clemson College for five days at the rifle range there. A pup tent city was established for housing, and a field mess was set up for chow.

Len Hicks located a vine-choked sycamore tree next to a creek behind the tent city. The vines were covered in a grapelike fruit called muscadine, of which Hicks picked a helmet's worth to supplement their Army chow. The fruit's smell and taste became very popular with the men of Fox Company, and soon trips to the sycamore tree for more of it became commonplace. The creek became a watering hole for the men of the company as well.

Lieutenant Tuck personally promised three cartons of cigarettes to any man in the company who qualified as an expert on the rifle range, in addition to the three-day passes offered by the company. Every man was expected to qualify at least as a marksman. To qualify as a sharpshooter was even better, but an expert was the most desired, not only for the rewards but also for bragging rights. There was a stiff sense of competition, as the men shot against each other on the range and also against the other companies that were shooting.

Scoring for the qualification was done in three shooting stances: standing, kneeling, and prone. A three-foot-round bull's-eye was shot "slow fire" at 200 and 300 yards, and "rapid fire" at 200 and 300 yards, and each firing stance was worth 100 points. Expert was a score of 250 or above, sharpshooter was a score of 200 or above, and marksman was 150 or above.

The rifle range shooting for Company F began on September 28 at 0900 with the men shooting slow fire at 200 yards prone, then 300 yards both sitting and kneeling. Rifles began to get sighted in, and the afternoon was spent practicing shooting rapid fire while kneeling at 200 yards. The following day was spent shooting rapid fire while prone at 300 yards.

The morning of September 30 was spent shooting slow fire at 200 yards prone and standing, then slow fire at 300 yards both prone and kneeling. A humid and warm afternoon led to sweaty riflemen shooting rapid fire while sitting at 200 yards, and prone at 300 yards. The final day of shooting, October 1, was spent shooting rapid fire at 300 yards while kneeling and prone. Confident in their rifles and shooting ability, the company finished on the range just before dark. No member failed to qualify.

The return to Toccoa and barracks life was a welcome change for the former pup tent riflemen. Bud Edwards wrote about it in October:

> We had a good time on the range but camp looked like paradise when we reached here. We have started wearing our O.D.'s (two piece fatigues) today. We also had an inspection today by the Battalion Commander. He didn't seem to like the condition that our rifles were in and a lot of the fellows are staying in camp on account of it. After lunch we put on our shorts and jump boots and went up the mountain. After not having any hard training for a week, that hike was sort of tough.

The weather became colder in the fall at Toccoa, often freezing at night. Men began to wear sweaters under their fatigues to battle the chill, and the two blankets and sheet set on their bunks barely kept them barely comfortable. The bunks in the barracks were made into double bunks to make room for a much-needed stove and for a rifle rack.

LEN HICKS • *One morning F Company was out for a speed march. A day or so previous it had rained, then turned cold. We made our first rest stop near some scrub oak, the frost so heavy it looked like snow. In this scrub oak thicket were two large hornet nests. Some of the young city boys hopped over the fence and cut the nests down and carried them on to the camp, still cold. This was not in my barracks, thank God. When things warmed up that evening with the stove going good, so did the hornets. It's doubtful if a couple of grenades could have emptied the barracks any quicker. It was a day or two before all of the hornets were disposed of and a few days for all the lumps to go down.*

The officers were able to complete their parachute training while still at Camp Toccoa, but the enlisted men had to wait until arriving at Fort Benning.

VINCE OCCHIPINTI • *The officers had to be parachutists before we ever got to Fort Benning and that was weeks in the future. But we managed to see these jumps from a distance, and the next day we'd hear from an officer that yesterday he'd made five parachute jumps to qualify as a parachutist and now he was sporting a pair of parachute wings. Big deal!*

The men resented the fact that the officer had won the coveted wings without having to endure all the training that they did.

On Armistice (now Veterans) Day, November 11, the men of Fox Company traveled to nearby Seneca, South Carolina, for a parade. According to Vince Occhipinti, "We were the parade. This was mostly to give these small-town residents a thrill to see what these guys who were running around mucking up all their beautiful fields could do, a chance to see how they look when they're dressed up first class." Bud Edwards added while writing home: "The Company Commander told us that our company was picked to represent the camp in a parade on Armistice Day at some small town in South Carolina. The Commander said we were picked because we had taken all the honors in the parades here at camp. Our Officers are really a swell bunch of men."

Tom Alley's mother and his girlfriend, Louise Morrison, had taken a train from Charlotte, North Carolina, to meet up with Tom in Seneca after the parade. "We were having lunch at a local soda shop when another member of the company walked in. Unaware who the women were, he asked me how I had managed to find two gals for myself in town so quickly. I explained they were my mother and girlfriend, and the poor guy quickly walked from the shop red faced and embarrassed."

The pace of the physical training, jump training, drill, and speed marches continued. More emphasis was added in the maneuvers, also known as field problems. Even with wool gloves, long johns, and wool sweaters under their coveralls, the night chill froze the men. Many field problems lasted all night, with Fox Company not returning to camp until late morning. Night compass courses continued as well, testing the squads with orienteering from six different compass bearings to six posts hidden in the woods.

A Friday night road march on November 13 was planned for twenty-five miles. Of all the men in the company, Tom Alley was especially excited to get to the finish, as he had a two-day weekend pass waiting for him: "My girlfriend Louise had stayed in Georgia after the Armistice Day parade, and we planned to get married. First Sergeant Willie Morris had obtained permission for me to get married over the weekend, and obtain the pass. The march ended up as a disaster, with some wrong turns being made. We marched thirty-five miles and arrived in camp just before daylight, instead of the middle of the night."

Exhausted but determined, Alley went into the showers and sat on the floor with all six shower heads blasting him with water. After an hour he felt revived, and went to the barracks, dressed, and headed off to meet his bride-to-be. After an all-day bus ride at 35 mph to York, South Carolina, to the only local justice of the peace in the area, they were married. On Monday morning the newlywed was back training with the outfit.

A three-day field problem started on Thursday, November 26—Thanksgiving Day. For their holiday dinner, the men of Fox Company and the rest of the Second Battalion ate cold K-rations, which came in small cardboard boxes not much larger than a box of Cracker Jacks. One canteen of water was allowed for each man for the entire weekend. On Friday night the company camp, or "bivouac," was set up near a small lake when orders came to strip to coveralls only. A dirt dam was at one end of the lake, and strung across it was barbed wire about thirteen inches above the ground. Covering the ground was a truck load of pig entrails and their contents. Len Hicks crawled first through the smelly course, soon followed by Bill True, who described it as "a slimy, bloody goo." It was never forgotten by the troops and always remembered as the "Hog Innards Problem." The training did not end, as on return to camp a midnight mock gas attack exercise occurred.

MARION GRODOWSKI ● *I think the Hogs Innards Problem was Colonel [Robert] Strayer's idea. He was battalion commander. Crawling through all that I felt like I was going to puke, and realistically I could see no rational reason for that training.*

Finally the men hunkered down for a cold night in the field. The following day they returned to camp and arrived in late morning. After a shower and a change of clothes, Fox Company finally settled down to a real Thanksgiving dinner. The meal was outstanding: roast turkey, dressing and giblets gravy, cranberry sauce, snowflake potatoes, buttered peas, baked squash, stuffed celery, tomato salad, hot rolls and butter, pumpkin pie, apple pie, chocolate marshmallow sundae, apples, oranges, and grapes. Coffee, ice cream, and cocoa were available, as well as candies, cigarettes, and nuts.

A series of physical training tests were given to the men at Toccoa, with points awarded for each and an overall cutoff established for the minimum qualifications. Bud Edwards wrote of some of the standards in a letter home to his parents, in Madera, California:

Obstacle Course	run in 3 minutes, 45 seconds or less
Chin Ups	7 no time limit
Push Ups	30 no time limit
Duck Walk	50 yards in 30 seconds
100 Yard Dash	13 seconds or less
1 Mile Run	7 minutes 30 seconds

Lieutenant Tuck added a few as well in a letter he wrote home:

25' Rope Climb	10 seconds (no leg use)
6 mile run	Up and back down mountain in 70 minutes
	1st 1/2 mile 3.5 minutes, 1st mile 7.5 minutes

The First Battalion (A, B, and C Companies) of the 506th was set to head for jump school, and on their last night in camp some pranks turned downright ugly.

LEN HICKS • *Since First Battalion was a week ahead of us, it was time for them to leave Camp Toccoa and go to Fort Benning. The last night the First Battalion was in camp, they had some time on their hands, and some figured this might be a good time to even the score with F Company, for F Company had been the outstanding company throughout our twelve to thirteen weeks of training. I'll have to give them credit—they tried. Their first attack was to run through three or four F Company barracks trying to dump some of the double bunks. That did not work so good, but they did knock down some stove pipes, and then they exited the rear door, but not without a kick or two. We in F Company would have let it go, but they were not satisfied. So, when we heard some loud yelling in the street separating us from First Battalion, I grabbed my pick mattock handle and so did some others in my barracks. It got a little hairy, but they never crossed to our sidewalk.*

I do not know who, but probably our officer of the guard had machine guns and crews set up at the head of our street with orders to shoot anyone

attempting to cross. They did not have to fire a shot! The first trucks pulled
out early loaded with the First Battalion men heading for Fort Benning.

Colonel Sink assembled the men of the Second Battalion (D, E, and F Companies) and told them about a record time and distance set by Japanese troops during a forced march in Malaysia. He explained he was determined to prove his men were better soldiers. The plan was for the Second Battalion to march from Toccoa to Atlanta, a distance of approximately 120 miles, in three days. The troops would then take a train from Atlanta to Fort Benning for jump school. The Third Battalion (G, H, and I Companies) would take the train to Atlanta from Toccoa, then march a longer distance from Atlanta to Fort Benning.

The Second Battalion (about six hundred men) left Toccoa wearing full gear and carrying their rifles. About eight miles from Camp Toccoa, bad weather caught up with them. Cold winds blew, rain fell, then snow, and eventually icy rain. On the now muddy back roads, the first stop was in Cornelia for lunch, where a field mess had been set up to serve rain-soaked chow. With only ten-minute breaks each hour, the men continued on until they reached mile forty after dark, where they stopped for the night.

With no rain but with strong winds, the cooks tried to get warm chow for the men while they pitched pup tents for the night. After no success heating the chow, sandwiches were provided. Because of the elements, building small campfires next to the tents became futile, so the tired troopers crawled into their pup tents for a miserably cold and windy night of much-needed rest. The following morning was, according to Len Hicks, "colder than a witch's tit," though movement around the bivouac area was essential for circulation and to generate body heat. Some of the men's boots that had been removed during the night had frozen. Tom Alley had a painful walk for over an hour in his frozen boots before they thawed out enough to even be laced up. After forming up, Fox Company headed out along with its sister companies, and soon reached blacktop roadways, which lasted for the remainder of the march.

The Second Battalion moved through Gainesville, Georgia, marching with a sense of pride. Moving on to a total of thirty-eight miles that day, the dog-tired soldiers stopped to bivouac in a pine grove, complete with a thick pine-needle ground cover. Without much banter or activity, the troops slide into their pup tents.

Day three seemed to last forever, but after being on the move for thirty-seven miles, the Second Battalion marched onto the campus of Oglethorpe College, about nine miles outside of Atlanta. Third Platoon's Ferris Rice had won a bet with Lieutenant Tuck. Normally during the march, men took turns in each squad carrying the heavy crew-served weapons, such as the 60mm mortar and the .30-caliber machine gun, which weighed thirty-one pounds. Ferris Rice carried not only the machine gun the entire route, but its heavy tripod as well. This earned Rice a steak dinner and five bottles of scotch, which was the bet offered by Lieutenant Tuck prior to the march.

Len Hicks, who had been nursing a badly sprained ankle, was contacted by Lieutenant Colt. He had arranged for Hicks to be taken to a motel in Atlanta to soak his leg in a hot bath. Many of the others took cabs into town for a hot bath and much-deserved hearty meal.

LEN HICKS ● *It did not take me long to get into that tub of hot water. After a while I began to look like a boiled lobster. After an hour of soaking, my foot felt better, as well as my leg and groin muscles. When I shaved and put on some clean clothes, things began to look a little bit brighter.*

After a few big meals and a few too many drinks, the men of Fox Company began to slowly filter back to the college campus.

The following morning the men of the Second Battalion geared up for their final day of marching, nine miles to the Five Points district of downtown Atlanta. After a few hours the group was parading down Peachtree Street in formation. Local high school bands moved in with each company and struck up a tune for the weary troops to march to. Pride and sense of accomplishment overpowered the pain that every man felt wracking his body. Some wept. The large crowds cheering and applauding their arrival as they marched down the street left an overwhelming sense of joy, an indescribable feeling. The mayor of Atlanta presented the battalion with a key to the city.

As the men of Fox boarded the train in Atlanta, they bought copies of the *Atlanta Constitution*, which had not only put the story on its front page but six subsequent pages. Colonel Sink, speaking of the march, was quoted as saying "Not a man fell out [dropped out of the march], and when they fell, they fell face forward."

The fatigued and aching, but proud, men headed off for their next challenge, jump school.

CHAPTER 2

PARACHUTE SCHOOL

The men of Fox 506th arrived at Fort Benning the first weekend of December 1942. With metal training towers 250 feet high looming in the distance, they were trucked past manicured lawns, two swimming pools, brick buildings, and a chapel. The sore and weary men were finally dropped off in front of a row of wooden barracks. The living conditions were worse than those at Camp Toccoa, and it could not be determined if their new homes were old and on the verge of falling apart or just hastily built. They were in a dusty area referred to as the Frying Pan because of its heat. Bud Edwards wrote home to his parents about their arrival, December 6:

> Well I am at Benning finally and it is really awful. It is the worst
> yet. When we arrived here I had a sore knee, feet, and ankle. All of
> us were in about the same condition. Yesterday morning we went
> down to the main theater and a Colonel gave us a welcome speech.
> He told us that we would finish our training in three weeks and
> that we were the first outfit to ever go through in three weeks. After
> all of us get our wings we all hope to go home on furlough.

For the usual recruits at the Parachute School, training lasted four weeks, which were called "stages" and were designated by letters. "A" stage was physical conditioning and infantry training from 0400 until dark. Due to the excellent, albeit battered, physical condition of the men from Toccoa, that stage was waived, and they started their training with "B" stage.

However, a new bunch of men would soon be joining the ranks of

Company F. Volunteers from around the country had signed up for the paratroops while at their basic training centers. After completion of basic training, they were placed on trains and later bused or trucked to Fort Benning. They would be known to the core of the company as the Parachute Training Replacements, or PTRs, and to them the original members were simply the Toccoa boys. The replacements filtered into Company F after jump school.

PTR John Taylor remembered the A-stage physical training as strict and rigid, with all movement around post at double time and with push-ups being dealt out by instructors for the most minor infractions. "I think every part of my body was sore—every muscle, every bone, and every joint, from the top of my head to the bottom of my feet. As our 'reward' on Saturday of the first week in A stage, we had to make a five-mile run in formation. If we did not finish in forty minutes, we would get to repeat that whole first week over."

A determined PTR, Robert Janes, wrote home about his first week at the Parachute School:

> I am going to be here for four weeks if I can take it and I believe I can. The first week we have physical training and lots of it. 8 hours a day for six days. We have to run obstacle courses, tumbling, jujitsu, and the last day of the week we have to run 9 miles in 90 minutes. They say if you can make the first week it isn't so tough then. If I drop out it is going to be flat on my face. The second week we pack parachutes most of the time. The third week we jump from the towers. These towers are 250 feet high. That's what is going to test my guts. I think I have the required amount though. The 4th week we make five jumps from the airplane. After you make five jumps you get your wings. This is sure a snappy, rugged outfit and it is really considered an honor. I am going to give them everything I got.

The Toccoa boys were not immune to the wrath and abuse of the training staff at the Parachute School. On the contrary, though they arrived in peak physical condition, the selective enforcement of physical discipline may have been worse than that subjected to the PTRs.

LEN HICKS • *We skipped 'A' stage because they found out we were in better physical condition than they, the staff were. Anything they could do, we could do it better and in less time. One morning in 'B' stage, I became the target of our instructor for no reason. His command was to 'get down and give me 25.' We all knew that meant get down and give twenty-five push-ups. Like a little rubber ball, I did them and stood up. He said I did not count them, so I had to get down and do them again. I did. Again he disqualified them for some reason or another. This happened over and over again. Some F Company members had counted I had done over four hundred pushups; others said five hundred. I knew that I had done some pushups, but I was not going to quit for that bastard. The officer in charge of these jokers finally walked over and told him to knock it off.*

The food at the mess hall at the Parachute School was a drastic change from that at Camp Toccoa. Len Hicks recalled: "Every morning our company officers took us out before breakfast for a nine-mile run, quite often in the cold rain. We were in our blue trunks, cold, and came back in for breakfast. I cannot remember even one breakfast in the Frying Pan area that was fit to feed a pig. The same went for the other two meals a day."

"B" stage was the ground training for parachuting, which involved parachute packing, jump commands, parachute steering, tumbling and landing, and jumping from a forty-foot tower.

MARION GRODOWSKI • *I was very interested in the parachute packing. All the small details, like there were twenty-eight panels, and the length of the parachute with suspension lines was seventy-two feet—the whole packing process was fascinating. All in all though, you could really just ball the parachute up and pack it. It would still open.*

Merlin Shennum penciled detailed notes in his issued pocket-size "Blue Horse" notebook:

Fort Benning, GA / Monday Assignment NO's 1, 2, 6

T-5 Assembly includes the TM1 and the TR1 of the troop training type harness. There are three main parts to a parachute assembly.
1) The canopy assembly
   (a) Canopy
   (b) Suspension lines

(c) Connector links
2) Pack assembly
    (a) Pack tray assembly
    (b) Pack cover assembly
3) Troop training type harness
The top center panel is the panel between suspension 1 & 28. The bottom center panel is the panel between lines 14 & 15.

After the T-5 parachute assembly lecture, Shennum continued his notes with parachute malfunctions and packing. Reminders were scribbled concerning the parachute packing process:

A "twist" is the improper crossing of suspension lines within their own respective groups. To remove an inside-out twist tumble backwards. To remove an outside twist tumble forward. A tangle is the improper crossing of suspension lines outside of their own respective groups.

The purpose of inspection is to prolong life & maintain the reliability of the parachute assembly.

Lay out parachute properly
    a) Straighten lines at apex
Fold panel
Right group lines over left
Left hand positions right palm towards apex
Lay panels out on the table properly
Straighten lines at the apex again
Close channel
Sweep panels out
Remove silk from panel by pulling out bottom panel
Dress the skirt

The jump commands, steering, and tower was nothing new to the Toccoa men, as they had been drilled on each numerous times while at their previous camp. However, they still had to go through the training process at Fort Benning, as did the PTRs. The tower was a mock airplane fuselage elevated approximately forty feet above ground. A set of wooden steps led to a platform that served as the floor of the mock plane, where an instructor waited inside. The trainee was clad in a parachute harness with a dummy reserve parachute snapped on his chest but without suspension lines or a parachute in his backpack.

A pulley outside the tower was attached to a cable that sloped gradually from the tower to the ground. The instructor snapped the riser webbing from the pulley to D rings on the trainee's harness and had him stand in the door. After making sure his left foot was forward with its toes out the door, his knees were bent, his head was up, and his hands were outside on the door frame, the instructor had the trainee yell out his name to another instructor on the ground below. On the command of "Go!" the trainee stepped off the platform and yelled out, marking time. He would bounce several times as the riser webbing became taut with the pulley above, and would then roll down the cable toward the ground. Trainees were told to keep their legs together and hands on the sides of their reserve parachute as they dangled in their harness and slid toward a sawdust pit at the cables end. A parachute landing fall, or PLF, was attempted as they made contact with the sawdust pit, and instructors were on hand to disconnect the trainee and grade him on his overall performance. Then the trainee went back to the tower and waited in line for another chance to practice his door exit and landing.

"C" stage began the following week. On the first day the troopers learned how to collapse their parachutes once on the ground and in high wind. The training was established to keep troopers from being dragged to their deaths in high-wind landings. The process involved placing a trooper into a parachute harness with an open parachute attached. To simulate the wind, an airplane engine had been mounted inside a safety cage, and the open parachute was billowed into its propeller blast. The trooper was then dragged across the ground by his inflated parachute. Trainees were taught to pull their risers to partially collapse their parachute, thus allowing them to get to their feet and out of their harness. The longer it took to complete the process, the more battered and bruised the troopers became. Confident but sore, the men of Fox 506th moved on to their next challenge, the 250-foot towers.

"Control tower" training came first. A trooper was pulled up in his harness while lying horizontal and facing down. The tower staff would lift him on a cable between 50 and 200 feet off the ground. On command the trooper would pull a rip cord that released his body from the horizontal position and allowed him to fall until his riser lines became taut with the cable overhead. The exercise was supposed to help with the fear of heights and the sensation of falling before the parachute opens.

Bob Janes described the control tower training in a letter to his parents:

On the control towers they have a rig that they strap you in to in a horizontal position and then pull you up and away about two hundred feet. The ground looks sort of funny hanging up there face down. Then you pull a rip cord and drop about twenty feet before the slack is taken up. It gave me a quick thrill but it was a lot of fun. While you are falling that twenty feet you have to count 1000, 2000, 3000, and change your rip cord from your right hand to your left hand. You really have to think fast to do that.

JOHN TAYLOR ● *In a typical drill, the first thing we did when we got to the tower was to put on a harness and lay flat on a mat. We would then be hoisted up the tower. Some guys were hoisted all the way, some 200 feet, some 125 feet. It was my luck to be carried all the way to the top for my first drop. From that height, the mat down on the ground looked like a cigarette paper. One, two, three, pull the rip cord and drop about fifteen feet so that you are caught in the harness. Then you're supposed to change the rip cord from your right hand to your left hand, and you'd better not drop it! This was quite an unnerving experience, but it was exciting, and we had a lot of fun doing it. Of course, we realized that our controlled falls from the tower, with our being tethered to a fed-out safety line, would be a little different than the real thing out of an airplane. It was good preparation nonetheless.*

After two trips up in the horizontal harness and once with a buddy on a bench seat, the troopers then moved on from the control tower to the free towers. The latter had four arms that protruded from the top horizontally. A trooper would be placed in a harness with an open parachute, which was fed into a lift hoop and attached to a cable. The trooper would be hoisted up 250 feet and up to two troopers could be hoisted and released at the same time from the tower arms, depending on wind direction. Once at the top the parachute canopy would be partially inflated due to the hoop assembly.

A public address system asked if the trooper was ready and released him moments later. The partially inflated parachute would drop a few feet and inflate. It was then the trooper's job to listen to the instructors below, while steering and maneuvering his parachute down to the ground below.

On approaching the quickly rising earth, the troopers were instructed to look at the horizon, not down, and to prepare for their landing. Once they were on the ground, the process was repeated of lifting and dropping pairs of soldiers from the tower. Bud Edwards described his first time on the free tower in a letter home in December:

> Monday afternoon we went off of the 250-foot towers. They took me to the top and released me. The greatest thrill was going up to the top. I will bet anybody that my stomach did at least two loops and maybe three. When you are coming down you have no sensation of falling. When you land you don't hit as hard as you do jumping from a four-foot platform.

The tower jumps continued into the evening darkness, and inadequate spotlights added to the surreal experience of the recruits as they were hoisted up and drifted down to earth. It was impossible to determine the exact direction to turn or when exactly they would land, so the recruits told each other to just keep their feet together and pray that they did not come in backwards. Marion Grodowski doubled his jumps from the tower when he agreed to jump twice for a friend who was fearful of the tower.

MARION GRODOWSKI ● *It was so dark out that faces could not be seen well. The instructors at the school did not know us, and I was able to pass through two extra times using the other guy's name. I was thrilled by the jumps, and it did not scare me a bit, so I had no problem going again for someone else.*

After completion of the tower jumps came the week of D stage: parachuting from an aircraft in flight. The first jump for Company F was on December 21, 1942. Clad in their steel helmets, coveralls, and jump boots, the nervous company of men walked to the rigger shed and picked up their previously packed main parachutes and reserve parachutes. They then donned them in a second nearby shed and went through inspection by a "rigger," a soldier trained to pack, maintain, and repair parachutes. The main and reserve parachutes were checked for damage, improper assembly, or any other visible problem that would keep them from opening properly and might injure the jumper. After being assigned into groups for jumping called "sticks," the men waited for their group to be called, then waddled off to a waiting C-47 and climbed aboard.

After brief instructions by their jumpmaster on board the plane, it lifted off. On command the men in the first stick stood up and hooked their static lines' attached hook fasteners to the cable running down inside the length of the aircraft. The jump would be just as trained in Toccoa, but instead of a practice exit a few feet out to the ground, the jump was from 1,200 feet. For most of the men in the company, not only was it to be their first jump from an airplane, but their first time in an airplane as well.

During a combat jump, paratroopers exit an aircraft as fast as possible so that the unit is not widely scattered. The parachuting at jump school was different. For their first few jumps, each man would move to the open door at the back of the plane and stand there. With a left boot toe on the door frame, his right leg back, and his hands cupped around the outside of the door, the nervous jumper took his time, staring wide-eyed at the horizon.

On command, which included a jumpmaster's slap on the leg, the jumpers exited the aircraft at a rate of one man every five to six seconds. As they accumulated jumps and progressed in training, exiting an entire stick of men in a matter of seconds became routine. For every man the jump was both a frightening and exhilarating experience.

RAUL OCHOA • *I enjoyed the silence. It was peaceful. It was amazing looking all around you, the parachutes in the air, and the people on the ground— really a wonderful sensation.*

MARION GRODOWSKI • *Standing in the door of the plane, I made the mistake of looking down at the ground and not at the horizon. I thought to myself, "Holy mackerel, what have I got myself into?" When I was told to go, I went out the door, and as my parachute snapped open I yelled a big "whoopee" or something like that. It was really a great feeling. I began to watch the boys below me in their parachutes, drifting down to the ground, as was I. My landing was not too hard, and once the jump was completed, I was totally elated.*

Bud Edwards wrote home about the first jump experience later that evening:

Dear Mother & Dad

I have just made my first jump and have only four more to go. That was the greatest thrill I ever had. We went over to the hangars about 10 o'clock this morning and got our chutes. We had to wait until five minutes to twelve before we could get a plane. I never had any sensation what so ever until I left the plane. I didn't get scared at all for some reason or other. I was the number six man in the first twelve men to leave the plane. When I left that plane I had no sensation of falling. When the prop blast caught the canopy I really got a jolt. That jolt was the best feeling I ever felt. You can't realize the feeling you get when you look up at the open canopy.

We have to go back to the shed and pack parachutes. We are supposed to make two jumps tomorrow. When I got within a hundred feet of the ground it seemed to come up faster than all get out.

I have to sign off now . . .

Love, Bud

While the men repacked their parachutes for their second jump, one jumper became complacent, believing an instructor's advice that you could ball up a parachute and it would still open. Gus Patruno decided to stuff his parachute into the pack without its usual intricate folding procedure. On the second jump for Fox Company on 22 December, Patruno's parachute remarkably opened with no problems. Confident that the folding procedure was a waste of time, Patruno again balled up his parachute and stuffed it into his pack tray. Jump three was made on the 23rd, and Patruno was not as lucky as before. The violent stress to the parachute on opening blew out three sections and caused more air to whistle through. Patruno's landing was much faster and harder than usual. Patruno decided it would be best to go back to meticulous parachute packing. With a new parachute, he completed another jump the same day without incident.

Fox Company's fifth and final jump was on Christmas Eve, 24 December 1942. Bud Edwards wrote home about his jump school completion after returning to the barracks:

I made my fifth and final qualifying jump today and it really felt good to have my feet on terra firma again. The first jumps you don't know what you are doing. The second jump you are a little leery. The third jump you know what you are doing and you wonder why you are doing it. The fourth and fifth jumps are just repeats. The main worry is getting out the door. When you get that opening shock of that canopy that is the greatest thrill a man ever felt. They give us our wings tomorrow.

TOM ALLEY ● *I really did not know what to expect from the jumps, but once I made my first one, I always felt like I was walking on clouds. I had injured my ankle on my fourth jump, a severe sprain. But I hid it from the instructors and made my fifth jump. I was determined to get those wings, and receiving them was my best day in the Army.*

VINCE OCCHIPINTI ● *We completed our training at Fort Benning, made our five parachute jumps, and on December 25th we had a giant parade of the 506th Infantry. We all received our wings, pinned on by officers at ceremonies that took a little more than an hour. In that short time, hundreds of people received their "wings."*

Captain Mulvey pinned the hard-earned Parachutist Badges—"Jump Wings"—on each member of the company during the ceremony. Afterward the men were treated to Christmas dinner with all the trimmings. A festively printed holiday menu was handed out that included the company rosters for the Second Battalion and a detailed list of the evening's fare. The dinner was lavish and delicious, compared to the usually horrible food at the mess hall:

CHRISTMAS DINNER DECEMBER 25, 1942

Fruit Cocktail	Wine	Cream of Celery Soup
Olives	Mixed Pickles	Celery Hearts
Roast Turkey	Oyster Dressing	Baked Ham
Cranberry Sauce	Giblet Gravy	Sweet Potatoes
Rice	Carrot and Peas	Creamed Corn
	Sliced Tomatoes on Lettuce	
Mincemeat Pie	Ice Cream	Assorted Cookies

Crackers	Hot Rolls	Butter
Oranges	Apples	Grapes
	Coffee Lemonade	

COMPANY "F"
COMPANY OFFICERS

Captain Thomas P. Mulvey
COMMANDING

First Lieut. Carl B. MacDowell
EXECUTIVE OFFICER

1st Lieut. Norman J. McFaddin	2nd Lieut. Andrew E. Tuck
1st Lieut. Freeling T. Colt	2nd Lieut. Frank J. McFadden
1st Lieut. Kenith J. Havorka	2nd Lieut. Eugene D. Brierre

FIRST SERGEANT
Willie A. Morris

STAFF SERGEANTS

Birmingham, Peter C.	Lane, Herman L.	Long, Dallas L.

SERGEANTS

Anderson, Wilford O.	Houck, Julius A.	Mercier, Kenneth D.
	Tamkun, Victor W.	

CORPORALS

Barnson, Macrae L.	Mather, Gordon E.	Roller, George E.
Malley, Charles R.	Robertson, Clifford E.	Werts, William H.

PRIVATES FIRST CLASS

Aebischer, Ray R.	Henderson, Charles	Replogle, Donald H.
Brooks, Paul	Hicks, Leonard F.	Roth, Douglas G.
Borden, Hugh G.	Kissel, Walter F.	Summers, Alan W.
Brown, Linus E.	Olanie, William G.	Supco, John
Chappelle, Joseph G.	Ott, Ray A.	Swafford, James R.
Gaston, Eldridge G.	Patruno, Mario J.	Wadman, Harold G.
Griffin, Frank D., Jr	Porter, Huber G.	Wolford, Thomas B.
	Zerbe, Roy E.	

PRIVATES

Adams, Gaston
Adams, Orval C.
Allan, Jack B.
Alley, Thomas H., Jr
Bailey, William J.
Baker, Thomas H., Jr
Bellow, Raymond L.
Beauchamp, A. R.
Beck, Henry B.
Boduck, Stanley G.
Botscheller, Gus V.
Brennen, Edward F.
Brewer, Raymond D.
Buchter, Richard K.
Burton, Louis F.
Carlino, Matthew J.
Casey, Patrick D.
Clardy, Eugene C.
Clemens, William D.
Cioni, Louis W.
Cortese, Nicholas J.
Crawford, Marvin F.
Cummings, George L.
Curry, Henry L.
Dickerson, Jack D.
Edwards, David W.
Egolf, Virgil L.
Elliott, George L.
Emelander, Donald A.
Farley, Gerald F.
Fink, George C.
Finkelstein, Morris M.
Fitshenry, Joseph L.
Flick, Joseph E.
Gates, Robert E.

Gillespie, John G.
Goodman, Chester R.
Green, William D.
Grodowski, Marion J.
Haney, Manning G.
Hanson, Arthur H.
Hegland, Lester T.
Harms, Donald R.
Henson, Donald G.
Hull, Kenneth A.
Hurst, William L.
Jacobs, Charles
Jackson, John E.
Johnson, Vern M.
Jones, Daniel P.
Kelley, Courtney E.
Knudsen, Richard
Krutys, Edward G.
Kudlicka, Robert M.
Kuntz, Wendelin G.
Lev, Orel H.
Lindsey, Leonard A.
Lucero, Alfred E.
Lutz, Robert W.
Mackay, Otto W.
Mackey, James W.
Maddock, Jack
Mann, Robert E.
Martin, George
May, Otto W.
Morrissey, Phillip J.
Mullinax, Charles E.
Nestler, Martin A.
Nocera, Frank
Occipinti, Vincent F.

O'Grady, Daniel F.
O'Hara, James R.
Pustola, Stephen
Rasmussen, Loy O.
Reese, Charles H.
Reese, George R.
Rice, Farris
Riddick, Robert E.
Robbins, Ralph
Scheurich, Charles H.
Schwenk, Russell A.
Sharp, Willard A.
Shennum, Merlin J.
Shropshire, Robert O.
Sims, Marvin D.
Snedden, Donald G.
Sopher, John G.
Spiewak, Stanley
Stanford, Clarence R.
Stewart, Kenneth E.
Stone, Robert E.
Strunk, Alfred
Tindall, Leslie L.
True, Willaim
Tucker, Willaim H., Jr
Uplinger, George W.
Valleries, Clifford F.
Villa, Jose L.
Vogel, Robert E.
Waters, James F.
Webster, David K.
Wilson, Alvin W.
Wood, Donald E.
Wright, Calvin L.
Wynne, Albert J.

Following the celebration for the completion of the Parachute School, the entire company was given a furlough. The proud new paratroopers spread out around the country for a relaxing visit with family and friends. For those who lived on the West Coast, travel by train would allow them only a two-day visit at home before they had to start back to Fort Benning. For a few, the time spent would be worth the effort to go. For one member of the company, the trip would result in unfortunate life-long consequences.

CHAPTER 3

FURLOUGHS, CAMP MACKALL, AND THE TENNESSEE MANEUVERS

After completion of the Parachute School, the men were finally issued a furlough, a leave of absence for ten days. Normally the length allowed off post was only a weekend pass. However, as a reward for the hard work and accomplishment, the minivacation was granted to the entire company. Most returned home to visit family. One had an interesting meeting in Chicago.

VINCE OCCHIPINTI ● *I can remember a colonel came up to me in an airport in Chicago and said, "Soldier, I've never seen a uniform like yours." We wore our jump boots with pants tucked in (bloused) and those smart caps, plus the insignia on our caps was not worn by the average GI. "What type of outfit is that?" he asked me. I snapped to attention and told him we were parachutists. "Well, you sure make fine looking soldiers," he said. "If you guys do as well in service, we've got the war won." I said, beaming, "Oh, yes, sir!"*

Marion Grodowski returned to his South Chicago neighborhood and became the topic of talk as he proudly strolled to his home on South Ada Street. Children circled around him, peppering him with questions about his uniform, his wings, and his shiny jump boots. Upon hearing he was a paratrooper, and then realizing what that meant, his mother nearly fainted. Though Grodowski had told his family he had joined the Army, he made no mention of the paratroops in his letters home. After his mother recovered from the shock, he received a pat on the back from his father and much praise from his impressed mother. His mother later showed him off like a prize turkey before Sunday services at nearby St. John of God Church.

All around the country, families and sweethearts greeted their para-troopers as they arrived home. Having to wear their uniforms throughout their visits, they stood out and were the talk of their towns. If the unique insignia, uniform, and boots were new to the military, they were even newer to the general public.

But after the evening meals, visits, dates, and trips to the movies, the men had to begin saying their goodbyes and climb onto trains to head back to Fort Benning. The time had gone by quickly, and many allowed them-selves a few extra days before going back, not realizing they were going to be AWOL (absent without leave).

On arrival to Fort Benning, those who were late from the furlough soon found that the Army was not going to be as forgiving as they thought. Those who had rank lost a stripe, were fined, and put on company punishment. This informal punishment, such as extra guard duty or extra kitchen police duty, does not go into a soldier's permanent record and he avoids a court martial. For the last men in the 506th to arrive late, however, Colonel Sink had a special punishment awaiting them: a drumming-out ceremony.

For Fox Company, the unfortunate soldier was Alfred Lucero. On 19 January 1943, the entire regiment was assembled with the men in full dress uniforms. They fell into their company formations at attention, and as a drummer tapped out a slow roll, names were called out—in the case of Company F, Pvt. Alfred E. Lucero. Lucero was escorted to the front of his unit. The drumming changed from a slow roll to a quick tap, and Private Lucero was stripped of his wings, having them torn from his jacket, and was made to take his trousers' legs from inside his boots. He was then es-corted from the field, to be transferred to a non-Airborne unit.

ROY "JOSH" ZERBE • *It was the most revolting thing about being in the Army, watching that ceremony. Terrible.*

MARION GRODOWSKI • *It was the most chickenshit thing to do to someone. It was horrible. We could not believe that it happened over being late from the furlough. Even our company officers were disgusted with the ceremony. We were all disgusted with it. But if that was the way Colonel*

Sink wanted it, then that was the way it was going to be. It was his outfit. Lucero was a good guy, and everyone in the company liked him. The whole deal was just chicken shit.

Bud Edwards, who had been on company punishment himself for arriving back to Fort Benning late, wrote home about the ceremony in a letter home:

Dear Mother & Dad
They have been keeping me so busy that I haven't been able to write a letter since the last one I wrote you. I have had fire guard three nights now and it robs you out of an hour and a half sleep. All that you have to do is go around and see that none of the barracks catch on fire. We had Monday off and went on the range Sunday. We fired the Sub-Thompson, carbine, and the Garand rifle. I did fairly well. When I said we had Monday off I mean the rest of the Company. I had K.P. (kitchen police) which was just a little extra duty. It wasn't so bad though because we did a lot of loafing around. I will probably keep getting extra detail until we get out of here, and we are moving out very soon. I don't know where we are going or when. Why I haven't any extra detail tonight I'll never know.
    I am getting more disgusted with this outfit as the days go by. Today we saw a little ceremony that made me think that this outfit is very crap. They call it the drumming out. They have the Major and his staff standing out in front of the battalion with a drummer and they call some of the men out of ranks who went A.W.O.L. a little too long. While he is marching out of the ranks with two Sergeants, one in front and one in back with a machinegun. When they get in front of the Major the Sergeant pulls the patches off of his cap and his coat. I have to sign off for now.
                                                        Love, Bud

Everyone was sickened by the event. However, there would be no more late arrivals on future furloughs. The example had been made, and it left its mark on the men of Company F.
    Intense training soon took the minds of the soldiers from drumming-out ceremonies to the business at hand—preparing for war. In late January

the company began platoon-size maneuvers on the combat range, and company maneuvers in the field. Tactics were practiced continually in the afternoons, along with compass courses, and field problems. Nine-mile runs were the normal routine in the mornings.

On 6 February, using custom-made Airborne stationery, Johnny Supco wrote home to his little brother Anthony back in Pottstown, Pennsylvania, describing Company F's latest training and adventure:

Hi-ya Anthony,
We're leaving this frying pan area on Monday morning at 9 O'clock; we are going to march with one full field pack and weapons to a camp in Alabama. It's only about 12 miles from here. I'm going to pack up after I finish this letter.

We had a big basketball game here last night between our Company and E Company. Our officers and men had about $500.00 dollars bet on the game, one first Sgt, had $60.00 bet himself. Our Company lost. The score was 25 to 26 it was a nip and tuck game all the way.

We had a busy day today. We played softball all morning and were showed how to camouflage yourself and different weapons in the afternoon. Some of the experiments were good, you could walk on top of them and you would not have been able to notice them.

I got paid last week & I got $96 bucks. Well that's about all I got to say.

So Long,
Johnny

On 8 February the men marched from the Frying Pan section of the post over to the Alabama side. Bud Edwards described the new accommodations in a letter home the next day:

Dear Mother & Dad,
I have been intending to write for the last week and haven't done it. I am in Alabama now and I am writing this letter from a pup tent where I shall sleep the night. We left the frying pan Monday at 10:00 am and arrived here at 12:15pm. This is a very good place. We have better barracks, mess halls, and orderly rooms. Everything about this place is better. The reason we are sleeping [in] pup tents tonight is because we were

issued some old mattresses, cots, and pillows and they found some bed bugs in them.

So they are fumigating them and we have to stay out of the barracks for twenty four hours. You should see the mess hall it holds the whole battalion and they serve the battalion in fifteen minutes. The wood on the inside is all burnt and it looks very nice. They have a juke box in the mess hall which will make it very nice for when we want to hold a party.

We have been having quite a bit of recreation lately like volleyball, basketball, and baseball. I played volleyball last night and managed to get a slight sprained ankle. I went on sick call this morning and had it taped up and it is feeling O.K.

You asked me in your last letter what "Currahee" means. It is the name of the mountain that we ran at Toccoa. Currahee is an Indian name and it means the same as Stand Alone. It is the regiment's battle cry. I imagine that is what you would define it as. I have to sign off now because I have to mark my clothing and equipment.

With All My Love,
Bud

Indelible ink was used to mark the clothing, web gear, and canvas covers of the soldiers' equipment. Metal stamps were used to emboss items such as canteens, mess kits, leather slings, and leather holsters. The marking for an item was the first initial of the soldier's last name and last four numbers of his serial number. Bud Edwards, #39392467, would have marked his gear E-2467. Army regulations dictated that each issued item be marked in a specific location. Several days were spent marking clothing.

After a barracks inspection to confirm all the bedbugs were dead, the men of Company F packed a blanket along with their shelter half (half of a pup tent) and headed into the field for overnight maneuvers. The entire weekend was spent on night maneuvers and in pup tents.

All of 18 February was devoted to the battalion's sixth jump. Fox Company had no refusals to jump, but the other two companies saw a total of six refusals. Those who refused to jump were transferred out of the Airborne. Fox Company would not be immune to jump refusals later, but on that Thursday they came out looking good.

The training continued until 25 February, when the company was sent to Camp Mackall, near Hoffman, North Carolina—a twenty-four-hour trip by truck and train. Their barracks there had bug-free mattresses on double bunk beds, with an entire platoon of forty-eight enlisted men in each building.

After the men settled into their new accommodations, a week of field maneuvers began with the company spending 5 March in foxholes. During the night a cold rain fell, and the men feebly attempted to use the shelter halves to keep the cold rain from falling into the foxholes. After a miserable night, the muddy company of men marched back into camp, then showered and spent their afternoon cleaning their equipment. A show inspection of the barracks and newly cleaned uniforms, gear, and weapons followed.

Road marches of twenty-five miles a day began in addition to the usual field problems. A new game was devised by the company officers, a two-man hundred-yard dash. A soldier would pick a man of equal or larger size, put him on his back, and run a hundred yards. The game seemed awkward and foolish at the time but would later be a lifesaver in combat.

On a $300 bet, Lt. Andy Tuck, Charlie Malley, Don Replogle, Charlie Jacobs, and George Martin decided to walk the hundred miles from Hoffman to Charlotte in thirty-five hours. Colonel Strayer allowed the event and gave the men three-day passes to be off post. A medic tagged along to treat their blisters, aches, and pains.

They set off in the afternoon after filling their jumpsuits' many pockets with rations, filling a canteen on their pistol belt, and coating their feet with benzoin to protect their skin. With Lieutenant Tuck arranging for egg sandwiches and coffee along the way, the men stopped only for short rest and food breaks. They went from Hoffman to Rockingham, to Wadesboro, then to Camp Sutton for breakfast, and on through Monroe. On the outskirts of Charlotte, the men only had twelve miles to go and just over six hours left when they stopped for another break. When they did, their muscles cramped, and they could go no further. The bet was lost.

While the Second Battalion was at Camp Mackall, word went out that Colonel Strayer wanted a battalion mascot. He offered a three-day pass and ten dollars to any man who could obtain a "wildcat" for such use. Other parachute units were already using dogs as their mascots, having them parachute in custom-made jump harnesses. Colonel Strayer apparently thought that a parachuting wildcat trumped a parachuting dog.

One night after drinking in town, Sgt. Charlie Malley and Sgt. Don

Replogle stole a caged bobcat from a roadside zoo right off post. In the middle of the night they brought it by taxi to Colonel Strayer's quarters. He awarded Malley and Replogle the passes and cash.

Gus Patruno built a cage for the bobcat eight feet long, four feet wide, and six feet tall, with an eighteen-inch door at one end. Gus had a natural way with animals and in no time was able to go inside the cage and pet the animal. The benefit to being the caretaker of the battalion mascot was that Gus was routinely called from maneuvers and brought back to camp by jeep to tend to the bobcat and its special food allotment from the officers' mess.

GUS PATRUNO ● *I was able to go to the officers' mess hall and order a steak, cooked medium. I would take the steak and later eat most of it, and give the scraps to the bobcat. I also had boots and a parachute harness made for it. One Saturday we decided to try to put them on. Lieutenant Colt had obtained some chloroform from the dispensary. Tommy Wolford and I entered the cage and held the cat while Lieutenant Colt gassed it with the chloroform. Once it was asleep, we laid the cat on a bench inside the cage and began to put the boots and harness on him. All of a sudden the cat jumped up about two to three feet in the air, and the three of us shot out the narrow cage door at the same time. And that ended that. The cat was left for the next arriving paratrooper unit when Fox Company eventually left Camp Mackall.*

On Saturday the 21st, the battalion had a parade and a review for the brass, and then they were given passes for the remainder of the weekend. Most headed off to Greensboro, North Carolina, by any means of transportation available. Some saw movies such as *The Crystal Ball* and *George Washington Slept Here*. Others went bowling, and some chased women. Merlin Shennum, Alan Summers, Marvin Sims, and Courtney Kelley rented a room at the King Cotton Hotel in Greensboro.

MERLIN SHENNUM ● *We rented a room and filled the bathtub with ice and beer. That was the only way to keep it real cold. We spent the weekend on the roof of the hotel drinking, and even threw some of our empty bottles off the roof of the building to the street below.*

The roof of the King Cotton Hotel was over 130 feet high, yet the partying paratroopers managed to avoid any trouble with the hotel staff and local police.

On return to Camp Mackall, the trips into the field for maneuvers continued. The drills went on every day and often into the night. On the 25th the men began night maneuvers in the rain. With only a blanket to each man and no pup tents being carried, the company was forced to take shelter under trees and wait out the night soaked. They returned to the barracks in the morning and cleaned their weapons. The hardships they faced on field maneuvers in training would be nothing compared to the misery they would later endure in combat, but they did help them prepare for their future.

The 30th of March saw the company complete their seventh jump. Bud Edwards wrote a lengthy letter home the next day describing the event:

Dear Mother & Dad,
We have been doing the usual thing lately, other than the jump we had yesterday. I don't believe I have ever described a jump to you yet. Well a jump day is usually an easy day. The Captain tells us the night before we jump that we are going to jump the next day. The next morning we get up and don our jump suits and jump boots. Then during the morning we take our rifles, machine guns and other equipment in equipment bundles. After getting those bundles rolled we get our rifle belt and make sure that the canteen, first aid pouch, and bayonet are all in the right place. We also make sure that we have our jump rope in case we get in a tree we can get down okay.

In the afternoon just before we jump they call our names off as to the respective position we will jump in and the plane we jump from. I was in the second plane and the twelfth man. After we line up we march down to the packing sheds and draw our chutes. When we get our chutes we adjust them and go down to the field. When our turn finally comes to get into the plane we put our equipment bundle in the plane and then we get on. This time it was the longest ride we ever had. The jump master we had for this plane was Lt. Brewer who is from California. He is 6'3" and weighs 213 lbs. The LT looks out the door and spots the field that we are going to jump in.

We then stand up and hook up. After we sound off for equipment check-up we close up to the door and go. There were two men who got air sick and vomited. One of these men didn't jump and it almost meant six months in the guard house for him but he jumped today. After we jumped we landed in a very soft field, it had just been plowed. When we got out of our harnesses we all rushed to our equipment bundle, got our rifles and took off to our platoon assembly area. When we get there we take off for our objective which happened to be a railroad bridge this time. We blew it up of course.

You ask about this camp. Well this is a fairly good sized place. There are two other parachute infantry outfits that I know of. The 511 which isn't qualified yet and the 508 which is qualified. There are also glider troops here. How many I don't know. They have one small P.X. (Post Exchange) for two regiments. We also have a theater. It is a fairly good theater. I went to the show tonight a very colorful musical with Mary Martin and Dick Powell.

Tomorrow we go into the field and stay out a couple of nights. It will most likely rain Friday night. Well I have been rambling on and not saying much so I had better sign off.

Love, Bud

The training varied in the following weeks. Days were spent on the rifle range, zeroing in and mastering their pieces. At a mock town, or "combat course," the troopers were able to move down streets, shoot at pop-up German soldier targets, and learn room-clearing techniques. They also practiced shooting at unknown distances and at odd angles. The urban warfare training and live-fire shooting built their confidence in not only their ability but their weapons as well.

In addition to the combat courses, the variety of weapons that they practiced with and mastered continued to broaden. The Thompson submachine gun was a popular shooter in the company. This was not only due to its looks and its cinematic fame but also its volume of ammunition and fully automatic fire ability. Besides the Thompson, they also practiced with the rocket-firing bazooka, the lightweight M1 carbine, and the Browning Automatic Rifle, or BAR.

Days of intense physical training included cross-country runs and the usual grueling calisthenics. Road marches of twenty-five miles in full gear became a tiring change of pace from the running. They started on Mondays at 0500 and usually lasted until the following day, with a field problem keeping the men training and digging foxholes along their route for well over twenty-four hours. Rain and soggy conditions often limited the sleep of the already tired paratroopers. And the return to camp only changed the sleeping conditions to the extent that down time was now spent cleaning gear and weapons. Long periods of warm, restful sleep were rare and cherished at Camp Mackall, and three-day passes were few and far between.

Most Thursdays, Fridays, and Saturdays were spent in the field on field problems. A march into the field on a Friday night would include night movement and land navigation problems. A mock attack would be staged before the sun came up on a designated "enemy position," usually a lake or bridge. Then foxholes would be dug and occupied until after sunrise. Fried eggs, oatmeal, fruit, and coffee would be dropped off in the field for a much appreciated company breakfast. Field rations would be the afternoon and evening fare, hastily eaten while attacks and counterattacks were practiced on their positions. Another night of maneuvers and land navigation problems would eventually bring the company back to their barracks to start the cleaning process on weapons and gear all over again. After a rifle inspection, they had the rest of the afternoon off.

A dramatic change to the company staffing occurred on 13 April. Over a dozen men were transferred from the unit for what was known as "Assignment X." Among those chosen to go were Bill True's chum Bill Tucker. Tucker had frequently butted heads with Lieutenant MacDowell, and rank having its privileges, MacDowell signed up Tucker for a transfer out of the unit. Morris Finkelstein, tired of constant abuse and bullying by James "Whitey" Swafford, volunteered for the mysterious assignment. Captain Mulvey tried to persuade Finkelstein to stay but granted his wish for a transfer. Assignment X turned out to be transfers to the 82nd Airborne and a trip to North Africa in preparation for the invasion of Sicily and Italy. Tucker and Finkelstein both ended up serving in the Third Battalion of the 505th Parachute Infantry Regiment.

After all the hard work, passes were handed out for the weekend of May 7, and that Saturday the men scrambled off to visit girlfriends, family, or see the sights anywhere but near Camp Mackall. The passes allowed the men to be free of the camp and training until Tuesday morning.

Vince Occhipinti and Bud Edwards bummed a ride in a fellow Fox Company man's car to Fayetteville, North Carolina, and then rode a train to Washington, D.C. On arrival they took in a game between the Washington Senators and the Boston Red Sox (Boston won, 2–1). Then touring around the area the duo passed by the White House on their way to a service club. For fifty cents each they got a bed for the night and a hot shower. After a quick shower and shave, the two were off on the town again, taking in the Washington Monument, the Lincoln Memorial, and the other usual tourist sights of the nation's capital. They arrived back at Camp Mackall at 2200 on Monday, not sure what was more tiring—Army training or fast-paced tourism.

On the men's return to Camp Mackall, the training continued, which included a parachute jump on 13 May. Ten-mile high-paced marches were the routine. Night maneuvers—good weather permitting—included sleeping out with no shelters or blankets. K-rations became the usual but disliked meal during the field problems. Another training parachute jump was made by the company on 19 May, which resulted in Tom Alley severely spraining both ankles. Jump injuries were not uncommon and usually resulted in men being restricted to quarters or placed on light-duty assignments until they could heal.

Maneuvers began in South Carolina the last week of May with Fox 506th making a parachute jump on the 27th in full gear with weapons. John Taylor had a rough time jumping with his .30-caliber machine gun for the first time, as it was secured under his reserve parachute, barrel down. When Taylor's parachute opened, he was supposed to turn the heavy weapon across the body to avoid injury when landing. However, on exiting the plane, Taylor had a brief collision with Lt. Bob Brewer, who was right in front of him at the door. Taylor exited head first and thus received a violent and stunning shock from his opening parachute. Before he could get his bearings, and still yet to maneuver his machine gun outward, Taylor landed in a group of trees against a stump. The impact forced the weapon's pistol grip up into his chin, knocking him senseless. Taylor came to more than a half hour later while hiking in column with the company. He had no recollection of how he got there.

For their assignment in the exercise, the men of Company F were to seize and hold a road intersection. Conducting roadblocks was an essential part of the paratroop doctrine. After holding their position until the following morning, the company rode in trucks to a nearby airfield and flew back to Camp Mackall. It was, for most men in the company, the first time they had climbed into a C-47 and actually landed in it later.

On their arrival back at camp, cleaning began and inspections of uniforms, barracks, webbing equipment, and rifles were held. Afterward the men packed parachutes and then helped pack all the company's equipment and supplies.

For the Second Battalion of the 506th, the first week of June was spent in long hours of preparation for a move to Kentucky and Tennessee for one of a series of large-scale war games called the Tennessee Maneuvers. Company F would "fight" with the blue army against the red army. Friday, 4 June, saw the company off on a train ride to Kentucky, traveling through Chattanooga and Nashville along the way.

Second Platoon's Bob Janes wrote home about their travels and training on Sunday, June 13, 1943:

Hello Folks,

I can't remember whether I have written to you since I have been out here in Kentucky on maneuvers or not but I will try and let you know what I have been doing in case I haven't.

Well to begin with we left Camp Mackall about a week ago Friday and had a nice long train ride here. We arrived here about 7:00am a week ago Sunday. We camped here by an airport living in pup tents, which doesn't appeal to me but has to be done. This place is near a town called Sturgis, Kentucky, and is about thirty five miles from, which may be on a map if you want to look and have a map, it will give you some idea of where I am. We use this place as a base camp for all operations against the red army. We jumped last week over Nashville, Tennessee. We had a two hour plane ride from here over there that I really enjoyed. You really get a bird's eye view of the country. This is really beautiful country.

They jumped us from about 550ft which is getting pretty low. I sure had a terrible body position when I left the plane door. I turned two complete summersaults before my chute opened. I didn't get much of an opening shock though. I just missed a fence by about two feet and expected to hit the ground real hard since I was loaded down with so much equipment but I landed very softly and didn't get hurt.

After we landed we went to our assembly point and then headed for our objective which was about five miles away. We reached our objective after a very grueling march and established a road block and held it for about twelve hours and then the red army surrounded us and captured us. They held us for about a day then took us by truck to Bowling Green, Tennessee and we slept on the ground there all night and then they picked us up and brought us back here by plane. We arrived back here Thursday and we have been lying around here resting up. We are going to pull out of here again tomorrow morning. We will probably jump over Tennessee again on a new problem. We are really going to be loaded down this jump. I guess if we had our footlockers with us they would have us jump with them tied on somewhere.

Boy these maneuvers teach you to rough it. We eat field rations, sleep on the ground without blankets, etc. I should be in pretty good shape by [the] time I get home on furlough. Well folks it is getting sort of late to write so I had better close for now. Will write again when I get time. It is damn hot here. The sweat is just rolling off me from just writing a letter. Hope you are feeling fine.

> Your Son,
> Bob

That same evening, Bud Edwards wrote home describing their diet of K-rations:

We ate our breakfast unit of our K rations. This breakfast unit consists of a small can of ham and eggs, two packages of compressed crackers which are harder than bricks, a small envelope of soluble coffee, a fruit bar, three lumps of sugar, one package of four cigarettes, and one stick of chewing gum. The supper and dinner units are similar with the exception of the ham and eggs and the drink. In the dinner unit you have a can of cheese and you have lemonade to drink. In the supper unit you have bouillon to drink and you have a can of some kind of cold meat.

The men of the company made another parachute jump on 15 June. Some of the planes they jumped from also towed gliders, which were cut loose prior to their arrival over the drop zone. This time a bridge was guarded. The men had a difficult time digging in because of rock just below the surface, and after digging a foxhole about one foot deep, all that was heard was the distinctive clank of metal on rock. The shale was impossible to get through, and Marion Grodowski broke his shovel trying to dig a decent foxhole. Piling rocks around the shallow foxholes was eventually the only option.

While Fox Company was in the field, supplies—usually rations and mail—were airdropped in canvas containers with parachutes. One supply drop included bags of hot coffee. But the smiles in anticipation of hot coffee turned to frowns when the men took their first sips from their canteen cups. The bags had left a terrible aftertaste in the coffee, and made it difficult for even the most devout coffee drinkers in the unit to swallow.

While acting as a company runner during the maneuvers, Len Hicks had an encounter with the red army one afternoon as he returned from delivering a message. Caught up in the beauty of the countryside and smelling a fence line of honeysuckle, Hicks walked right into a double-columned company of red army soldiers. Hicks was informed that he'd been captured, and moved into the roadway between the four long rows of soldiers. Then someone noticed his paratrooper carbine, which, unlike the standard M1 carbine, had a folding metal stock. Hicks walked down the middle of the column as soldiers kept asking about what type of weapon he was carrying and asked to see it. The bewildered group watched and questioned as Hicks walked right out the back of the column and sprinted off to freedom.

Maneuvers were not limited to parachuting and traditional field problems. One evening the unit used boats to cross a swollen Cumberland River during darkness. It was the company's first time using boats and, for some men, the first time in any boat. First the boats had to be carried over a mile to the riverbank, and after what seemed like an eternity on the swift water, the opposite bank was reached. The company then wandered through a cornfield and attacked a red army unit at daybreak.

Len Hicks had another interesting encounter while at the Tennessee Maneuvers. Near the company command post was a small cabin that was occupied by a man who was befriended by the company. The cabin had a well in its front yard, and the troopers were welcome to drink from it. Enjoying the visits of the soldiers, the man invited Hicks and his friends to eat lunch on the porch of his home and talk about fishing.

One afternoon after they finished eating, the man asked Hicks if he could look at his mess kit, which Hicks had noticed the man staring at. When it was issued to Hicks upon joining the Army at Fort MacArthur in California, the mess kit already had names, dates, and places scratched into its metal. The man looked it over silently. Then tears began to run down his face. The man said, "You will not believe this, but this mess kit was mine during the First World War. These names were my best friends. These places were battles we were in." Hicks asked the man if he would like the mess kit back as a souvenir, and he accepted. Hicks's only regret was that he had not scratched his own name into it as well.

During the mock battles and skirmishes at the Tennessee Maneuvers, the soldiers were under the constant eye of referees and umpires. Units and their members were designated as killed, wounded, or captured by the officials during "fights" with other units that for safety usually did not involve the use of live ammunition. Occasionally, however, officials would assign a unit a specific task which would involve live fire on a target or targets. One such incident involved mortar-man Frank Griffin.

As a member of the Second Platoon's mortar squad, Griffin was carrying the 60mm mortar tube and its bipod. The company was on one hillside firing at targets around a few shacks on another hillside, under the watchful eye of a group of referees and umpires. The mortar squads were told to knock out an outhouse near the shacks on the far hillside. Griffin could not locate the soldier with the heavy base plate for his mortar, but he did have an ammo carrier, which he used as a substitute. Griffin's team set up the mortar tube and fired off a round toward the outhouse; after making a quick adjustment, he fired a second round. The "crapper" was destroyed, much to the admiration of the officials. Apparently they had never seen the mortar fired without the base plate before. Fox Company eventually cut their base plates down to half size to save weight, but even so, the flat and heavy item was got "lost" frequently. Griffin, however, had displayed a unique skill that would later be repeated in combat, time and again.

TOM ALLEY • *The best thing about the maneuvers was that we fought like the Airborne was supposed to fight. We would jump in, take an objective, and hold it for a couple days. Then we went back to our base camp. All the other guys in the regular Army outfits were stuck in the field for the entire maneuvers.*

During these maneuvers, men were often given a pass into a nearby town for a break from the Army life. One afternoon Merlin Shennum was sent into town to retrieve three men from the Third Platoon who had failed to return on time. He found them in a military police station, being held on trumped-up charges.

MERLIN SHENNUM • *The MPs told me their passes were no good. I knew that was a lie and told that to the officer in charge. He demanded that I stand at attention in front of him inside his station. I told him like hell I was. He told me I was not in my chickenshit outfit anymore and was under his jurisdiction. When I refused to stand at attention he came over his desk and hit me in the head with a blackjack. I was then dragged by several other MPs into a holding room with my other troopers from the company.*

Well, the next morning these MPs took us outside and made us drill up and down the street for a while. Then they trucked us back to our unit. When we arrived, Captain Mulvey asked what had happened. I explained about the MPs claiming the passes were no good, how one guy had hit me, and that they said our unit was chickenshit. Mulvey said he would "fix their butts." That night he and Lieutenant Tuck went into town on a late night raid and cleaned out that station. They really tore it up good.

At the close of the Tennessee Maneuvers, the men of Second Battalion ended their exercise in Kentucky, on the outskirts of Camp Breckinridge. Company F spent more time on the firing range honing marksmanship skills. Then, finally, furloughs began to be issued in platoon-size allotments. The men headed out for ten days of family visits and rest.

CHAPTER 4

FORT BRAGG, CAMP SHANKS, AND THE HMS *SAMARIA*

Those not lucky enough to obtain furloughs at the end of the maneuvers had a dirty forty-hour train ride back to Fort Bragg. The only blessing of the trip was good meals on the train, which included meat and potatoes for dinner, with all the chocolate milk they could drink. On 16 July 1943, they marched into a camp with new two-story barracks—luxury accommodations compared to the pup tents, foxholes, and chigger-infested ditches they had been sleeping in during the Tennessee Maneuvers.

On the 28th the men paraded before the Fort Bragg brass in full dress uniforms in honor of the 506th Parachute Infantry Regiment being officially recognized as part of the 101st Airborne Division. It had been assigned to the 101st on 1 June, but it was not until after the Tennessee Maneuvers that the official ceremony was completed.

On 30 July, another scorching summer day, the men of the 506th were on parade again, this time for a quartet of generals including Lt. Gen. Lloyd Fredendall. Fredendall, who had been relieved of command in North Africa, was now commander of the Central Defense Command in the United States. Drenched in sweat, with ashen, burning feet, the men of the company finished their "dog and pony show" and marched back to their barracks for a shower, a change of clothes, and some sleep.

Inspections intensified at Fort Bragg during August, with physical training intensifying as well. Men were issued new equipment and spent time cleaning their fatigues, uniforms made of herringbone cotton twill. Two sets had been issued to each man, a jumpsuit and two-piece uniform, and two sets were expected to be clean and pressed. A panoramic photograph of the company in the jumpsuits was taken the week of August 20, and most of the men of Fox 506th managed to make it into the picture. Those on pass, such as Bill True, and those who were ill, such as Robert Janes, missed out.

With the influx of replacements to the company came a rise in theft. New members were suspected of stealing cigarettes, fountain pens, and other personal items from bunks and open footlockers. The suspicion that cloaked the new replacements would take some time to fade away. Every non-Toccoa man was suspect.

One evening prior to shipping out from Fort Bragg, Colonel Strayer assembled the Second Battalion. With all the men together, he proceeded to give a raving pep talk and motivational speech about the ability and future promise of the men of 2/506th. At the end, Strayer opened the floor to questions and answers. The room was silent. Strayer peered nervously into the crowd.

After a few minutes of low whispers by the assembled battalion, one lone hand rose from the group. It was Pvt. Henry Beck of Fox Company. With some relief, Colonel Strayer said, "Okay, son, tell us who you are and where you are from, then advise of your question." Beck stood up and nervously looked about the room. In a thick Scandinavian accent, he responded, "Sir, maw name is Hen-ray Beck, an Ah-am from Meena-sooda." The room exploded in laughter. Laughter soon turned into pandemonium by the entire Second Battalion. Beck eventually sat down, red-faced and confused, and the pep rally ended with no further questions.

After being issued new gear, cleaning weapons, and standing for multiple inspections, 2/506th moved out to Camp Shanks, in New York near the Hudson River and not far from New York City. As a break from the hard work, Fox 506th watched an exhibition baseball game on August 31 between the Red Sox and the best baseball team the 101st could muster. The 101st lost eleven to one.

Normally the men would be checked for venereal disease in what was called a "short arm inspection." Routinely throughout their training, they were rousted from sleep and forced to fall into formation in boots, raincoat, and helmet. A personal manipulation of their genitals by the inspecting medical staff would reveal a contracted case of VD. However, at Camp Shanks they performed a "running short arm inspection."

MERLIN SHENNUM • *Instead of the usual formation inspection that was up close and personal, we were forced to strip and run naked in a line past the medical staff. They counted the incident as an official inspection, and we got out of an up close and personal look. Everyone, no matter their medical reason, was getting on the boat heading to England.*

On 6 September 1942, the men of Fox Company fell out with their barracks bags packed. They soon found themselves ferried into New York Harbor from Camp Shanks. After gulping down a cup of coffee and a donut from the Red Cross, they were climbing the gangplank of the HMS *Samaria*, a six-hundred-foot cruise ship converted to a troop transport. An observer looking closely at the line of olive drab troopers climbing the plank would have seen that one carried an American Indian–style bow and arrow along with his cumbersome bag and rifle, and that another was wearing a raccoon cap under his helmet. Both apparently eccentric soldiers would soon make history with the 101st Airborne.

On board the overcrowded *Samaria*, each soldier was assigned a bunk belowdecks along with a trooper from another unit. The double-booked vessel resorted to having one group of enlisted men sleep on deck at night, while a second group slept in the quadruple-stacked bunks.

Each day the sleeping arrangement was alternated, but the above-deck living soon won favor over the sardine-like life below. Life jackets were issued and had to be worn at all times. Once settled on board, the ship raised anchor and with tugboat support headed out toward the Atlantic. The paratroopers caught their last glimpse of that amazing symbol of freedom, the Statue of Liberty. All hoped to return soon to family and friends, but for some it would be the last glimpse of America they would ever have.

The *Samaria* being a British vessel, its crew and its mess were uniquely British as well. There was no American "chow" on the messdeck, and the food was difficult for even the most hardened soldier to stomach. Boiled fish, stewed green tomatoes, herring, and powdered eggs were served twice a day. For a more traditional GI breakfast, an effort was made to choke down corn flakes soaked in powdered milk. Coffee was horrible, tea tolerable, and fresh bread with jam was the unit's favorite "meal." With time Roy Zerbe actually began to like the bizarre new diet, and Bill True managed to stomach a bit of the new menu as well. Most, like Gus Patruno, resorted to buying candy bars and other snacks from the commissary on the boat.

As the ship swayed and bobbed, zigzagging across the Atlantic, sea-sickness spread like wild fire. Like flying in an airplane, for many in the 506th, being at sea was also a first-time event. Art Peterson and James "Rebel" Waters turned as green as pickles, became violently ill, and remained incapacitated for the entire trip. The enclosed decks quickly were wet with vomit, creating a stench that, combined with body odors and the smell from clogged toilets, made the open decks the place to be.

However, for some the excitement of the voyage kept them active and occupied. Marion Grodowski, invigorated by his trip to sea, spent his days standing near the prow of the ship, watching the deck rise and fall with the waves, feeling the mist and spray of the ocean on his face. Inspections of weapons, lifeboat drills, and company assemblies broke the monotony of voyage. Craps and poker games started, and money changed hands each day. Manning Haney would arrive in England almost $3,000 richer than when he left New York. He seemed to always be lucky.

Showers became a topic of discussion among the troops. Saltwater was used for the enlisted men's showers, and with the almost impossible task of maintaining a supply of hot water, it was usually cold as well. Officers encouraged the men to shower, even though their soap barely made a lather when combined with saltwater. Most managed to get three showers during the voyage, but one trooper, much to the disgust of the company, never showered at all.

The *Samaria*, along with the cluster of other transport ships and escorts it had traveled with, arrived in Liverpool on 15 September 15. After a day of delays, the troops disembarked and, once again overburdened with gear, marched to a railway station.

A train took them from Liverpool to the county of Wiltshire, about seventy-five miles west of London. From there blacked-out trucks drove them to their new home in the small, picturesque village of Aldbourne.

CHAPTER 5

ENGLAND

After arrival in the storybook-like village of Aldbourne, the men of Company F found themselves calling a row of Nissen huts home. Companies D and E mainly had horse stalls for their barracks. Headquarters Company and the medical detachment also drew the Nissen huts.

Located on a swampy skirt of town, the Nissen huts were concrete slab–floored shelters with roofs and walls made of an overlapping half circle of corrugated steel. There were doors on each end, as well as a pair of windows. To the untrained eye it looked identical to the American version, the familiar Quonset hut. Sixteen men shared a hut, which contained eight wooden double bunk beds and a small stove. The stove burned coke, a porous and cheaper version of coal. Between the coke and the size of the stove, hut heating became either an art form or an exercise in futility, depending on the quality of the kindling for the rationed coke.

The men were issued mattress covers and led to a nearby haystack. After filling the covers with hay, the company trudged back to the huts with the mattresses stuffed like ticks. Many of the men woke in the morning to a half-inch layer of cold water on the floors of their huts. They soon learned to live with the minor flooding and wet concrete.

During the following days, they made improvements to their new barracks. After a heavy dusting, shelves and racks were built for clothing and gear. Marion Grodowski and Johnny Jackson were tasked with going into the town of Swindon to pick up some paint. A taxi took them not only for their paint but to several pubs as well. After numerous pints of warm beer, the duo returned by taxi, along with their paint cans, to their home in Aldbourne. After stumbling from their cab, paint cans in hand, they staggered past their company in formation. The two were quickly put to bed. Manning Haney brought the two trays of food from the mess hall later in the evening, as they were too ill to get out of bed.

Hut interiors were painted in the limited four color choices available to Jackson and Grodowski. The Second Platoon's interior was as red as a whorehouse, and the Third Platoon's preference was dark blue walls with a sky-blue ceiling. Battling cold weather and rainy days, Gus Patruno led a group in laying bricks in front of the huts and building walkways to keep their boots and the troops from the soggy ground. Cabinet-style radios were privately purchased in nearby Swindon for the barracks, and a few pinup pictures were put up. Men were issued two weeks' worth of personal rations to stow in their barracks as well, consisting of fourteen packs of cigarettes, six candy bars, a tube of shaving cream, and two packs of razor blades.

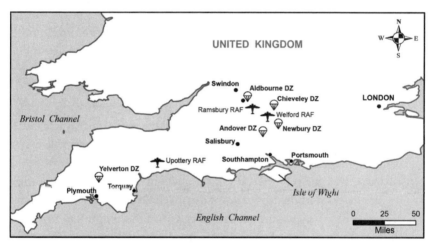

UK TRAINING

The Second Platoon's Bob Janes wrote home about the new experience in England in early October, a drastic but fascinating change from his life growing up in the woods of Oregon and Washington:

"Somewhere in England"

Dear Mom & Dad,

I imagine you have heard the old saying, "There will always be an England" but I hope I always won't be in England. As luck would have it I arrived over here just at the wrong time as the nasty weather is just beginning. I am wearing more clothes right now than I ever did at home in the middle of winter.

I imagine you are wondering about the customs, etc of the English. Well to begin with as you probably already know, they drive on the left side of the road and their cars are about the size of an Austin or a little bigger. But, this is very practical as everything else I have seen over here, since these small cars are very easy on gas and very maneuverable in the narrow places that you find in these cramped cities. All their houses, I mean the houses that I have seen in the villages, have thatched roofs made of straw. These villages are very neat and tidy as everything else that I have seen on the island.

Nothing is thrown away or wasted. The money exchange is very different and confusing. To start with they have the half penny, penny, three pence, six pence, then the shilling which is about twenty cents in our money, half crown (.50) and crown ($1.00) and the pound note which is about four dollars in American money. There are many other coins and notes but I don't thoroughly understand them yet, so you can see I couldn't explain them to you.

All the villages seem to have their share of pubs where the old fogies go to play dominoes, darts, and drink ale and stout which tastes something like that home brew Dad used to make. I haven't had many connections with the English yet but those that I have met in the local village seem to be very nice, but right down in their hearts I think they resent the boisterous, forward, loud spoken American whose soldiers are paid three times as much as theirs. I am not going to go into this subject anymore until I find out for myself just what it's all about. As far as I'm concerned the Limies are nice people.

All the fellows in the hutment that I live in chipped in two pounds ($8.00) apiece and bought a radio the other day. It cost $128.00. It isn't half as nice as the radios that you could buy in the U.S. for that price, but I think I have had my two pounds of enjoyment out of it already. We get mostly foreign stations and the best dance music is from a German station. The German version of American swing isn't too bad either.

Well folks I hope this letter finds you all feeling fine. Please don't worry about me because I am feeling fine. I have an enormous appetite and should get fat, but paratroopers get plenty of exercise you know! Tell everyone hello, with all my love.

Your Son, Bob

Maneuvers soon began on 6 October, and the 7th saw the company involved in regiment-size field problems with mock attacks of a town. After marching two and a half miles from town and setting up camp, it was involved in battalion-size maneuvers on the 12th and 13th. The next two days were spent with maneuvers at the platoon level. On the 15th the company returned to the relative comfort and luxury of hot meals, Nissen huts, and bunk beds.

The tough training was rewarded with weekend passes, and the men left in small groups for Swindon and London. One member of the First Platoon, Pvt. Iver Odegaard, went AWOL while on pass in London on the 21st. "Odie," as he was known to his platoon mates, had found himself a well-to-do British Army widow and moved in with her. He remained there until 21 November when, feeling guilty, he returned. However, Odie did not return without a plan. He went into the moors and dirtied and tore his uniform, scratched himself up, and made himself look generally the worse for wear. He then turned himself in, claiming he had no recollection of what had happened or where he had been. He was immediately taken to the hospital for what the company's morning report referred to as "Possible Concussion of Brain followed by Amnesia." "Odie" stuck to his amnesia story throughout a battery of doctors' interviews and medical exams, and returned to the unit on 13 December with no disciplinary action having been taken. His secret was concealed by the men of the First Platoon.

During the early morning hours of 16 November, Fox Company climbed into trucks and rode thirty miles to an airfield. The men geared up in parachutes, completed their prejump equipment checks, and climbed into C-47 transports at 0700. After a forty-minute plane ride, the company jumped in the area of Andover. After assembly, trucks took the men back to Aldbourne, now a short eighteen miles away. Noted in the company's morning report, prepared by 1st Lt. Freeling Colt that day, unit morale was "excellent."

In early December, field maneuvers continued as the unit trained as mechanized infantry. With a tank unit in support, Company F spent the second week riding on tanks and in armored vehicles, learning how to safely and quickly jump clear of their ride and maneuver around the battlefield. Coordination was also practiced in radio communication, hand signals, and joint fire and maneuver combat tactics. This brief training would be critical in combat.

Training on other topics continued as well, including first aid, chemical and gas warfare, map and compass reading, and the use of sound-activated field phones. For some, their previous training had already brought them nearly to perfection in knowledge and practice. But for others the repetition was needed to hone their multitude of skills and make their reaction in training, and ability in action, second nature. Several men from each platoon also went off to Scotland for demolition training with British commandos. "Down time" from training for the rest of the company was spent on cross-country marches, physical training, and drill.

Another jump was planned for mid-December. Having traveled sixteen miles by truck, the company pulled into Welford Airfield at 0815. After the usual and now almost routine gearing up, the troopers climbed into transport planes and were in the air within a half hour. The flight took them down toward Yelverton (RAF Harrowbeer) near Plymouth, for a mock assault on a radar station. As they approached the drop zone, several men standing in the doors of their planes were shocked to see two fighter planes falling from the sky afire. Unknown to the paratroopers, two German fighter planes had moved in behind them to attack the defenseless formation. British fighters pounced on the two before they could act, and the hunters quickly became the hunted.

Not out of the danger for the day, the company did its lowest drop ever, at about two hundred feet. Parachutes opened as men exited their planes in rapid succession. As the paratroopers looked up to make sure their parachutes opened correctly, they hit the ground. One man passed through power lines with no problems, and the company had its tightest jump pattern to date. The astonished looks on the faces of the radar ground crew must have surely matched those of the paratroopers, who seemed to touch the ground seconds after jumping.

After assembling from the drop zone, the company completed its mock assault of the radar station and ended the maneuver before the noon hour was up. Captain Mulvey called the men together to explain the dogfight, and said that certain tragedy had been averted by the Royal Air Force. Instructions were then given not to speak about the incident or their jump altitude until further notice. Toward evening they were flown back to Welford Airfield. Trucks took Company F back to Aldbourne for a late dinner in the mess hall.

Later that month Supreme Headquarters Allied Expeditionary Force (SHAEF) conducted a surprise inspection of the Second Battalion's camp at Aldbourne. Joe Flick had painted a realistic life-size image of Betty Grable on the exterior door of the First Platoon's hut. Identical to the famous pinup except that she was nude, the painting gave the appearance of a naked blond woman attempting to knock on the hut's door. Although the First Platoon's artwork was admired by the SHAEF staff, it was the Third Platoon that was noted as having the initiative desired by SHAEF. In addition to the two shades of blue paint used to adorn the inside, oak shelves held neatly stacked toiletries, and an ironing board was folded against the hut's interior door. The passes given as awards were well received by the men of the Third Platoon.

New Year's Day passed and left the men of Fox 506th like any other day in the daily fog and rain of England, but with the hope that by the following year they would all be back home with family and friends. The training and routine continued, however, with Vince Occhipinti returning from Bomb Reconnaissance School with the US First Army. Bud Edwards wrote home about camp conditions and a request for quality-of-life items.

Dear Mother & Dad,
I just got off of K.P. and decided to write to you before I turn in. I also might go down to the Red Cross Canteen here in camp and get cup of coffee and a sandwich. They also have a phonograph, magazines, books, and writing tables. It sure is a nice place to have.
Would you please send me some wool gloves, heavy work socks, a double edged razor, some cookies or candy, and can you also send some cigars? I believe that will do for now . . .

Love Bud

With all the hard training going on, the men looked forward to passes away from camp. When the pubs in Aldbourne filled, the party spilled over to Swindon and its surrounding area. After complaints by local pub owners, seven-day furloughs were even given to ship the boisterous men off to Birmingham and London. With plenty of cash, confidence, and youthful energy,

Company F members managed to get themselves into some sort of exciting event no matter where they wandered off to. Men had to be assigned once again to follow them around and try to keep them away from trouble. The Third Platoon's Art Peterson was on continual assignment to keep the boys in line and get them back to camp in one piece. A handsome Hispanic American of linebacker size, Peterson had the charisma to sweet-talk the happy drunks into trucks for the ride home, as well as the physical strength to toss the angry drunks in with them.

DAVID KENYON WEBSTER • *Well, now the second platoon of F Company has wrecked the Three Tuns pub in Swindon and somebody has just knocked out one of our British bus drivers. No wonder Atlanta, Columbus, Fayetteville, and Charlotte find the paratroopers a trifle wearing.*

Bob Janes wrote home in a January 1944 letter:

I was going to answer the nice V-Mail letters and the long Air Mail letter from you and Dad tonight but the C.O. just came up and told me that I was going to town tonight on C.P. duty (Chutist Police). So, I will answer them Monday night. All I have to do is go around to all the pubs and see that the troops are least able to leave the bar when they tear the joints up. I was in town last night and was going to buy a few drinks and come home, but nine tenths of the soldiers in the ETO were there and what pubs weren't already sold out didn't even open. I will write a longer letter soon so don't worry about me and write often.

Not everyone in the company went looking for, or managed to get into, trouble. Raul Ochoa went to Swindon and watched movies at the theater. They were usually Westerns. As Ochoa was from southern Texas, the movies were a welcome escape, not only from training but from the pub fights as well. Merlin Shennum and Gus Patruno exercised horses for a family at a nearby estate, spending hours riding in the mist and fog, all the while rotating through the family's stock of horses.

Initiative and improvisation were taught both in the field and the classroom. It was drilled into the men to take every opportunity that presented itself, weigh the risks, and act with skilled aggression and speed. The heating of their barracks was no exception. The tiny stove in each hut was only a foot in diameter and a few feet high, and barely put off any heat. The trick was to get a good hot fire started using wood or for some, like Len Hicks, using small bits of plastic explosive, which burned like compressed fuel. After the fire started, coke was placed in the stove and could produce a tolerable amount of heat. Coal was what was needed, and Company F knew right where to get it.

On the roadside between Swindon and Aldbourne, a pile of coal was spotted and pilfered by the men of the First Platoon. The mess hall at Aldbourne also had an ample supply of coal for heating. The Third Platoon saw to it that the mess hall's coal vanished as well. After multiple complaints from all the coal's intended owners, the coal was traced to the majority of Company F's huts. Punishment was swift.

The men were told to assemble wearing their fatigues. A truck lumbered up to the company formation, its back full of buckets and wash tubs. Each man took either two buckets, or two men shared a wash tub. The company then marched seven miles to a railhead and a large pile of coal. The containers were filled, and the coal was carried the seven miles back to camp where it was piled. Hand distribution was the next mode of delivery to all the victims of the theft, which took days to complete. As an additional punishment, the company was forced to sleep for a week in pup tents in front of the huts. The row of tents soon became referred to as "Sticky Fingers Lane." Having been taught a lesson, the company returned to its barracks after a week of pup tent life. But the men soon fell back on their training for using initiative and improvisation, and the mess hall's coal disappeared again the following week. It was never located, but Fox Company's huts remained remarkably warm.

Coal was not the only thing that was misappropriated by the men of Company F. Country boys such as Roy Zerbe soon began shooting "the king's" rabbits while on field maneuvers. The rabbit was a delicious supplement to typical Army rations on overnight maneuvers. However, someone in the battalion's hierarchy caught wind of the unauthorized hunting, and those caught in possession of the rabbits ended up having to pay a fine. However, more rabbits were shot and eaten than paid for by the men of Company F, so the modest fine was worth the risk. The hunting, like the coal theft, continued.

Specialized training sent the Second Platoon's 2nd Lt. Charles Semon off to the Isle of Wight for a full three weeks of instruction at the Battle School in Shorwell. Then the company, along with eleven new replacements, was trucked to Ramsbury on 12 March for its first night jump. The men geared up and at 2100 found themselves jumping out into the night sky two miles west of Chieveley for a field problem. All did not go as planned.

JOHN TAYLOR • *The military had sent over new planes equipped with buzzers that went off to signal the paratroopers when it was time to jump. On the first drop, the planes were at some point in rendezvous getting the formation together when the buzzer went off unexpectedly. Some of the boys didn't have their chutes on all the way and some of them, like Dude Stone, went out with just one strap on. Lieutenant [Thomas "Dusty"] Rhodes had his reserve chute deploy accidentally, and it skinned his face up. Fortunately he was the last man out, so the reserve chute didn't bother the other jumpers.*

All the men made it out of the plane all right. When I jumped, I couldn't see a thing. The first thing I knew, I skidded head first into the ground. I got a mouth full of dirt, and my helmet came down and skinned my nose all up. Trying to see down, I guess I had pulled my feet out of the way, and leaning over my feet I must have landed in a prone position. It didn't hurt me, but shook me up pretty good.

Bill True discovered later that the plane had actually lost power in one of its engines and the buzzer had been activated as a bailout warning as the plane fell in altitude. The men had exited at five hundred feet over a wooded area, but all landed without injury. Dude Stone had snapped on one harness strap and his reserve across his chest, and jumped without hooking up to the static line but used the smaller reserve parachute on his chest to bring him to the ground. He was lucky to not have been pulled from out his harness when his parachute deployed. The stick of lucky troopers also missed the main drop zone and thus managed to avoid the maneuvers in the field. One paratrooper had a humorous experience after the emergency jump.

TOM ALLEY • *I had just landed after our emergency low-altitude jump when a jeep drove up with two astonished British soldiers riding inside. Apparently several jeeps from the airfield and soldiers in the area watched what had happened with our jump from the crippled C-47 and drove out to find us. When the jeep pulled up, one soldier explained he had just spoken with another paratrooper down the road who was only wearing his backpack parachute, and it was still packed tight and never deployed. And he was not injured in any way! The jumper, Dude Stone, told the soldiers we were so well trained and conditioned for emergency jumps, that using the parachute was optional. I confirmed his story, and after I refused a ride, the jeep drove off with two wide-eyed, astonished soldiers inside.*

The truth was that Dude Stone had caught his reserve parachute in a tree on his landing, and unable to free it, left it behind. When he walked out on the road with his main parachute on, he could not resist telling a tall tale to the British jeep crew. When the story later circulated, a good laugh was had by all the members of the First Platoon. The remainder of the company made their jumps without incident. And after moving north and completing a night of training, the rest of the company took trucks from Beedon back to Aldbourne.

Three-day passes followed the maneuvers for the bulk of the company. On return to Aldbourne, they were sent back into the field for a cross-country trek that involved training in river crossing. In boats the men practiced ferrying squads across a small river using ropes, which involved reconnaissance of the riverbanks, deploying on both banks, and supporting each other in the process. The practice crossings, although in a much smaller river, worked better than their previous "amphibious maneuvers" back in Tennessee.

Men of Fox Company were still being shipped off for specialized training. Some went to receive orientation on the Pathfinder program. Pathfinders were specialized teams of paratroopers trained to parachute in front of a larger invasion force and set up drop zones using lights and radio equipment. Charlie Malley and Stevie Pustola were the two Fox Company men who eventually completed the program. Jerry Farley had already gone off to the 327th Fighter Control Squadron to learn how to be a forward air controller, using a radio to direct Allied air attacks on enemy ground positions.

On 23 March the entire Second and Third Battalions of the 506th, along with the 506th Regimental Headquarters and the 377th Parachute Field Artillery Battalion, made a mass jump for a grandstand of high-ranking officials. The 506th's First Battalion remained on the ground for an inspection by the reviewing staff. Watching the jump that day was Prime Minister Winston Churchill, Gen. Dwight Eisenhower, Lt. Gen. Omar

Bradley, and the 101st's own Maj. Gen. Maxwell Taylor, Brig. Gen. Don Pratt, and Brig. Gen. Anthony McAuliffe.

John Taylor was jumpmaster on this flight—"the Churchill jump"— the first time in his Army career to do so. Being in charge of the men in the plane and determining when they jumped was a thrill. Even more exciting was seeing Eisenhower and Churchill close up as they mingled with the men after they landed. The view from both in the air drifting down and watching the massive drop from the ground was impressive for all involved. The experience inside the plane prior to the jump was detailed in a letter home by the Second Platoon's Bob Janes:

> I can't tell you how many jumps I have now but everyone knows that I am in the paratroops, and the paratroops jump, so I guess it won't hurt to tell you about one of my jumps. Well to start with I happened to be in one of the last two trucks that got lost on the way to the airport. I think we toured all of England that night and arrived at the airport in just enough time to put chutes on and climb into the airplane. I like it that way as it gives a fellow less time to sit and sweat them out.
>
> After waiting about five minutes they raised the load of crazy paratroopers up into that great place they call space, and headed for a field somewhere in England that was going to receive a bunch of fearless men from Mars.
>
> I was sitting there chain smoking a few packages of cigarettes knowing that the only way I was going to get out of that plane was through that little small door in the rear of the plane via a thing called a parachute. I was also thinking about what you folks were doing at the time, thinking about my wife, and looking at that wedding band she gave me that I have never removed since the day she gave it to me, and use it for a good luck piece.
>
> Well it didn't seem like we had been in the air but a few moments when the jumpmaster says get ready. I take a long drag on that good old Lucky Strike and grasp my static line hook fastener and wait for the order, "Stand Up and Hook Up." "Stand Up and Hook Up" yells the jumpmaster. I managed to stand up and hook up to the cable on the top of the plane. Then we check each other's chute and wait for the pay off order which is "Let's go!" I guess I

forgot to tell you but I am the number four man which is closest I have been to the door since my first jump when I was number one man in the door.

About that time the jumpmaster yells "Is everybody happy?" and everybody yells "Yes" lying like hell. Well that green light comes on and the jump happy jumpmaster yells "Let's Go!" and the next thing I know I am out the door counting one thousand, two thousand, three— whoomph and there is that big beautiful parachute dangling me a few hundred feet above the ground. When I say a few hundred feet I mean it too, because if they start dropping us any lower I will start drawing submarine pay.

Well the first thing you do after your chute opens is check your canopy for blown panels, or thrown suspension lines. After doing this you start looking for a place to land. Check the wind drift and made a left body turn and then I was right in the middle of a turnip patch. I landed like a bomber with its wheels up due to a ground wind, but I was lucky and did not even get a scratch. . . .

Sunday services were available to all the men at Aldbourne, but only the truly devoted seemed to have the motivation after a night of drinking to get up early and go to church. One Sunday, Dick Knudsen and Bob Janes found it difficult to roust the remaining sleepy paratroopers for church. Chester Nakelski was asleep in his bunk still clothed and wearing his jump boots from the night before. So, the duo coated his boots with a heavy layer of shoe polish. Then they went outside and nosed a bazooka rocket into a soggy ditch alongside their hut, and ran wire from the bazooka back into the barrack and attached it to a flashlight. They then set Nakelski's shoe polish-coated boots on fire. When the hot-footed Chester sprang from his bunk, they detonated the bazooka round using the flashlight's switch. Between Nakelski's yelling and the mud-splattering explosion outside, the hut's occupants were up and alert in no time, if not heading off to church.

Two days later the men took an afternoon ride by truck to the British Army's Imber Range. A bivouac was established, and the following morning was spent on live fire field problems using every weapon in the company's arsenal, including the bazooka. The excitement of the live fire exercises ended later that night with a truck ride back to Aldbourne, followed by a day of routine weapon cleaning and inspection.

Len Hicks had been assigned as the company armorer-artificer in the headquarters section. Two large crates in which American glider planes had been shipped to England arrived at the camp for Hicks to use as an armory and weapon repair shop. Hicks was able to miss out occasionally on maneuvers and field problems due to his work in the repair shop. One afternoon 1st Lt. Carl MacDowell, the company's executive officer, stopped in on Hicks in his "shop" carrying a package under his arm. When MacDowell asked Hicks for a can opener, he told the lieutenant that he only had his trench knife. MacDowell closed the shop door behind him and locked it. Then he produced from the package a large can labeled "Florida Orange Juice." After a few holes were poked into the can, MacDowell challenged the Californian Hicks to see how Florida orange juice compared with California's. A taste led Hicks to the conclusion that the juice from the two states was remarkably different. MacDowell's brother, who was the president of the Florida Citrus Fruit Growers, had actually canned his sibling's favorite booze in the can. Hicks kept the contents a secret, and MacDowell was able to keep his stock away from the other company officers. It was a victory for both men, who were able to share several cans of "juice" over the next few months.

On Easter Sunday, 9 April 1944, the company was off to church for traditional holiday services. During the service, the congregation read "The Paratroopers' Easter Prayer," written by Protestant chaplain Tildon McGee:

Lord, as we worship Thee on this Easter Morning, fortify us, we pray Thee, against the many perils that lay ahead. We humbly face Thee with true penitence for our sins, and we wholly dedicate ourselves to Thee. Lord, when to the battle we go, as over the enemy we fly with shells bursting around us, save us from undue concern and give us firm control over all our fears, knowing that Thou art near. And when we jump from giant transports in the sky quickly to descend into the midst of hostile fire, help us, Lord, perfectly to trust in Thee. To those of us who must perish in the fight, grant us peace of soul and rest with Thee; and to those of us these dangers do survive, Lord, God of Hosts, give us strength our mission to accomplish.

The unit was soon alerted for departure, so the men prepared for what they suspected would be another large maneuver or field problem. During the early morning hours of 25 April, trucks were boarded and a one-hour ride was taken to Newbury. By 0630 the men had boarded train cars and were off to Torquay, over 180 miles away, near the southwestern tip of England. After their pleasant ride the men marched for three miles to the Hydro Hotel in Paignton, where they were billeted for the evening. A fantastic meal awaited them that evening in the hotel: pork chops, potatoes, peas, and dessert. Early in the morning the company again climbed into trucks and rode thirty miles to where a camp was established. They then prepared to participate in the largest exercise for the upcoming invasion.

Using trucks to simulate planes, the men made "tailgate jumps" onto the battlefield, with sticks being disbursed in a typical drop pattern. The exercise, on 27 April, went from 0230 until 2100, with the company securing roads, crossroads, and small towns. The company spent the following day acting as an outpost for the 101st Airborne Division's command post. The maneuvers continued into the next night when trucks took the company to a train station in Dartmouth. The weary troopers climbed aboard a row of train cars that took them through the night 180 miles to Hungerford's train station, from which trucks drove them into Aldbourne.

Passes to Swindon were welcomed by the men of Fox Company and with "latrine rumors" of the impending invasion of Europe running rampant, the troopers headed off to their favorite pubs for a beer. Regardless of the men's activity—chasing girls, playing darts, drinking, or simply eating a bag of fish and chips—their thoughts and conversations were about the invasion and where it might be. Everyone had his own theory, but France was generally considered the best bet.

The feeling and tone of activity around Aldbourne took on a more serious and hectic pace than ever before. At the roll call after Sunday services on 7 May and during the morning roll call formation on the 8th, the company was read a notice from division headquarters. It included the following:

Article of War.58 DESERTION
Any person subject to military law who deserts or attempts to desert the service of the United States shall, if the offense be committed in a time of war, suffer death, or such other punishment as a court-martial may direct. . . .

The following day three medics from the 506th Medical Detachment were assigned to Company F, with one responsible for each platoon: Bill Baird, Millard Moore, and Joe Droogan. The same day, the usual truck-to-train routine began again, and a late afternoon train ride took the battalion back to the far southwestern corner of England, to Camp Upottery at Upottery Airfield. Over the following two days, the men prepared for another night jump. This time they would be jumping near Newbury with full gear and equipment, including equipment bundles full of supplies.

On 11 May at 2115, the heavily burdened troops "chuted up," climbed into the all too familiar transport planes, and took off for their night jump exercise. This time the planes flew back in the direction of Aldbourne, and the jump was made at 0100. Jumpmasters released parachute cargo bundles just prior to the troopers' exit. Inside the bundles were rations, water, medical supplies, radio equipment, ammunition, and heavy weapons. The bundles had red lights attached to them that the troopers were supposed to watch for as they descended so they could locate them on the ground.

John Taylor landed on a roadway, striking his head on the ground and knocking a head full of stars into his view. He had been watching the red lights on the cargo bundles and did not pay attention to how low he was getting to the ground. Once he saw the red lights stop moving, it was too late to make any adjustments with his parachute, and his body made a rapid introduction to the hard-packed road.

Marion Grodowski somersaulted through his parachute as he stepped out the door into the darkness that night. With the opening shock of the parachute, he lost his helmet and caught his foot in a riser line, causing him to be hung upside down in his parachute.

MARION GRODOWSKI • *I struggled to free myself and could not get my boot loose. As I was hanging there, I saw another paratrooper drift past silhouetted by the moon. It reminded me of Halloween, with a witch flying past the moon on a broomstick. Funny the things you think about when hanging upside down in parachute.*

Grodowski's landing, however—like Taylor's—lacked any comedy. Hanging upside down caused him to land on his head, knocking himself out in the process. When he came to, he had a terrible headache. It was daylight as well, and the unit had already assembled and moved out. It took several hours for him to catch up with the company.

The First Platoon's Cliff Vallieres unfortunately made a tree landing and was badly injured when his chute broke free and he crashed through the branches to the ground forty feet below. His injuries ended his career with the Airborne.

Overall, the remainder of the company had an excellent night jump. The men had been briefed to assemble on a light in the drop zone. The Second Squad of the Second Platoon initially confused the drop zone light with two girls on bicycles, one of which had a bright white headlamp, but after such misidentified lights in the area were abandoned, the company made assembly in record time for a night drop.

Field problems rounded out the day, and then trucks took them back to Aldbourne. On arrival to camp, news spread that Paul Peterson of the Second Platoon had been injured badly enough in the night jump to be taken to the hospital. He would eventually be shipped home due to his injuries.

Colonel Sink assembled and spoke to the battalion in formation, praising the men of Fox Company: "If all the men jumped like Fox Company, the 506th would be a jumping regiment." He was impressed with the company's ability to jump in a tight group and to assemble quickly, and made this known to the rest of the Second Battalion. It was a welcome comment and a proud moment for the company—recognition of their hard work in training.

The camp activity intensified. Marvin Sims was transferred to the 101st's 81st antitank/antiaircraft unit, Lt. John C. Williams left for regimental headquarters, and a new lieutenant joined the company with the First Platoon, William Brooks. The desertion notice was read again to the company formation. White spade figures, the 506th's designated identification symbol, were painted on the sides of their steel helmets. Paperwork was finalized for payroll and life insurance. Damaged gear was turned in for new issue, and jumpsuits were impregnated with an antigas solution. Weapons were inspected down to every spring, pin, and part, and the company's lone sharpening stone ran all day long putting a razor's edge on fighting knives and bayonets.

Preparation for war was not without its moments of laughter and excitement. The Second Platoon decided to borrow the company motorcycle for a little off-road riding. It was usually reserved for headquarters members to use for messenger service, but it was assumed no one would mind. After several members took their turn riding the motorcycle around on the parade ground, Matthew Carlino asked if he could ride.

The Long Island native had never ridden a motorcycle before. After a quick instruction on how to start and ride, Carlino took off. The bike accelerated in a wide circle, while Carlino repeatedly yelled, "How do I stop it?" After several sweeping high-speed passes, Carlino ran the bike into a ditch and then into the side of a hut, launching himself up onto the side of the dwelling. He was not hurt, at least not physically, but according to Marion Grodowski, "As a fellow choirboy I was shocked to hear the language that came out of his mouth after he crashed. He thought up and said some words that even growing up in Chicago I had never heard before."

The town of Aldbourne saw the entire Second Battalion off. They had fresh crew cuts, were clad in their jumpsuits, sported newly issued helmet nets, and had the division's Screaming Eagle patches on their shoulders. Never before seeing the men all wearing the same complete uniforms, the townspeople sensed that this was really going to be a real goodbye. Handkerchiefs waved, girlfriends gave final hugs and kisses, and tears rolled down cheeks as the convoy of trucks pulled away. From Company F's 28–29 May morning report:

> The Co. entrucked and left Camp Aldbourne 1600 arrived at Hungerford 1620 hours total distance traveled by truck 9 miles entrained and left Hungerford at 1700 arrived at Camp at 2100 total distance traveled by rail 120 miles. Forward Station: Camp Williams, Devonshire

The Second Battalion's new accommodations at Camp Williams were a change from the huts, stables, and bunk beds of Aldbourne. The housing consisted of pyramidal squad tents, similar to those used back in the unit's first days at Toccoa. Men were briefed on the day's events and assigned billeting in the tents. Gear was dropped on cots, mess kits removed from duffle bags, and the men fell in at the mess tent for chow. Crates filled with supplies and ammunition were covered and draped in camouflage netting. The camp was ringed with barbed wire, and armed guards were posted twenty-four hours a day.

Fox Company was scheduled first for chow that day, but E Company was already lined up at the Battalion Mess Tent. 1st Sgt. Willie Morris went over and spoke to E Company's first sergeant, William Evans, questioning why his company was in line to eat first. Not pleased with Evans's answer,

Morris punched Evans, knocking him onto a table. "It was like something from a Western," recalled Bob Janes, "like a cowboy sliding down a bar full of drinks." The fight was over before it started, and Fox Company took its slot back at the front of the mess hall line.

Meals in the marshaling area turned out to be the best the men had ever had in the Army. Although many recognized it as being "fattened up for slaughter," the chow was much appreciated. Dinners consisted of steaks, chops, roast beef, and fruit cocktail. They had pancakes, bacon, real fried eggs, hot cereal, juice, and coffee for breakfast.

The day after the company's arrival, its officers attended briefings on the upcoming invasion. In a guarded tent they were told of the objectives of each company, battalion, and regiment in the 101st Airborne Division. Aerial photographs, maps, and scale models, also known as sand tables, were shown to inform the officers of each task assigned to them for the operation. The rumors of where they were going to fight ended: they would be parachuting into Normandy, France.

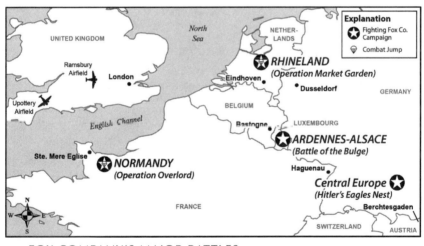

FOX COMPANY'S MAJOR BATTLES

Later that day the noncommissioned officers (NCOs) were briefed on their role in the liberation of Normandy.

JOHN TAYLOR • *My first view of everything was with the company commander, the platoon leaders, and the NCOs in the long, narrow briefing tent. This tent was about one hundred feet long, eight feet wide, and ten feet high. Inside were sand tables with miniature buildings and vegetation which modeled the terrain of the area, along with maps, air photos, and schematic drawings of the place. Throughout the week we would visit the briefing area with our squads and were given time to familiarize ourselves with the entire mission. It was then that we formulated our plans as to how our squad would complete its particular part of the picture. We knew at this time where we were going and what we were going to do. We did not know at this time when we were going.*

On 30 May the entire company was briefed, and every man in each platoon learned of their specific role in the invasion.

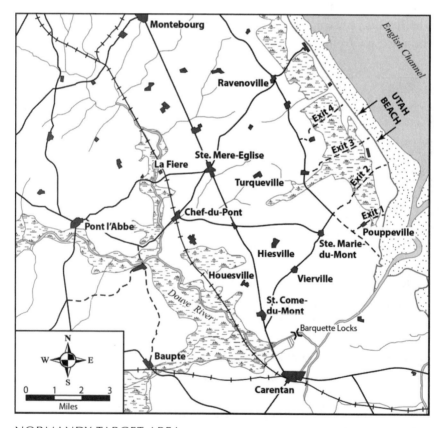

NORMANDY TARGET AREA

ROY ZERBE ● *They had made some very well constructed sand tables, with every road, river, house and tree displayed. The tables were each about ten feet by twenty and covered the tasks for the entire airborne invasion right down to our own specific objective.*

The company had the important role of taking and securing Pouppeville, a small village consisting of a couple dozen homes. It was just a short distance from Utah Beach, where one of the two US seaborne armies would be coming ashore. One of the roads that led from the beach ran directly into Pouppeville, so it was essential that Company F hold the town to stop any German reinforcements from making it to the beach, but also to wipe out any German soldiers who may have been fleeing back from the beach. The role was just one of dozens of small objectives for the 506th that, combined, would be crucial in securing the land behind the beach during the invasion. They were informed that their participation in the invasion was expected to last seventy-two hours.

Parachute equipment bundles were packed with medical supplies, weapons, spare parts, rations, and cans of ammunition. Men were issued ammunition for their personal weapons, and the remainder of the day was spent loading and adjusting their gear, filling magazines with cartridges, and sharpening knives and bayonets. The company's one wheeled sharpening stone ran continually over the next few days. Gus Patruno sharpened his knife so much that it took off a noticeable portion of the blade. Others used hand-held stones from their personal collections.

A number of the men removed from their duffle bags weapons that had been mailed from home and stowed them in gear bags and among the many pockets of their jumpsuits. Brass knuckles, garrotes made with piano wire, blackjacks, and an assortment of pistols flashed about the tents as men prepared for the unknown fight. Corporals were issued bolt-action M1903 Springfield rifles, grenade launchers, and rifle grenades. It did not go over well with many of the men who wanted firepower, not single-shot rifles. In addition to their stock of ammunition cartridges, each corporal was given a box of blank cartridges to use to launch the grenades off the end of their rifles. Marion Grodowski complained not only about the single-shot handicap of the Springfield but also his lack of training in its grenade launching function. But he was issued a .45-caliber semiautomatic pistol and hip holster, and sent on his way.

The following day was spent loading the equipment bundles onto the planes and fitting parachute harnesses to each man's preference. Weapons were inspected down to each pin, spring, and part. Any worn or damaged part was replaced. Weapons were cleaned, oiled, and reassembled.

Maps were issued to NCOs along with compasses. Officers had the same detailed maps, as well as escape kits with a silk map, a saw blade, and a tiny button-size compass. Some maps were based on an aerial photo of the drop zone and had the roads drawn on them.

Briefings over the sand tables continued daily. Eventually the men knew each road junction, key feature, and village's name in their invasion sector. Pouppeville's location was only one of many towns they could soon identify on a blank Normandy map. Other towns such as Sainte-Marie-du-Mont, Carentan, Hiesville, Houesville, Angoville-au-Plain, Holdy, Vierville, Sainte-Mère-Église, and Saint-Côme-du-Mont were put to memory as well. "We knew it all like the back of our hand," remembered bazooka-man Robert Noody.

On 3 June the men were each issued ten dollars' worth of "invasion money." It was in the form of French francs newly printed by the Allied military and was to be the temporary currency of a liberated France. The notes were small, colorful, and square, resembling play money from a child's board game, and had a small French flag on the back. Men were allowed to cash in their British money for the francs as well. Inevitably craps and poker games started, with invasion money as the ante and pot. Richard Buchter walked away at the end of one gambling session with 635 francs, pocketed with the hope of spending it in France.

One member of the company, Edgar Bishop, was seen flashing his newly acquired invasion money the next day to the cooks in the mess tent. The cooks were not part of the Airborne operation, and some in the unit felt Bishop may have been leaking sensitive information to personnel of less than credible integrity. Rumors were that company officers ordered Bishop to be disciplined for a breach of security. Some said that what happened occurred strictly because of enlisted men's peer pressure. Regardless, Bishop was beaten to a bloody pulp by four of the company's biggest and best fighters. He did not fight back. Bishop's injuries would not only send him to the camp hospital but also scratch him from the Company roster.

On the 4th the company was called to formation, and the jump rosters were read to the men. One trooper in the First Platoon, Ray Kermode, did not hear his name read. He protested, and Captain Mulvey relented, penciling him in for the jump. The plan was to leave that evening and parachute during the early morning hours into Normandy, but high winds forced the jump to be scrapped. The men remembered that the evening meal was fried chicken with strawberry ice cream for dessert, the first ice cream they had been served by the Army since their arrival in England. Men wrote letters home, sharpened knives, cleaned weapons, and with mixed feelings waited for the inevitable "go" order.

The following afternoon, while the men returned from the showers, the order was given. They would go to Normandy that night. Faces fresh from the shower were blackened with grease paint, burned cork, and ashes. After a final meal in the mess tent, the men headed off to locations about the camp for religious services for their respective denominations.

A short time later the company formed up wearing cotton underwear, wool shirts and pants, and jumpsuits. The tacky antigas chemical now coating the jumpsuits' fabric made them extremely warm and uncomfortable, especially for those soldiers who wore woolen long johns over their cotton underwear as well. Paper armbands treated with a gas-detecting paint were handed out and pulled onto right arms and attached at the epaulet.

The company made the quick trip to the airfield. The final placement of gear and parachutes began. The latter, previously drawn and adjusted, were stored inside each man's assigned aircraft. They were removed and, along with an inflatable life vest, were handed out to each man. The men's weapons and three days' worth of supplies, which they were to carry, included the following:

M1 rifle (disassembled into three pieces and enclosed in a canvas "Griswold bag").

M1 carbine, Thompson submachine gun, or Springfield M1903 rifle with grenade launcher.

Minimum of 96 rounds of ammunition for the M1 rifle, 300 rounds for the Thompson (in twenty-round magazines), 175 rounds for the M1 carbine, and 145 rounds for the M1903.

Four hand grenades.

Helmet with camouflage net. Some men put treated burlap cloth strips in the net, removed from camouflage netting at the camp.

Bayonet if carrying the M1 rifle.

Entrenching tool (folding shovel).

M3 fighting knife.

Gas mask and pouch.

Canteen of water (one quart).

Pistol belt or cartridge (pouched) belt.

Suspenders.

Musette bag containing one Hawkins mine, a raincoat (most tied it below the bag), underwear, toilet articles, and two cartons of cigarettes.

In pockets were four D-ration chocolate bars, six K-rations, a bottle of water purification tablets, maps, two British battle dressings, waterproof-cased matches, goggles, and condoms.

Let-down rope.

Switchblade knife (placed in a zippered pocket near the jumpsuit collar).

Wool or leather gloves.

Metal "cricket" (child's toy used for night identification by clicking)

First-aid pouch with Carlisle bandage and sulfa pills.

Parachutist first-aid kit (waxed bandage, morphine syrette, and tourniquet in a cloth pouch), typically tied to a boot.

Main backpack parachute and reserve (chest-pack) parachute.

Men with specialized assignments carried different or additional equipment:

Calvin Wright, wire-man:

Two spools of phone wire and sound powered phones in a British leg bag.

Robert Noody, bazooka-man:

Bazooka in a British leg bag with a bag containing three rockets.

Three rockets slung in a second bag over shoulder.

Ray Aebischer, machine gunner:

Machine gun and tripod in British leg bag with his loaded web gear and carbine.

One can of ammunition tied to his leg and another secured in a rigger-made bag.

Robert Stone, mortar-man:

Bipod (in a pouch between the web gear and reserve parachute).

Three mortar shells in a musette bag.

Gus Patruno, mortar-man:

Mortar tube in British leg bag with six mortar shells.

Land mine in a musette bag.

Alvin Wilson, mortar-man:

> Mortar base plate (in a pouch between the web gear and reserve parachute).
>
> Three mortar shells in a musette bag.

Louis Burton, radio-man:

> SCR-536 walkie-talkie (in a pouch strapped to leg).
>
> Nine sets of batteries (bagged).

Harry Ostrander, rifle-grenadier:

> Grenade launcher.
>
> Ten rifle grenades (six high-explosive, four antitank).

Joe Droogan, medic:

> Marine kit (large bag containing collapsible litter, bandages, pills).
>
> First-aid kit (morphine, sulfa powder, surgical instruments).

Len Hicks, armorer-artificer:

> Spare parts for all company firearms and three spare machine gun parts kits.
>
> Small tool set (all parts and tools carried in a British leg bag).

Those who did not have to carry specialized weapons or equipment carried either an extra can of machine gun ammunition or a mortar round in their musette bag. Smoke grenades were handed out to NCOs and all those who did not appear to be carrying enough already. Robert Janes was given a demolition bag filled with blocks of TNT.

The British leg bags were issued the day before, and no instructions were given on weight limitations for them. Only a few had made jumps with them before, while training with the British Army. The bag was a knee-high canvas pouch that had a fifteen-foot let-down rope attached and leg straps. The bag was meant to be attached to the wearer's leg with his foot inserted into a strap or slot on the bottom of the bag. It was designed so that on exiting the plane, the trooper would pull a cord that released the leg straps and dropped the bag below. The hanging bag was secured to the soldier by the let-down rope. Robert Noody, not wanting to be so close to his bazooka-filled bag when he landed, attached a second let-down rope to his harness and then secured it to the rope on the leg bag.

Each man was also given a copy of a letter from Colonel Sink and one from General Eisenhower:

OFFICE OF THE REGIMENTAL COMMANDER

Soldiers of the Regiment   D-Day

Today, as you read this, you are enroute to that great adventure for which you have trained for over two years.

Tonight is the night of nights.

Tomorrow throughout the whole of our homeland and the Allied world the bells will ring out the tidings that you have arrived, and the invasion for liberation has begun.

The hopes and the prayers of your dear ones accompany you. The confidence of your high Commanders go with you. The fears of the Germans are about to become a reality.

Let us strike hard. When the going is tough, let us go harder. Imbued with faith in the rightness of our cause, and the power of our might, let us annihilate the enemy where found.

May God be with each of you fine soldiers. By your actions let us justify His faith in us.

Robert Sink
Colonel

Eisenhower's letter:

Supreme Headquarters
Allied Expeditionary Force

SOLDIERS, SAILORS, AIRMEN OF THE
ALLIED EXPEDITIONARY FORCE

You are about to embark upon the Great Crusade, toward which we have striven these many months. The eyes of the world are upon you. The hopes and prayers of liberty-loving people everywhere march with you. In company with our brave Allies and brothers-in-arms on other Fronts, you will bring about the destruction of the German War machine, the elimination of Nazi tyranny over the oppressed peoples of Europe, and security for ourselves in a free world.

Your task will not be an easy one. Your enemy is well-trained, well-equipped and battle hardened. He will fight savagely.

But this is the year 1944! Much has happened since the Nazi triumphs of 1940–41. The United Nations have inflicted upon the Germans great defeats, in open battles, man-to-man. Our air offensive has seriously reduced their strength in the air and their capacity to wage war on the ground. Our Home Fronts have given us an overwhelming superiority in weapons and munitions of war, and placed at our disposal great reserves of trained fighting men. The tide has turned! The free men of the world are marching together to Victory!

I have full confidence in your courage, devotion to duty and skill in battle. We will accept nothing less than full Victory!

Good Luck! And let us all beseech the blessing of Almighty God upon this great and noble undertaking.

Dwight D. Eisenhower

The troopers pocketed their letters and made last minute adjustments to their gear and parachute harnesses. Motion sickness pills were handed out and taken. Like ducks they then waddled up to the doors of their assigned C-47s, planes #74 to #81 of the 439th Troop Carrier Group. The single step ladder that mounted off the plane's only door was extremely difficult to climb with all the extra equipment being carried. Many had to be boosted by fellow troopers and Army Air Corps crewmen. Those with the British leg bag were last to board and had a very difficult time lifting their overburdened leg. Some bags had been loaded with almost one hundred pounds of supplies. Once they were aboard, paper ice cream buckets were distributed in case of airsickness, and men were given a second motion sickness pill to take during the flight.

They were off to war.

CHAPTER 6

D-DAY FLIGHT

<hr>

The engines of the C-47s sputtered to life with their usual cough of smoke and oil. The planes began to taxi and, one by one, lumbered into the air. Before midnight the air armada of transports had joined up and was on its way to Normandy. The eight aircraft carrying the men of Company F were part of serial #12 which comprised thirty-six planes carrying the entire Second Battalion of the 506th. A total of 425 planes carried almost seven thousand paratroopers of the 101st, 120 of which carried the men of the 506th.

The aircraft for serial #12 were piloted by members of the 91st Squadron, 439th Troop Carrier Group, 9th Air Force, and flew in what is referred to as a "V of Vs." This allowed the planes to remain in a tight formation for a close drop of the paratroopers on their drop zone. The Second Battalion of the 506th was grouped as follows:

<hr>

BATTALION HQ			#46		
		#48	#47		
	#52		#49		
#54	#53	#51	#50		

<hr>

D COMPANY			#55		
		#57	#56		
	#61		#58		
#63	#62	#60	#59		

E COMPANY			#64			
		#66		#65		
	#70			#67		
#72		#71		#69	#68

F COMPANY			#73			
(#74–#81)			#75	#74		
	#79			#76		
#81		#80		#78	#77

In strict radio silence and at five hundred feet over the English Channel, the planes flew a counterclockwise route from England to the western coast of the France. Clearing it, they rose to fifteen hundred feet, still in tight flying formation, heading eastward at 088 degrees. As it gained altitude, the formation flew into a thick cloud bank, which forced the pilots to spread out to avoid a collision. Some dropped below the clouds to find other moonlit aircraft to form up with, some above—all the while trying to keep on their heading.

Antiaircraft artillery began sending strings of tracers whipping their way up toward the lumbering transport planes. Explosions flashed around the flying Vs and peppered those planes lost and flying alone. Most of the aircraft lacked a navigator as well as any equipment for homing in on the beacons placed on the drop zones by the Pathfinders minutes before. Fox Company's Charlie Malley and Stevie Pustola were Pathfinders on plane #4 and were supposed to be part of the operation to ready Drop Zone C with lights and set up a homing beacon. However, their plane had engine trouble and was forced to crash-land in the channel. They would be picked up by the British destroyer HMS *Tartar*, but their lack of presence ahead on the drop zone helped put the air operation in disarray

The pilot of Fox Company's far-left C-47 in the V formation described the problems with the flight that morning:

RUSSELL HENNICKE • *As we approached the turn towards the Cotentin Peninsula, we began encountering clouds. In the turn I was momentarily losing sight of the plane whose wing I was on. The turn got sharper, and I had to throttle all the way back to keep from overrunning him. I lost flying speed and had to drop the nose and add throttle to keep from spinning in.*

Immediately I was in a dense cloud and had to continue the turn on instruments. I didn't know what rate of turn we had been making, because you never take your eyes off the plane whose wing you are on. I had to guess (and feel) it.

My copilot reminded me of my compass heading (088 degrees) at which we were to make the approach to the drop zone, so I rolled out of the turn on that heading. Right then we broke out of the clouds (at about six or seven hundred feet of altitude).

Immediately a searchlight came on, illuminating a parachute falling directly into my path. Obviously we were over the drop zone. I gave the signal for the paratroopers to stand up and hook up to the cable overhead. At the same instant I had to make a violent left turn to avoid that parachute.

I'm sure the paratroopers didn't appreciate that just when they were trying to stand up. Immediately the tracers started up towards us, seemingly a safe distance ahead but then curving right towards us and hitting us. I had throttled back the left engine for the troopers' exit and was leaning forward to see upward and ahead for any other chutes.

By now the searchlight was out (shot out by a RCAF plane we found out later). Now it was not easy to see any other chutes. The crew chief reported all the paratroopers jumped OK.

Hennicke's plane had one engine shot up during the incident. Flying alone, on one engine, he made it back to the channel where a forced landing was made on the Isle of Wight. Other members of Fox Company described their experiences:

VINCE OCCHIPINTI (in stick #75) • *While we were flying over at a steady pace, you could see out the window across from you, occasionally a plane over on the right or left. We could not see the big picture though, and I'm not sure we would have wanted to.*

The soldiers sat there, some quietly, some talking with each other, others half asleep. I doubt they were sleeping, though. I had Lieutenant Rhodes on my right, and a soldier—I can't recall who it was—on my left who leaned over and said to me, "Would you tell the lieutenant to get rid of that cigar?" He wasn't really smoking it, but half of the cigar was gone, and it was lit. The smoke was not bad, but at this stage it annoyed people. This was not a practice jump, and there were understandably some queasy stomachs. I don't think the cigar smell helped.

I leaned over to the lieutenant and asked him if he minded putting out the cigar. He said, "Oh, I'm sorry, does it bother somebody?" "Well, some of the boys are bothered by it," I said. He said OK, and he found a little hole, a two-inch hole with a stopper in it, in the window. He pulled out the stopper and threw the cigar out. Everybody was comfortable then. We sat there and enjoyed the ride as best we could.

By this time we were approaching land on the Cherbourg Peninsula, and by now I could see flashes of firing guns. I also saw an occasional fire on the ground. I couldn't distinguish the fires because our sight was limited, but some of the fires were from earlier bombings by the Air Force. Some of it was caused by planes ahead of us that had been shot down.

Eventually, the order came to stand up and hook up. This usually comes about three to four minutes before the green [light]. But I think the jumpmaster, the lieutenant in charge, probably gave the signal early because it seemed like an endless four minutes. Someone in the cockpit signaled to him that we were getting close: the door was opened, and we could see a bit of what was happening on the ground.

Near the door is the red light for "stand up and hook up." Alongside it is the green light. All of a sudden, the green light goes on, and he says, "Go!" Now everyone in back is pushing at the man in front of him— not hard, just to sort of egg him on. Maybe the front five or six guys hear that, and numbers two, three, and four are instantly out with number one.

It's nothing like you see in the movies where someone is at the door yelling "go" and one person jumps and a few seconds later, the person at the door says "Go!" again and another person jumps. Films show a trooper coming to the door, surveying the countryside, finishing a cigarette and jumping. No way.

We knew that plane could be shot down at any minute, and the last thing anybody wanted was to be in it at the time. Out the door we went. Eighteen guys out of the plane in six to ten seconds.

GEORGE YOCHUM (in stick #76) ● *I looked around the plane and found everyone looking relaxed. I noticed that some of the men had their eyes closed. This was not unusual, as they were trying to catch a little sleep. The crew chief informed us that we were now heading for France and then removed the exit door. I looked out the door, and the sight of all the planes was awe inspiring. It reminded me of Christmas with all the blinking of red and green wing lights that carpeted the sky. The crew chief bellowed out that we were five minutes from the coast of France. "Stand up, hook up" was the next order given by our jumpmaster. In unison, we stood up and snapped our static line hooks to the cable that ran the entire length of the plane. "Sound off for equipment check." We inspected each other's gear—"one okay, two okay, three okay"—until everyone was checked. Our jumpmaster (Captain Mulvey) was leaning out the door looking for the coast. Then he turned to us and said, "There it is!" As we crossed the coast, the plane was suddenly enveloped in bursts of flak. It sounded like someone throwing rocks on a tin roof.*

Our plane twisted and turned. It was difficult for us to hold our footing. To the rear of the plane a streak of white light shot from the floor to the ceiling, and with that I fell to the floor. The emergency bell was ringing, and on this signal everyone started bailing out. I couldn't get up because of the weight and the gyrations of the plane. I clutched at anything my hand could grab and pulled myself to the edge of the door. With one final pull I dropped headfirst into the night.

MARION GRODOWSKI (in stick #77) • *The motion sickness pills we had been given made me feel excited. Sitting in the plane on the way over, with all that excitement, I felt invincible. As we approached the coast, we were met by heavy ground fire, and our plane went into a series of tight turns. I remember asking what the hell was going on, and Ralph Robbins answered, "Evasive action." To me it meant we would jump in the wrong place. As the plane banked back and forth, we had to lean or hold onto the bulkhead to keep our balance.*

JOHN TAYLOR • *The guys on the plane seemed fairly relaxed going over. Most of us took one motion sickness pill about an hour before we took off and another one just before takeoff. I know I had butterflies, but I had made up my mind at the beginning that if I had any doubts about not jumping, it was going to be before I got on the plane. Once I got on the plane, I was there and the commitment was made, and I could pretty well settle down to whatever we would hit.*

On the way over I could not see any outward anxieties or displays of emotions that were contrary to what I would call normal. In fact, because we'd taken motion sickness medicine, there was some dozing during the trip. I know I slept a little bit, until I was told we would be coming up on the coast of France.

It took a little over two hours to get to our destination. We did not fly in the most direct route over Utah Beach. Instead we flew around the tip of the Cherbourg Peninsula and came in around "the back side." As we approached the coast of France, we could see tracers and quite a bit of firepower coming up in the sky. We were flying at approximately seven to eight hundred feet, or we were supposed to be at any rate. I assumed we were pretty close to it.

It was upsetting to look out the window and see flashes of light, knowing that this plane or that had gone down in a fireball and crashed, or possibly had exploded in the air. I did not notice anything that indicated a problem with our plane, but it sure was bouncing around. As we approached France, we flew through a solid wall of fire and did not have the luxury of dodging those bullets. Naturally, we all wanted to get the hell out of that airplane. We preferred to take our chances on the ground.

Our destination called for us to fly eleven minutes over enemy territory before the jump. Our plane bounced around like a Piper Cub in a gale. Of course it did not take long for those minutes to go by. We got the red light several minutes before the green one, and we were pumped up and ready to go. The green light came on, and as I was one of the last ones to jump, I thought the exit from the plane was very fast.

ROBERT JANES (in stick #78) • *Sitting in the plane and looking around it appeared as though everyone was calm. There was some joking, some prayers being said, and a lot of cigarette smoking. It was exciting, and I was resolved to do the job I had been trained to do. As we passed over the coast of France we began to receive antiaircraft fire, but the pilot seemed to take no action or change in course. The flight seemed no different to me than one in England, or Tennessee for that matter. The movement and speed of the plane seemed routine.*

Once we hooked up you could really see the tracer fire outside, you could hear the bullets making a snapping noise as they passed. I could not wait to go and get out and jump. I looked over and saw the plane's crew chief standing in the back of the plane. I really felt sorry for him. We were going to be out of the plane, and that poor guy would have to stay on board and fly through all that stuff back to England.

ROY ZERBE (in stick #79) ● *On the flight over I did not take my air sickness pill. We started taking flak from the islands when we approached the coast of France. Lieutenant Colt had us stand up and hook then. We were less of a target that way I guess. Outside the tracer fire was everywhere, making it look like a Fourth of July celebration. We jumped on the green light at about five hundred feet.*

MERLIN SHENNUM ● *There were times when you felt like you could go to sleep in that plane. Those pills made you want to sleep. We started to get flak at the islands near the French coast, and it sounded like popcorn popping outside of the plane. There were all kinds of tracer fire going by the plane making a bunch of goddamned noise. We stood up, hooked up, and counted off. I do not remember feeling any fear. I just wanted to get to the jump. No one wanted to stay in that plane.*

ARTHUR PETERSON ● *It was dark. I was scared. Well, not really scared but uneasy. I kept wondering what was going to happen, what was it all going to be like. There was a lot of firing going on, there was flak, explosions, and the sky was filled with tracers.*

HENRY BECK (in stick #80) ● *We were flying rather low over the water. I was amazed at the number of ships in the channel. There is no way to know how many ships, but they were as far as the eye could see. It was amazing. The air sickness pills they gave me made me nauseous and sick.*

ROBERT NOODY (in stick #81) ● *The motion sickness pills they gave me made me drowsy, and I was quite sleepy for a while. Then I got nauseous and someone handed me one of the cardboard ice cream buckets that had been set in the plane. I got sick and ended up throwing up into that bucket. When we flew over the coast of France, the whole sky was ablaze with tracer fire. There was so much shooting and so many explosions going off, it lit up the interior of the plane. I really was unprepared for all of it and had no idea at the time what all the activity outside the plane was. It had not really sunk in yet that I was at war.*

TOM ALLEY ● *I could hear the plane being peppered with flak and see the flashes outside the plane from the enemy fire. I don't remember being scared, but I really wanted to get out of that plane.*

The eight planes that carried the men of Fox 506th were broken from their original formation due to the cloud cover and flak. Planes 74, 75, 76, 78, 79, and 81 remained in sight of each other and dropped their troopers in the same general area, in and around the small town of Sainte-Mère-Église. Planes 77 and 80 were farther south, closer to their intended drop zone.

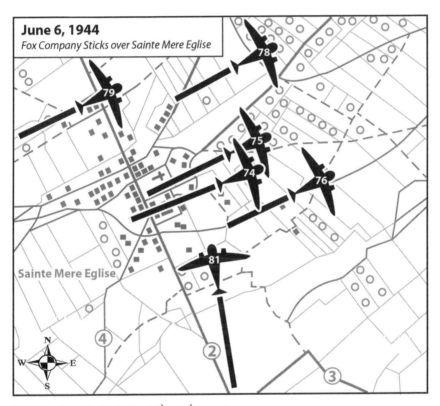

June 6, 1944
Fox Company Sticks over Sainte Mere Eglise

Sainte Mere Eglise

STICKS OVER SAINTE-MÈRE-ÉGLISE

For most of the men, the war had just begun as they leaped out the transports' doors and into the chaotic battle below. For a few other members of the company, their war would be over before they touched foot on French soil.

CHAPTER 7

D-DAY NIGHT JUMP

Lt. Andrew Tuck's stick #74 parachuted directly over Sainte-Mère-Église, and the location of the troopers standing in the plane determined who would live or die during the jump moments later. With

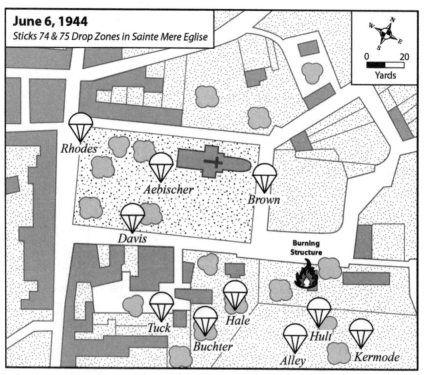

DROP LOCATIONS OF STICKS #75 AND #75, SAINTE-MÈRE-ÉGLISE

church bells ringing and tracer fire whipping across the sky, the troopers quickly exited and parachuted over the town from west to east. They were easy targets that evening, as a structure at the southeastern corner of the square was ablaze, illuminating the sky.

Tuck managed to get his parachute caught on the chimney of the Sainte-Mère-Église school, just south of the town square. Pfc. Don Davis landed in the street in the southwestern corner of the square. German soldiers quickly swarmed Davis, who pretended to be dead. After turning him over and kicking him a few times, the German soldiers left. Davis's ruse had worked. Pfc. Richard Buchter drifted down with $635 in French francs in his pocket. He would never get the chance to spend any of it. Buchter landed in a tree just east of the school. Suspended from the tree branches, he was shot and killed before he could get free from his parachute. He remained hanging dead in his harness for the remainder of the day.

The men who followed Buchter closely out the door were also unlucky. Pfc. William Hale and Pvt. Walter Hult were also killed in their parachutes as they landed among the trees near a grassy field just east of Buchter. Ray Kermode landed nearby as well but avoided the gunfire. However, he soon disappeared, never to be seen alive again by anyone in the company.

Stick #75 was flying parallel to the left wing of stick #74 and spilled its troopers directly over the church and square of Sainte-Mère-Église. With Lieutenant Rhodes landing on the western edge of the square, the remaining troopers parachuted from west to east over the church.

THOMAS RHODES • *I was hit as I went out the door over Sainte-Mère-Église but was able to count seven chutes following me before I hit the ground. I did land in the town square. I had been hit in the mouth and was bleeding rather profusely. A few minutes after landing, two French civilians helped me to my feet and prevented a German soldier from shooting me on the spot.*

They then laid me down and all ran toward the fire a short distance away. I started getting out of my chute when a group of ten or twelve Germans came up and started looking me over, at which time I played dead. The Germans took some of my equipment and left. I then got out of my parachute, ran across the square, down an alley, and into a house.

While laying on the ground in the square, I saw some of the 82nd Airborne troopers jump. Anyway, after getting into the house, I found

*a back entrance and headed for the 82nd's drop zone nearby. Somewhere
along the line, I passed out.*

*Coming to about daylight, I spotted some 82nd troopers and joined up
with them. The lieutenant in charge took me to the battalion aid station. I
was evacuated back to England.*

A defenseless Pfc. Ray Aebischer from Stick 75 landed next to the front
door of the church. His overloaded leg bag and all his weapons and supplies
had been torn off during the jump.

RAY AEBISCHER • *The church bells were constantly ringing, drowning
out any hopes of communicating with other members of my unit. Not seeing
any movement in the moonlight by any person, friend, or enemy, I felt very
much alone. Trying the church door, I found it locked. Not wanting to
attract attention or be a living target for some German soldier, I crawled
around the church to the rear, then along a high cement wall which
surrounded the church grounds.*

*At the same time a machine gun was firing down the street. As another
wave of friendly aircraft flew over, the machine gun was directed towards the
planes. This appeared a good time to make a run for it, so I dashed across the
street into an orchard.*

*As the planes flew off in the distance, the machine gun began firing
down the street again. One man, whose chute had gotten caught high in the
trees in the churchyard, was hanging there lifeless. He had been either shot
while descending or upon being trapped in the tree. In the moonlight, I could
see another trooper, still in his parachute, lying on the street, obviously caught
in the gunfire—no movement and no sound for help.*

*As it was urgent to get on with the mission assigned, my only thought for
the moment was how to defend myself against an enemy soldier without any
weapon but this one trench knife. I kept a firm grip on it, realizing that I
would have to be quick to survive.*

Pfc. Linus Brown landed along some trees near a water pump at the
eastern end of the church square. He noticed a French civilian standing
nearby and a house on fire a short distance away. Brown quickly exited his
harness, ran north past the church, and vaulted over a stone wall into the
surrounding housing.

TOM ALLEY • *I have a vivid memory of the church bells ringing even to this day. I saw the fire near the square at Sainte-Mère-Église. I don't know if it was a house or a barn. I slipped my chute to the right, as hard as I could do so safely to avoid landing in the fire. The machine gun tracers were so thick it was like you could walk down them to the ground. I landed in a pasture or an orchard—an open field really. I was illuminated by the burning building just a few hundred feet to my north. I stayed low, pulled out my trench knife and the bag holding my rifle. I put the rifle together as it was in three pieces for the jump. As I did so, I watched the occasional plane pass over with men jumping out.*

After about fifteen minutes another large group of planes passed heading east, with a lot of paratroopers jumping out over the town. I think it was the 82nd Airborne. After I assembled my rifle, I crawled over to a nearby hedgerow.

Pfc. Bud Edwards parachuted into an orchard just east of town and managed to tangle himself during his first tree landing, in an apple orchard.

BUD EDWARDS • *I was a short distance off the ground but in a tangled mess of straps and suspension lines. I struggled for about thirty minutes and could not get out of my harness or the tree. Three troopers from the 82nd arrived and asked if I needed some help. I told them I did, and they cut me out of my harness and helped me down. We moved over to a hedge with trees on top, and one of the troopers yelled, "Hey, Joe! Is that you?" I looked up, and about thirty feet off the ground in a tree was another 82nd trooper. As the trio went to work again to rescue another trooper, I thanked them and headed off for my objective.*

VINCE OCCHIPINTI • *As I was coming down, I could look around. We weren't very high. I estimated we jumped at about four hundred feet, which is quite low. We didn't mind, though, because that's plenty of time for the main chute to open and not much time (although seconds seemed like a lifetime) for us to be floating in the air with bullets racing past us. It still gave us time for the reserve chute to open, but the important thing is that there isn't a lot of time before we hit the ground. No one wanted to be a target for the enemy any longer than he had to be.*

And by this time, out there with the chute opened, I could tell there were a lot of things going on below me. There was a tremendous noise, and I could see tracer bullets coming up after me. In fact, I knew that all the German soldiers on the ground had seen me jump and had targeted all their guns in my direction. On every fifth to seventh machine gun bullet, anyone can see the tracer, meaning you can see where it is going and improve your aim. I couldn't see the other bullets in between. Here came another tracer and another and another. I could see them coming at me from all directions. What was most horrifying was that in between each of those tracers were five or six other bullets.

I could tell I was low because I could already make out signs of the horizon, trees and buildings off in the distance. Within an area of two to three hundred yards, I could see a huge fire. I thought I could make out the activity, but I didn't pay much attention to it since it wasn't beneath me. In the air I could see other chutes coming down. There was nobody immediately next to me. The nearest parachute was about seventy-five feet away.

Suddenly the ground was there, and bam I hit. What I had noticed when I was coming down was that my harness had become very tight. It was like being in a straightjacket. I lay there on the ground and started to work on the fasteners that connected the harness at my groin.

If I could get these loose, then there was a snap fastener that could relieve the reserve chute off my chest, and once I got that done I could remove the rest of the harness and the package that contained my rifle. My idea was to get at that first, put the rifle together, and load up. I found, however, that I could not get the harness loose because I couldn't reach under the chute to get it disengaged. I struggled with both for quite some time. I reached to get my dagger underneath my equipment but couldn't reach it.

It was a cloudy night, but the moon broke through occasionally to help us see. I could see hedgerows and trees surrounding the field I was in. I heard a noise not to far from my left. Suddenly, a large shape loomed nearby. It said, "Moo." A cow just stood there looking at me.

The paratroopers in stick #76 exited due east of the town square at Sainte-Mère-Église. When Pfc. Bill True exited, he could see a fire off to his left and assumed it was a Pathfinder signal. It was actually the house fire at the edge of the town square. They were over four miles north of their drop zone.

GUS PATRUNO • *I can remember passing over Sainte-Mère-Église. As*

1ST PLATOON, 1ST SQUAD
(Back row, L to R) Mackey, Supco, Valliers, Navarro, Vogel; Lovell, Wallace, Hult, Kermode; Mather, Buchter, Davis, Hale

1ST PLATOON, 2ND SQUAD
(Back row, L to R) Gilley, Temco, Ours, May; Alley, Sullivan, Edwards, Steinke; Occhipinti, Brown, Aebischer, Clemens

1ST PLATOON, 3RD SQUAD + HQ *(Back row, L to R)* Roth, Cortese, Orosco, Odegaard; Napieralski, Stone, Replogle, Droogan (Medic), Stewart; Wilson, Jackson, Flick, True

2ND PLATOON, 1ST SQUAD *(Back row, L to R)* Tom, Trimble, Bettelyoun, Robbins, Grodowski; Watkins, Hogenmiller, Passino, Ochoa; Taylor, Waters, Haney, Provenzano

2ND PLATOON, 2ND SQUAD *(Back row, L to R)* Baird (Medic), Psar, Martin; Peterson, Dickey, Knudsen, Trepelka; Nakelski, Janes, Lev, Bell; Jacobs, McNeese, Hull, Carlino

2ND PLATOON, 3RD SQUAD + HQ *(Back row, L to R)* Gillespie, Moore (Medic), Borden; Pusker, Jeffers, Sharp, Cauvin; Griffin, Olanie, Casey, Swafford

3RD PLATOON, 1ST SQUAD
(Back row, L to R) Schwenk, Rivenbark, Petersen, Summers, Oakley, Hurst; Peniak, Shennum, Vick, O'Hara; Rice, Byrne, Wolford

3RD PLATOON, 2ND SQUAD
(Back row, L to R) Riddick, Newhouse, Davenport, Reese; Crawford, Clark, Mika, Dickerson; Mackay, Kelley, Balleu, Gaston

3RD PLATOON, 3RD SQUAD
(Back row, L to R) Patruno; Malatich, Zurbe, Beauchamp, Chappelle; Beck, Jones

HQ + 3RD PLATOON *(Back row, L to R)*
Reese, Porter, Colt, Schwenk, Brooks;
Emelander, Malatich, Green, Chappelle;
Morris, Rivenbark, Pein, Payne

FOX COMPANY OFFICERS
(Back row, L to R)
Mulvey, MacDowell, Colt, Tuck;
Semon, Rhodes, Brooks, Hall

CORPORALS
(Back row, L to R)
Mackay, Vogel, Martin;
Wolford, May, Grodowski

Toccoa
training
amphitheater.

Toccoa
instruction.

Toccoa
obstacle
course.

Toccoa jump tower.

Toccoa mock plane.

Pop Clark
in the door.

OFFICERS AND NCOs 1943

Back row, L to R: Cpls. Green, Emelander, Malatich, Haney, Mather, Jacobs, Gaston, Roth, Wolford; *middle row:* Sgts. Cortese, Tamkun, Schwenk, Houck, Porter, Reese, Griffin, Flick, Borden, Occhipinti; *front row:* SSgt. Mercier, 1 Sgt. Morris, Lt. Brewer, Lt. McFadden, Lt. Hovorka, Cpt. Mulvey, Lt. MacDowell, Lt. Colt, Lt. Tuck, SSgt. Byrnes, SSgt. Maley

Quote reads: "Here's the team that made Company F, 506 Parachute Troopers what they are today. The best damned outfit in the whole United States Army. August 18, 1943 Ft. Bragg"

Marion Grodowski

Tom Alley

Bill True

Art Peterson

Waldren Bettelyoun

Carll MacDowell

Mario "Gus" Patruno

Bill Green

Don Replogle

Richard Buchter

Bob Janes

Harvey Morehead

Don Emelander

Les Hicks

Bob Noody

Gaston "Rebel" Adams

Orel Lev

Manning Haney

David "Bud" Edwards

Tom Alley and E.B. Wallace

Joe Hogenmiller

John Taylor

Ken Hull

Les Hegland

Raul Ochoa

Tommy Wolford

Merlin 'Goat' Shennum

Ralph Provenzano

Roy Zerbe

Homer Smith

Bernard Tom

John Supco

Capt. Dean and 1st Sgt. Malley

Vince Occhipinti and Bud Edwards

Pustola, Himelrick, and Vogel

Bill Hisamoto

Tommy Psar

Below: Practice jump, May 1944.
L to R standing: Olanie, Sharp,
Griffin, Jacobs, Swafford, Nakelski,
McNeece, Provenzano, Grodoski;
kneeling: Robbins, Haney, Janes,
Pusker, Psar; *front:* Carlino

Willie Morris shooting a machine gun over the heads of fellow soldiers, Toccoa, GA.

Participants in the "Ike Jump."

I jumped I could see a church, and a house burning. It did not seem long before I hit the ground, quite hard. I think it was due to the heavy leg bag I had. It was torn off my boot during the jump but was dangling below me, swinging. My chute was swinging, I was swinging, and the bag was swinging. I think I hit the ground first, followed by my leg bag, then the parachute.

Stick #78 dropped its troopers just northeast of Sainte-Mère-Église. Richard Knudsen, who was carrying a bazooka in his leg bag, was the second man to jump, right behind 1st Lt. Russell Hall. In addition to the bazooka in the leg bag, Knudsen carried nine bazooka rounds contained in three separate pouches inside the bag. As he exited the plane, the sky was filled with tracer fire, and his parachute was filled with bullet holes. A panel was blown out of the parachute, and he hit the ground before he was able to release the leg bag. Landing hard in a small field, surrounded by hedgerows, Knudsen was in pain. He was four hundred yards from town, severely injured, and alone.

ROBERT JANES • *The first thing I thought of when my chute opened was to go to the ground as quickly as possible because the Germans had machine guns in two corners of our field, filling the air with plenty of lead. I reached up and grabbed my back risers and slipped my chute as hard as possible to get down quick. I don't think I ever let up on slipping my chute, because I hit the ground like a sack of cement and saw plenty of stars. It did not even hurt me. I was too damn scared. I remember hearing church bells ringing and a siren wailing off in the distance.*

For those in stick #79, their jump would place them just northwest of Sainte-Mère-Église. On exit, Pfc. Merlin Shennum saw a set of lights off in a distant field, which he assumed were Pathfinder drop zone lights. He drifted into a large hedgerow-bordered field and landed near a row of trees. He quickly removed his rifle, assembled it, and fixed bayonet.

ROY ZERBE • *The sky was filled with fire, and it looked like the Fourth of July. I would guess we were low, at about five hundred feet. I could see fires off in the distance. I managed to land in an apple tree and was suspended only a few inches above the ground. As I tried to free myself,*

I heard what sounded like an army approaching from behind me in the orchard. My carbine was in a hip pouch, and I struggled to get to it. I looked back towards noise and much to my relief saw it was a group of cows, curiously approaching.

Pvt. Art Peterson was oscillating during his descent and landed hard and backwards. He quickly pulled out his assembled rifle and found himself alone in a small field. He headed off for the nearby town, using the glow of fire and church bells for reference.

The last plane to spill its troopers near Sainte-Mère-Église was stick #81's. When pilot Russell Hennicke banked hard left to avoid a paratrooper in his flight path, he turned north, and the men jumped from south to north toward the town.

With his overloaded leg bag, T/5 Len Hicks jumped right behind Lieutenant MacDowell. Within seconds from exit, the bag tore away from his boot, the rope stretched taught, broke, and the bag dropped out of sight below him. Staring at the stub of rope hanging from his harness, Hicks was mildly relieved. At least he would not have to carry all that gear anymore. Following Hicks out the door, also with a leg bag, was rifle grenadier Cpl. Les Hegland. Hegland managed to keep his bag attached and landed on the opposite side of the roadway from Hicks, the Cherbourg–Carentan highway. Pfc. Bob Noody jumped next.

ROBERT NOODY • *When I jumped, I released my leg bag. I had tied on a let-down rope of over thirty feet to the end of the rope that was attached to the leg bag. Even though the bag was heavy with the bazooka and rockets, the extra rope seemed to stretch out and take the strain. I tried to swing the bag out from below me to keep from landing on it. I was not successful. I landed in a ditch along a hedge, and my butt hit right on that damn bazooka's sight. Boy did that hurt! Planes were flying all over. Parachutes were all over the air. There was gunfire, and with all that was going on, strangely I was afraid of nothing.*

For those men in sticks #77 and #80, their pilots' course when clearing the cloudbank sent them much farther southeast than the rest of their flight. For stick #77 the green light came on just west of the tiny village of Houesville, over the railroad track between Carentan and Cherbourg. The drop location would be just as tragic as for those who jumped over Sainte-Mère-Église.

With the jump light switching from red to green, the Second Platoon's 2nd Lt. Charles Semon exited stick #77 followed by his two overloaded machine gunners, Pfc. Manning Haney and Pfc. James "Rebel" Waters. As the men rushed out and felt the violent shock of their opening parachutes, a danger became immediately apparent. Water!

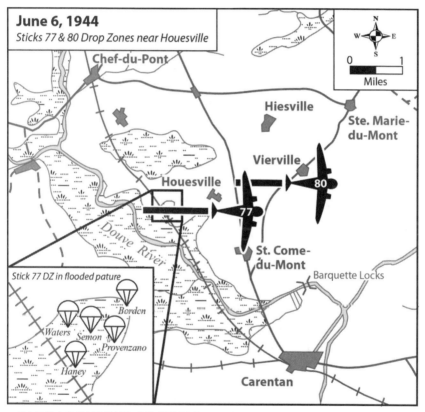

DROP LOCATIONS OF STICKS #77 AND #80 NEAR HOUESVILLE

Overloaded with ammunition and supplies, a water landing without the ability to quickly free oneself from two parachutes, a harness, a web gear buckles and straps would result in a terrible death by drowning. Even a few feet of water would be enough to drown an overburdened paratrooper, and every man drifting down from stick #77 knew it.

RALPH ROBBINS • *Lieutenant Semon was first, then Haney, Waters, Ralph Provenzano, then me. I guess we jumped at a thousand feet. I passed through a cloud, which I thought was ground fog, expecting to land at any moment. However, after passing through the cloud, I could see the moonlight reflecting on a large body of water. There was land nearby but no wind. I could see I was definitely going to land in the water, which I thought was the English Channel. I had come to the conclusion that I was going to have to jettison my equipment to avoid drowning. I was literally jerked towards the land by a surface wind so strong it must have taken me at a 45 degree angle from vertical. If it hadn't been for that wind, I don't think Provenzano or I would be alive today. Provenzano landed in shallow water, and I was the first to fall on dry land. The wind was so strong I had difficulty in collapsing my chute.*

MARION GRODOWSKI • *I had a violent opening shock. A .45 pistol that I had holstered on my hip, as well as my canteen, tore away. I looked up and saw a blown panel in my parachute. I would be falling faster because of it and hitting a little harder on landing. I could see the reflection of water below me and began to slip my chute hard to avoid it. With the blown panel and violent movement of my parachute, I had a very hard landing. The impact on dry land was so hard that I thought I had broken my leg.*

Unable to avoid the water, Lieutenant Semon splashed into a flooded field just east of the railroad, as did the overloaded Waters. Drifting down to the moonlit water, Haney acted quickly to save himself and avoid the water. Pulling out his razor-sharp fighting knife, he cut away his musette bag, machine gun, and bagged can of ammunition. He even discarded his helmet.

He then slipped his chute back and forth, and managed to land right on the raised railroad tracks that ran through the flooded waters. He was lucky. The lieutenant and Waters were not. They landed in a flooded pasture, known to locals as the Cul-de-Fer. Both drowned.

JOHN TAYLOR • *I got out good, my chute opened, and I checked it. Just the regular things you do without thinking. I looked down and saw a haze. I assumed this haze was on the ground and braced myself to land. When I passed through the haze, to my surprise I was still a good six hundred feet up.*

At that point, I could see what looked like spots on the ground and a mirror—a large area of water. We were directly over this area of water, and I knew we were in trouble. My first thought was to try to get my equipment off of me, and I reached for the knife on my leg. It was not there! I knew I could not cut the equipment off of me, and I just slipped the chute as much as I could away from the big body of water. I thought my time had come. I landed on a narrow piece of land barely twenty-five feet from it.

I hit the ground hard. The box of machine gun ammo I had swung down on my right leg smacked me on the leg when I landed. I really thought I was in trouble for a few minutes there. I thought my leg was broken, and it seemed like it took thirty minutes to get out of my chute.

The men of stick #80 would land the nearest to their drop zone but still off course and over a mile away. They jumped east of Houesville over the Cherbourg–Carentan highway.

HENRY BECK ● *The opening shock tore off my musette bag and my clicker. I landed in a field alongside a roadway. Five other members of my plane landed in the field as well. I remember with the moonlight I could see a road sign mounted nearby, listing the distance to Sainte-Mère-Église. Since I lost my clicker, I was forced to use the password to identify friend and foe.*

CHAPTER 8

CHAOS, CONFUSION, AND FIRST BLOOD

Once on the ground, the men tried to free themselves as quickly as possible from their parachute harnesses and locate others from their sticks. Down in Houesville, the men of stick #77 tried to find each other while facing death for the first time in combat. Unfortunately it was their own who were the dead.

Marion Grodowski had never bothered to sharpen his fighting knife. His harness was too tight to unsnap, and it took him over fifteen minutes to cut through the cotton straps. He had jumped with one of the Springfield rifles and had a grenade launcher attached. The end of its barrel was shrouded with a condom to keep out water and dirt, and a second condom knotted around it to hold it in place. He removed them to ready his weapon, comically wondering what the French would think when his harness was found in a field with two condoms.

Grodowski crept over to a fence where he met up with Raul Ochoa, Ralph Robbins, and a soaked Ralph "Pro" Provenzano. Robbins had just come from the flooded Cul-de-Fer where the wind had blown his parachute toward the bank. He told the group that he had pulled it in, with a floating Lieutenant Semon attached. Semon felt cold, and Robbins attempted to revive him but to no avail. The lieutenant was dead.

The group returned to their platoon leader's body and tried to take as much of his weapons and gear as they could use. Grodowski replaced the canteen he lost in the jump, and Robbins took Semon's pistol and holster. Scout Joe Hogenmiller arrived, and the six men headed off from the swamp, sadly leaving behind their dead leader. A second parachute was seen floating off in the distance as they left the Cul-de-Fer.

The group walked to the first home they saw, a one-room dwelling at the western edge of Houesville known as Le Pommier. They slowly opened the door, and Grodowski slipped in, hoping to surprise any Germans inside. He startled the home's only occupants, Auguste Benoist, his wife Germaine, and their young daughter Antoinette. Grodowski began to ask the man questions, using French he had memorized from an issued language guide. Hogenmiller walked inside and tried to help calm the family by pointing to the small cloth American flag on his jacket's sleeve.

"*Je suis un American. Où sont les boches?*" he asked. Grodowski had no idea what Benoist's answer really was, but by his gestures it seemed as though the Germans were in numerous locations, all outside of town. The man then stood in the doorway of his home and pointed around outside, repeating his explanation. Unsure if anything was accomplished and wishing he understood more French, Grodowski left the home saying "*Merci.*" The men assembled and headed east.

A short distance away they met Pvt. Ray Passino, Pvt. Norman Trimble, Pvt. Joe Watkins, and a soaking wet SSgt. Hugh Borden. Borden had landed in the flooded area as well and had cut away his equipment to avoid drowning in five feet of water. He was forced to dive down to recover his Thompson submachine gun and three muddy stick magazines. Everything else was left at the bottom of the swamp.

Grodowski's ankle was injured in the jump, and he thought it may have been broken. As he began to hobble along, he remarked to Provenzano that it may be best to loosen his boot. Provenzano, who had an injured ankle as well, suggested against it, advising that leaving it tight would keep the swelling down. Ochoa was also injured. The farther east the group moved, the slower their progress. Borden decided that the injured men should be left behind to move at their own pace. It was essential that those who were able to should get to their objective as fast as possible, which had been the orders issued prior to the jump. So, after a few brief words of encouragement, Borden, Hogenmiller, Watkins, Passino, and Trimble moved on without the three injured men. As the group walked away, Provenzano checked the time. His watch was waterlogged from his landing and had stopped. It showed 0120.

A battered Sgt. John Taylor met up with three men in the field where he had landed. Cpl. Joe Gillespie, Fox Company's runner-liaison with headquarters, had badly broken his ankle on landing. He was made comfortable and hidden away in the field. Pfc. Bernard Tom and Pfc. Ray "Tiger" Cauvin headed out with Taylor.

JOHN TAYLOR • *In this type of situation a person can sense things. The water was not supposed to be there. If we had dropped too late we would have been in the English Channel. So, we knew we had dropped early and worked from that point to orient ourselves. Planes were passing over from the paratroop serials behind us. I judged their flight as being about ninety degrees. I got into a hole and covered up with a raincoat. Using a flashlight to study a map, we figured our position roughly, and with the aid of a compass we began to move in the direction of Utah Beach.*

Crossing several hedgerows, we approached a little road. We eased up to the road listening and observing for enemy troops. Seeing another intersection to our left and in the moonlight, we found a sign indicating Houesville not far away. Back into another hole, cover up and re-evaluate the maps. We were moving the correct way. Turning northeast, we continued. When I left this hole, I made a mistake and left the flashlight. No way that we could find the hole again. Forget the flashlight.

Taylor, Tom, and Cauvin continued northeast. After waiting and observing no activity for several minutes, they carefully crossed the Cherbourg–Carentan highway.

———

After his landing just outside Sainte-Mère-Église, Sgt. Occhipinti struggled to free himself from his parachute harness. Out of the darkness loomed a dagger-wielding man. Occhipinti could make out that the man was a paratrooper whose pockets were ripped open, and he appeared stripped of his weapon, ammunition, and grenades. Only his musette bag dangled from his harness. Occhipinti assumed the rest had been torn off the trooper's body in the jump.

VINCE OCCHIPINTI • *He came over to me, and he was actually in better shape than I was. After all, he had a dagger, and I was sitting there tied up like a mummy. He came over, put his knee on my chest, his dagger to my throat, and asked, "What side are you on?"*

I recognized him. He was a sergeant in E Company. I was a sergeant in F Company. I had observed him train his squad in England. His name was Sergeant Guarnere. The reason I could remember his name was that I knew he was a fellow Italian, although we never socialized. In fact, I don't think we had ever said hello to each other, a fact I regretted at the moment.

Anyway, I said, "I'm Sergeant Occhipinti, F Company. You're Sergeant Guarnere, E Company." He said, "Yeah, yeah, that's right, but what side are you on?" I quickly surmised that when he had lost all his equipment, he lost some of his ability to reason momentarily. Really, it's understandable. After all, a dagger isn't much to be floating around enemy territory with.

After a couple more exchanges of this very valuable information, I said my name, his name, with him repeatedly asking what side I was on. Finally, he must have come to his senses. He took his dagger and started cutting loose my harness straps. I got my rifle out, which he asked for. I quickly refused but agreed to give him a few grenades. He took the grenades and took off looking for a rifle.

After the encounter with Sgt. William Guarnere, Occhipinti moved across the field he had landed in and met up with two others from his stick, one being his assistant squad leader, Cpl. Otto May. The trio moved to the cover of a nearby hedgerow and attempted to orient themselves with map and compass. However, because they had no visual points for reference, the task was cancelled. They decided to wait in the foliage along the hedgerow for it to get light enough to see.

———

Pfc. Gus Patruno gathered up his mortar tube, ammunition, and supplies from his leg bag. He had jumped with his rifle in two pieces, with the stock and the rest of the rifle shoved separately through the belly band of his parachute harness. Patruno had placed the trigger group on his rifle, with a clip of cartridges in the rifle. That way he could fire the rifle in an emergency, even without the stock attached. With no danger immediately apparent, Patruno quickly assembled his rifle and moved out.

Patruno used his clicker and immediately met with another trooper, whom he realized was in a completely different regiment than his, the 501st. The trooper's rifle stock had unfortunately split in half on landing. Patruno carried a roll of adhesive tape that he used to silence his gear buckles and other squeaky equipment. He quickly went to work and using the whole roll, managed to get the stock repaired and the rifle taped back into a useable condition.

The pair then scrambled onto a hard-packed road and crossed paths with a group of eighteen men from the 82nd Airborne en route to Sainte-Mère-Église. Patruno and his companion were quickly put on the flanks to work as security for the group as it moved down the road. Patruno told the lieutenant leading the men that he needed to get to Utah Beach and that he was moving away from his objective by traveling with them. After a quick debate, Patruno left his mortar tube and six mortar rounds with the men from the 82nd. Patruno was happy to lighten his load. He and his fellow Screaming Eagle then headed east on the roadway, away from the group and back toward their own objectives.

After traveling east for a short distance, they saw a Frenchman pedaling toward them on a bicycle. Patruno stopped the man and asked him the direction to Pouppeville. The man sat straddling his bicycle, gesturing as though he did not know the answer and wanting nothing to do with the two paratroopers. Patruno began to argue with the man when three trucks filled with German soldiers came barreling down the road toward them. The two paratroopers dove off into the cover of the closest hedge.

With lights on and traveling at forty to fifty miles an hour, the trucks raced past. Shocked, Patruno and his comrade watched as the Frenchman on the bicycle began waving at the trucks as they passed, frantically pointing and yelling toward the two paratroopers hiding in the nearby hedge. As each truck passed, the man became more animated in trying to point out the men and flag the trucks down. Either oblivious to the Frenchman or following orders, the drivers sped on toward Sainte-Mère-Église.

The two Americans breathed sighs of relief and watched as the Frenchman began pedaling away, bathed in the moonlight. Patruno raised his M1, took aim, and squeezed off one shot. The Frenchman flipped violently off his bicycle and fell dead into a roadside ditch.

After moving a short distance farther east, the two walked up to a signpost. They glanced at the names posted there. Patruno recalled the sand table briefings back in England and realized he was far north of where he was supposed to be. He needed to head south by southeast. He took a deep breath in disgust, and the two headed out to the sound of nearby gunfire.

The pair quickly shuffled down the road toward an intersection. A wild firefight was under way. Men were shouting and yelling, and sporadic tracer fire crossed back and forth down the lanes. Patruno and the other trooper moved to each side of the roadway and headed toward the corner of the intersection. Trying to figure out what was going on and from where, Patruno crossed the road. A German stood up at the corner and from less than fifteen feet, fired off a shot at Patruno. As the bullet snapped past him, Patruno quickly fired a shot back. Patruno missed as well. Heart pounding, Patruno turned to face his opponent, both raising their rifles to attempt a better-aimed shot. But the German was ahead of him. Patruno heard the trigger pull on the German's rifle, followed by a click. The rifle was empty. Patruno took aim as the German frantically opened his rifle bolt and attempted to load. Patruno took his time and aimed. His rifle bucked from the recoil of the shot, and the German dropped dead at the corner of the roadway.

With the firefight ending, Patruno found himself with a group of forty to fifty men from another 101st regiment, led by a major who was wielding a .45 pistol. A dozen German soldiers lay dead about the roadway and the surrounding ditches. Finally among his friends, Patruno's companion fell in with his unit, and the major told Patruno he needed to fall in with them as well. Patruno protested, explaining his assigned objective. The major ordered Patruno to stay with them. So, in a column of two, the group moved out, and an angry Gus Patruno moved along with them.

Never to be outdone, Patruno figured a way to avoid remaining with the group of troopers. As they took two steps forward, Patruno took one step forward and one step back. Within minutes he was at the rear of the column and able to slip unnoticed into a nearby field. On his own again, Patruno cut through several fields. Soon he stepped out on another road. Using his compass he headed in the general direction of his objective and walked into the outskirts of the town of Turqueville.

––––––––

T/5 Len Hicks moved from the edge of the road he landed on and crept off into a nearby field. Seeing a shadow moving by some nearby trees, he clicked once. From the shadow he heard two clicks in response. "Who's there?" he whispered. "It's me, Jellesed" was the response. Hicks had met up with fellow Fox Company trooper Pvt. Andrew Jellesed. Happy to have company, Hicks headed over to a nearby fence with Jellesed following close behind.

Moments later they walked up on an officer from another outfit who was as confused about their present location as they were. While the trio tried to determine just exactly where they were, Hicks heard footsteps. A helmet—a German one—was bobbing along the top of a nearby hedgerow. Hicks saw that the soldier was heading for some parachutes that could be seen hung up in some trees in the distance. Having received the order to try to use bayonets and knives only during the predawn hours, Hicks fixed his bayonet on the end of his rifle.

Hicks moved toward the German soldier, who was apparently oblivious to the trio of paratroopers standing nearby. He tripped up the soldier by forcing his bayonet and rifle tip between the man's legs. The moment the fallen soldier hit the ground, Hicks was on him with his bayonet plunging into the soldier's throat. The soldier's death was as quick as it was violent, and the only noise heard after the thrust was that of Hicks's heavy breathing. A quick search of the dead German yielded only one item, a small two-bladed aluminum jackknife. Hicks pocketed it and rejoined the lieutenant and Jellesed, who had watched the assault in astonishment.

Moving up through the field, they came to a roadway intersection. After throwing some rocks and hearing no noise and seeing no movement, Hicks crossed the road. The others followed. A clicker was heard in the distance. Hicks responded with two clicks. Using the toy cricket noise like a beacon, Hicks moved over to the some thick foliage alongside a hedgerow. Crouching in the bushes were two Fox Company men, one of which was radioman Doug Roth. They hurried back toward the intersection and cut through a home's backyard garden. There they stumbled upon Cpl. Les Hegland, Lt. Carl MacDowell, and their medic, Joe Droogan.

MacDowell had injured his knee in the jump. When he stood, his leg swivelled around at the joint. In pain, the lieutenant ordered the men to help dig him a foxhole and leave him behind. Their orders were to move to their objective and leave those wounded or injured behind, but the men refused. They used the lieutenant's map to orient themselves and, with the church bells still ringing off in the distance, determined they were southeast of Sainte-Mère-Église. Carrying their leader, the group moved out.

After moving away from Sainte-Mère-Église, the group came upon a platoon-size group of American paratroopers led by Lt. Dick Winters of E Company of the 506th. The men fell in with Lieutenant Winters and recognized F Company's Nick Cortese, Art Peterson, and Sgt. Julius Houck among the soot-faced soldiers. Lieutenant MacDowell was loaded into a wagon full of horse saddles and was later pulled away from the group to an aid station.

———————

Pfc. James Mackey and Pfc. Jesse Orosco expected to quickly meet up with their stick shortly after their landing at Sainte-Mère-Église. Not having made any contact with others from their plane, the two moved toward the town, its church bells as reference. Hanging nearby in the trees were the lifeless bodies of several paratroopers. Orosco saw his friend Bill Hale suspended from a tree only a few inches above the ground. He was trying to free Hale from his harness when a machine gun opened up from the square. With bullets crackling past, Orosco left Hale behind, fleeing eastward away from town.

While Orosco had been dealing with Hale, Mackey searched for his best friend, Richard Buchter. Mackey found him. He too was hanging from a tree, just over the wall from a nearby building. As Mackey approached, he could see that Buchter was dead. He stood frozen, his heart pounding in shock. Trying to make sense of the surreal image in his mind, Mackey was devastated.

Only the rapid fire of the machine gun coming from the square forced him from his thoughts. He ran for his life back into the darkness away from town. The death of his close friend would change him forever.

———————

As Merlin Shennum was landing in a field west of Sainte-Mère-Église, he assumed by the drop zone lights he saw that he was only a field or two north of his intended original landing site. After moving around the hedgerows, he managed to find a way out of the field heading west. With gunfire lighting the sky and planes passing overhead, he crept into the next field and stumbled into an officer from the 82nd Airborne.

MERLIN SHENNUM • *The officer had injured his leg in the jump and asked me to help him into some shrubbery alongside a nearby hedgerow. I helped drag him over, and he thanked me, telling me he wanted to have a chance to get a few Germans before they got him.*

Shennum left the officer behind and headed out, still believing he was in the right area and going in the correct direction. After cautiously weaving through a maze of hedgerows and fields, he stumbled down an embankment and onto a railroad track. It was then he knew where he was—on the railroad line between Cherbourg and Carentan. Shennum had studied the sand tables and aerial photos while back in England and now realized he was not pointed in the right location. After a glance at his pocket watch–style compass, he headed south.

A short time later Shennum heard a loud noise coming from a roadway just south of his position. He got down prone on the tracks, fearing the sound was hobnailed German boots marching toward the railroad tracks. He pulled out a grenade, only to see that the noise was being made by horses' hooves.

Shennum breathed a sigh of relief. He put the grenade away, picked himself up, and headed onto the road. There he ran into a young lieutenant from the 82nd Airborne.

MERLIN SHENNUM ● *I talked to this officer, and he explained that I should just stay with him and head for his objective. The two of us began to walk east down the road and came to a bend or S turn in the roadway. Just as we made the bend, we heard a motorcycle coming in our direction. We stepped off the road, which was only about ten feet wide, and stepped into a small ditch. Around the bend came the motorcycle, a German motorcycle with a sidecar, with one guy riding, one in the sidecar. We let them get close, then opened up on them at point blank range. They crashed into the ditch across the roadway from us. Both were dead.*

As it began to get light, Shennum and the officer continued east toward the La Fière causeway.

———

After scrambling from distant firefights and the glow of the burning building in Sainte-Mère-Église, Tom Alley moved down a hedgerow and ran into a buck sergeant from the 82nd Airborne. The two headed north and moved out onto a small road. It was there he ran into two Fox Company men, privates E. B. Wallace and Edward Brennan. Wallace, like Alley, was from Charlotte, North Carolina. The three were happy to see each other's familiar faces.

They walked a short distance down the road. After picking up a few more unknown paratroopers, the group was halted by the sound of hooves and squeaky wagon wheels. They all quickly moved into the ditches that lined the road. While lurking in the shadows, they peered down the roadway. A half dozen Germans were walking toward them with a mule-drawn wagon.

TOM ALLEY • *We let them get close, then jumped out from the ditch, taking them totally by surprise. I looked in the wagon and saw it was filled with ammunition. The 82nd sergeant began to disarm all of the German soldiers, who had their hands in the air. I stepped back to cover him as he pulled a submachine gun from one German soldier's hands. The sergeant moved down to disarm the final soldier, a guy who was holding a leather strap used to lead the mule and wagon. The German then smacked the sergeant with the leather strap—he hit him hard. I do not know if it was fear or instinct, but I shot the German standing closest to me and dropped him dead. The other Germans broke and ran in the direction they had initially come, but were quickly mowed down by the sergeant using the German submachine gun he had obtained moments before.*

As Alley and the sergeant looked over the dead Germans sprawled in the roadway, they realized they were alone. The other paratroopers were gone! The two were slowly walking back toward their hiding place in the ditch when they heard someone whisper from the darkness "Hey, what happened?" Wallace explained to Alley that when all the shooting started, the others had heard the German gun firing and thought it was the Germans doing all the shooting. Discretion being the better part of valor, they had moved back into the concealment of the ditches.

———

Bazooka-man Bob Noody assembled with several other members of his stick just a few hundred yards south of Sainte-Mère-Église. He paired up with a close pal, Pvt. Harvey Morehead. The two stopped and saw a paratrooper hanging from a tree, over twenty feet off the ground. Pfc. Don Emelander was struggling to free himself and eventually cut himself from his harness. However, he fell at an odd angle and crashed to the ground, breaking his leg in the process. "I was surprised by how far he fell that he was not killed," recalled Noody.

Although made as comfortable as possible, Emelander had to be left behind. The remaining men moved out to the east. It would be getting light in only a few hours.

CHAPTER 9

FIRST DAY IN NORMANDY

W ith the frequent crack of a rifle shot, and thumps of artillery in the distance, the Second Platoon's Sgt. Hugh Borden led his small band of paratroopers toward the town of Sainte-Marie-du-Mont. Accompanying Borden were Cpl. Joe Hogenmiller, privates Ray Passino, Norman Trimble, Ralph Robbins, Joe Watkins, and their medic, Millard Moore. Moore had managed to join the group as it made its way out of Houesville. It was beginning to get light out, and the men had managed to skirt other villages and contact with the Germans, all the while heading east toward their objective at Pouppeville.

With Hogenmiller as scout, they encountered a Frenchman who left his nearby farmhouse to make contact with them. With gestures making up for a lack of translation, Hogenmiller understood a pilot was being hidden on the farm, so the group walked over to investigate.

It turned out that the family was harboring no pilot at all—it only wanted to celebrate its new freedom with the Americans. The farmer's wife and two daughters handed warm, fresh bread, thick with butter, to each trooper. A bottle of wine was provided for each man, which the farmer had retrieved from his cellar. There was a dome-topped steeple peeking above the trees in the distance, and Borden was able to confirm with the farmer that it was the church of Sainte-Marie-du-Mont. With wine bottles protruding from their jackets and packs, the seven troopers thanked the farmer and his family, and headed out toward the town.

As they neared it, they came up on a machine gun crew from another regiment. Borden asked what they were doing and why they did not go into Sainte-Marie-du-Mont. They were informed the town was "full of krauts" and that the crew was waiting for support. After being warned "you are nuts to go in—they will mow you down," Borden's group cut the communication wires from a roadside pole and headed into town.

Borden split the group in two. They crept toward the town using ditches on both sides of the road for cover and concealment. A wounded paratrooper was discovered in one of them, and the group paused as medic Moore dressed the trooper's wounds and gave him a shot of morphine. Leaving the wounded man behind, the group advanced.

As they carefully made their way into the edge of Sainte-Marie-du-Mont, they came under enemy small arms fire. Training kicked in. Using fire-and-maneuver tactics, the group moved door to door toward the town square. Each man would fire at the Germans as he reached the cover of a doorway or building. As he continued to fire, a man would move up one house or doorway and fire also. This shooting and leapfrog tactic allowed the troopers to reach the town square without injury.

Borden took cover at a corner of a building and ordered men to take the church. Hogenmiller led the attack, trailed by Watkins and Robbins.

JOE HOGENMILLER • *As I ran across the street, I fired at the church's front door. I forced the door open and entered, keeping the rest covered with fire until everyone was in.*

Four Screaming Eagles from other units made their way into the church after the trio of Fox Company men. The new arrivals took up positions to cover the entry doors on the ground floor of the church. Hogenmiller, Watkins, Robbins, and another 506th trooper found their way into the steeple, which gave them not only a 360-degree view of the town but also of miles of the surrounding area.

The confused Germans in Sainte-Marie-du-Mont began to withdraw from different areas of the town. Not sure of the paratroopers' locations, they began to move into the Americans' fields of fire. With Borden, Passino, and Trimble hidden around the square, a wild firefight ensued. Over a dozen Germans attempted to flee over a short wall from the square and were cut down by rifle fire. The men in the steeple began shooting at everyone approaching the town or trying to flee it. German machine gun fire peppered the church steeple, but Hogenmiller and his duo of supporters kept firing back.

A small German armored vehicle chugged slowly into the town square. Watkins responded with two well-placed rifle grenade shots into its front. With the second blast, the top hatch opened, and a soldier tried to climb out. Trimble dropped him with a head shot.

Germans attempted again to move into the square, this time with two horse-drawn artillery pieces and a wagon of ammunition and supplies. All of the paratroopers opened up with a deafening volume of fire and began to cut the arriving Germans down. A few Germans escaped and moved a machine gun into a nearby building. They soon began to fire back at the church.

From high in the steeple, Hogenmiller watched in the distance as an artillery piece was set up in a field outside town to the west. The piece fired at the steeple and missed, so Hogenmiller ordered the men downstairs immediately. As they moved down to the church's ground floor, a second shell fired made a direct hit on the steeple. Unknown to Hogenmiller at the time, the gun was being fired by other members of the 101st, who suspected that the steeple was occupied by Germans.

More paratroopers began to fight their way into the town, and the German machine gun crew fired back in an attempt to stop them. A gun battle ensued with neither side making any progress. Around noon, and after over four hours of fighting, American tanks edged up to the town. Low on ammunition, Borden and his men were grateful for their arrival. Borden ran to the first tank and spoke with a corporal who poked his head outside a hatch in the front of the tank. Borden pointed out the building from which the German machine gun crew had been harassing his group.

The tanks moved into town. After spreading out, they fired into the building pointed out by Borden. Surrounding homes were fired into as well, and the machine gun crew fell silent. After grenades were placed into the barrels of the abandoned German artillery pieces and detonated, the handful of Fox Company men left Sainte-Marie-du-Mont and headed for Pouppeville. They left behind a graphic but impressive tally for their fight: almost an entire platoon of dead German soldiers, a destroyed armored vehicle, a wrecked horse supply train, and two vandalized field pieces. For his valorous actions in Sainte-Marie-du-Mont, a Silver Star would later be awarded to Sgt. Hugh Borden.

Back near Sainte-Mère-Église, Sgt. Vince Occhipinti and Cpl. Otto May slid out from their hiding place along a hedgerow and moved toward the prominent steeple of a church in a nearby town. They ran into about a dozen troopers from the 82nd Airborne, who informed them of their location. Deciding to remain with the more numerous men of the 82nd, Occhipinti and May settled in to help defend the town.

VINCE OCCHIPINTI • *We were Screaming Eagles. Of course, we were on our own. So we sort of looked around for foxholes and places to dig in. We discovered a small orchard; the trees were not very big, but inside that orchard was a set of slit trench jagged teeth. You could walk back and forth along this. It was about seventy yards long, turned a corner, and then went about another forty yards. All of this was in the orchard so you couldn't see it from the air. The Germans, of course, knew it was there.*

Pvt. Roy Zerbe and Pfc. Armand Beauchamp moved slowly through a field, working away from Sainte-Mère-Église eastward toward the coast. As it began to get light, a rifle shot cracked between them. A German sniper was hidden in the lush foliage of a tree across the field from them and had missed his first shot at the two men. They rushed for concealment in the high grass and overhanging leaves of the closest hedgerow. Having an idea where the shot had come from, Zerbe decided they should assault the sniper in the tree.

ROY ZERBE • *We fell back on our training, and I immediately began to return fire at the sniper. I yelled for Beauchamp to move, and he rushed forward as I covered him with rapid fire.*

Then Beauchamp fired toward the sniper, and Zerbe moved past him to another position of cover in the field. Again Zerbe fired, and Beauchamp ran past him as another shot crackled by from the sniper. When Zerbe rushed forward, there was no return fire from the sniper but no covering fire from Beauchamp either. Zerbe dove for cover and looked back. Beauchamp had frozen in fear.

ROY ZERBE • *I was so mad at him that I began to yell at him for not helping me. I do not know if I hit the sniper or not, but we did not get any return fire from the tree after that. I decided to move out, and we left the field. I was really disappointed, as Beauchamp was a good friend, but I had the feeling that I could no longer trust him.*

Zerbe and Beauchamp moved out to a nearby road and soon came upon several more members of their unit, Sgt. Russ Schwenk, Cpl. Tommy Wolford, privates first class Alan Summers and Ed Peniak, privates James O'Hara and William Hurst, and unit drinker and boxer, Pvt. Horace Vick. Under Schwenk's leadership, the group moved toward its objective at Pouppeville. Along the way it picked up the Second Platoon's Sgt. Frank Griffin and Sgt. Charlie Jacobs. They arrived at Pouppeville at 1100, only to find the town and beach exit already in US paratroopers' hands.

Meanwhile, the jump-injured Grodowski, Provenzano, and Ochoa hobbled along just east of Houesville, wary of every odd noise and shadow. The day continued to get light, with the sun peeking over the distant trees, causing many of the suspicious shadows among the hedgerows to fade away. The quickly approaching hum of low-flying aircraft caused the men to move into a ditch by the roadside. Grodowski looked up as the cause of the noise came into view.

MARION GRODOWSKI ● *I looked up and saw two P-51 Mustangs along with a trailing clipped-wing British Spitfire. They began to circle us, or at least it appeared as though they were looking at us. They were very low, and as they circled, I kept pointing to my American flag armband, hoping they would see it. I'm not sure if it worked, or if they saw me, but I kept pointing, and Ochoa and Provenzano kept waving. After a few passes around us they flew off.*

The trio spread out about fifty feet apart and began to move out down the road again. A few minutes later, with Provenzano in the lead nearing a bend in the road, the group came to a halt. Provenzano pointed his rifle toward a nearby ditch. Grodowski motioned for him to come back, so Provenzano tiptoed back to report what he had observed. The report back was that there were Germans up ahead and too many for one rifle. Grodowski made a plan.

MARION GRODOWSKI ● *I was to take the inside of the hedgerow, which ran parallel to the road and reach the point where my hedgerow turned to the right. Pro was to go back to where he had been and wait for me to start shooting, then step in and help out.*

With Ochoa on rear guard, the two men moved out and headed down both sides of the hedge, with Grodowski in a field, and Provenzano still on the roadway. At the bend in the hedge, Grodowski stopped and peered through the hedge.

MARION GRODOWSKI • *I looked through the bushes and saw a German machine gun emplacement. One German was on his back in the ditch, smoking a cigarette, and looked right at me. I was sure he was staring at me, but he must have thought I was one of his boys because he never moved. I looked over to the next field, about seventy-five yards away, and it appeared as though the entire German Army was digging in. I decided we could not win that fight and fell back to get Provenzano.*

At the bend in the road, Provenzano had also observed all the Germans digging in and their machine gun position. He did not wait to be told to move back but did so knowing their survival depended on it. Once paired up again, the two men grabbed their rear guard, Ochoa, and moved off to skirt the German position. All the while, Ochoa asked questions about what they had observed.

After moving for about a mile, using the maze of ditches and hedgerows for cover, the three men stopped, and Grodowski looked over his map. Ochoa tapped him on his helmet, pointed over the hedge they were resting on, and whispered, "Krauts." The two peered over and found the backside of their hedge lined with German troops, also resting. The three men hobbled off again into the maze, away from the Germans, adding to their disorientation with every step. They were completely lost.

When John Taylor had crossed the Cherbourg–Carentan highway with Tiger Cauvin and Bernard Tom, they spent most of the night passing over a series of hedgerows. They heard voices in the distance and came up to a field with numerous gliders scattered about, some of which had crashed into the hedges. After moving into the field, Taylor inspected a crash site.

JOHN TAYLOR • *I looked into one of the crashed gliders and saw a dead general. It was Don Pratt, our assistant division commander, and he had been killed in the crash. He was the first dead American I saw in Normandy. There was an injured pilot stretched out on a broken off piece of the glider.*

After talking to the glider troopers and pilots for only a few minutes, the men headed out and continued for their objective, leaving behind thirty to forty men in the field. As the sun began to come up, they spotted two men at the edge of a hedgerow and crawled up a ditch to them. They directed the three to a nearby house that had been set up as a regimental headquarters by their well-respected commander, Col. Robert Sink.

JOHN TAYLOR • *We made our way up to this big house. It was an impressive estate surrounded by a large wall with barns and outbuildings. It had a grandiose lane leading up to it. Major Matheson, a regiment staff officer, greeted us and told us there was no word on our Second Battalion guys, or anyone else for that matter.*

At the command post we were told to help round up other troopers. To do this we would fan out like a clock in small groups and go in different directions till we found someone. Then we would direct them to "the big house."

The trio came up on a firefight near Holdy, with an attack being led by Captain Patch from the First Battalion of the 506th. He and a group of his men were dueling with a German machine gun crew, and he sent Taylor, Cauvin, and Tom to flank the position from one side, and about a half dozen men to do the same from the other. Taylor recalled the first shots he fired in the war as they flanked the Germans.

JOHN TAYLOR • *I could not see their faces, only their silhouettes. We took out a machine gun team of three men and some other soldiers with them. We had a total of eight to ten men, and they had close to this. We fired with our M1 rifles. We didn't stop to see the result. At that point I didn't have time to think about it, but it's not something I ever forgot.*

With the gun position knocked out, the men set up a defensive perimeter at the command post. Manning "Kentucky" Haney, Taylor's best friend, walked into the command post. He was a welcome sight. Haney had lost all of his equipment when he cut away his gear during his jump over the flooded Cul-de-Fer outside Houesville. He had landed on the railroad tracks and managed to find his way to the command post, minus his machine gun, his helmet, and all his extra gear. He did have his carbine, however, which had been folded in a hip holster. With his Kentucky drawl and sheepish grin, he filled the men in on his landing and overland adventure, reporting he never made contact with any Germans while en route. Haney was lucky.In a muddy cow pasture southeast of Sainte-Mère-Église, Bud Edwards and Harry "Dutch" Ostrander sat hidden in some high grass at the edge of the field. Alone, they stared toward the only gated entry to their hideaway and only access into the field. They waited patiently as the darkness faded away and the morning sunlight broke into the field

A few minutes later Ostrander had puzzled look on his face. Edwards asked what was wrong. Ostrander pointed at a bush, near the gate, that he did not remember being there before. Edwards had not noticed either. "Take a shot at it and find out," Ostrander said. Edwards raised his rifle, took careful aim, and squeezed off a shot. The arm of a German soldier toppled out from the bush. As the sun came up the first morning, Dick Knudsen was one of the members of Fox Company who lay injured from the jump. Unable to move with a broken hip, he was in a field just four hundred yards east of Sainte-Mère-Église. He had listened to the shooting all around him throughout the night. A lieutenant from the 82nd eventually came upon him and administered a shot of morphine. Knudsen told him where he had hidden his bazooka and shells, and the officer left to retrieve the items, promising to send help back for him. A short time later, two medics from the 82nd arrived with a stretcher and brought him into town to an aid station.

DICK KNUDSEN • *A French woman was waiting along a road as the medics brought me into town. She had picked some strawberries and offered them to me, repeatedly saying "Merci. Merci beaucoup."*

Pvt. Bob Janes made his way from outside Sainte-Mère-Église to the division headquarters near Hiesville, where he spotted Maj. Gen. Maxwell Taylor, the 101st commander. After remaining there for a short time, he volunteered for a patrol.

BOB JANES • *I ended up that morning going out on a patrol. There was a Hispanic sergeant from the 82nd and four other paratroopers. They said they were looking for a machine gunner. I told them I could shoot one. I thought, since I had lugged Manning Haney's machine gun on maneuvers and watched the guys shooting them, that I could manage. We took off on the patrol and startled three Germans in a ditch a short distance away.*

They surrendered without a shot and seemed pleased to have been captured.

We went down the road a way and came to an intersection. I set up the machine gun facing down the road, pointing it where the roadway made a bend out of view. Well, we were not there very long when a platoon of Germans came marching towards us from around the bend. They were in two columns and marching like they were in a parade or something. I let them get close and remained still in the middle of the road. They kept getting closer and closer, and then I opened up.

I sprayed both lines of troops with three long bursts. They tried to get into the ditches on both sides of the road, and I fired down the ditches at them as well. The sergeant yelled for us to go, so I picked up the machine gun and turned towards the sergeant who had been covering the German prisoners with his tommy gun.

One of the Germans yelled out, "Me nicht Nazi! Democrat!" He repeated it several times, and it sounded like something he had practiced. Well, the sergeant was not having any of it and mowed all three guys down at point blank range. I watched them as they fell only a few feet from me dead, into a ditch. I was shocked, and it had quite an impact on me. It was like it happened in slow motion. We ran back toward the command post and had to move around through several fields to avoid German troops. But we made it back with no casualties."

For Don Emelander, his broken leg had kept him in a field just a few hundred yards south of Sainte-Mère-Église. During the early morning hours he had removed his rifle stock from its action and trigger group, and fashioned a splint using the stock and his T-shirt to keep his leg immobilized. A German patrol came upon him and saw he was injured and without his weapon. After going through his pockets and removing his accessible supplies, one German pulled out his wallet and looked at a photograph inside. "Mudder?" the German asked, viewing a picture of Emelander's mother. He replied it was. The German handed back his wallet, and the group walked away to the south, leaving the bewildered paratrooper behind.

Len Hicks had continued on with the large group of 506th troopers accompanying Lieutenant Winters from E Company. In the group was still a handful of other Fox Company men, Sgt. Julius Houck, Cpl. Les Hegland, and privates Nick Cortese and Art Peterson. They had arrived at a small village called Le Grand Chemin. Lieutenant Winters was tasked with assaulting a battery on Brécourt manor near there that contained four German artillery pieces. Hicks wanted to go along for some action.

LEN HICKS • *There were more E Company troopers in this group, about twelve to fourteen. They were right by me when Winters was briefing them. I told Winters I would like to have some of that action. His reply was "Would anyone else like to go?" I walked over and asked for volunteers. Sgt. Julius "Rusty" Houck was the only one interested.*

As the assault began, Hicks and Houck moved in with the group in the trenches that led to the gun positions. As they progressed, they to moved on and fought for the last gun position. Hicks and Houck were prone a short distance from a German soldier in the gun pit when they decided their next move.

LEN HICKS • *We were lying very near each other when he suggested he would throw a grenade over to the #4 emplacement. I told him to be very careful; we did not have much cover in case they wanted to throw it back. I do not know if it was Rusty's grenade or my shot that got the guy.*

As Houck rose to throw his grenade, a burst of machine gun fire struck him in the upper body. He still managed to send the grenade into the gun position, then slumped dead.

LEN HICKS • *About two or three minutes later, Lieutenant Compton [of E Company] crawled up to check on us. After a few minutes he suggested that I try to work my way over to this fourth gun. The only way I could see was the trench between the two guns. For the first few feet I could walk bent over. Then the trench became too shallow. I had just started to get down when I was hit in the right shinbone. I stopped. Lieutenant Compton asked what was wrong. "I think I slowed one down a little" was my reply. Luckily I could walk back to a spot near him. He brought out his jump knife, ripped my pants leg up near the crotch, and proceeded to be the best aid man that ever worked on me. (Later I did have others.) He used all my bandages and some of his. Most of my calf muscles had been blown away, and I had started to bleed. He wanted me to lay down there, but I told him I only had two rounds left and would not be much help.*

Hicks crawled back in the trench up to Lieutenant Winters, who asked how bad his wound was and whether he could get out of the trench, as they were all low on ammo and were pulling back. Hicks told him he could. He continued crawling back and was passed by the remainder of the retreating troopers in the process. When he arrived at the end of the trench, Hicks found he did not have the strength left to pull himself from out of the four-feet-high trench system. After several tries, he sat with his back against the trench wall and waited for the Germans he assumed would soon come to kill him.

After a few minutes he heard someone coming. He readied his rifle. To his surprise, it was Virgil "Red" Kimberling from Headquarters Company. Kimberling had been left behind at the last gun emplacement when he did not hear the order to pull back, and no one realized he was still there. He only retreated when he ran out of ammunition. Kimberling pulled Hicks up and carried him from the trench, then ran him over to a fence line and rolled him under the wire. A second trooper provided cover fire, and Kimberling carried Hicks away from the emplacement and to safety. Hicks could not thank Kimberling enough. He owed him his life.

Gus Patruno had headed into Turqueville and noted the town sign seemed to read an awful lot like "Turkeyville." As he entered the town, a couple of the French residents began to wave "stop" at him from a window. One came outside and told Patruno, "Beaucoup boches" and pointed down the road in the direction he was headed. A small road was pointed out that went due south, so Patruno headed down it. After about a mile of walking, he realized he was going the wrong way and needed to head east. Patruno hopped over a hedge and moved into a large field that contained what appeared to be a half dozen cavalry horses and a very large barn.

GUS PATRUNO • *It was a very large barn—a hundred feet by about sixty to eighty-feet wide. So I sneaked into the barn, and there was a German guard at one end and another at a central entrance in the middle of the barn. So I went in and got a bridle and went back out to the horses. I picked out a white one.*

It had to be a white one, because that is what all the good guys in the Westerns rode. I put the bridle on him and wondered how I was going to get up on the horse. It was almost five feet tall, and here I am loaded with hand grenades and carrying a rifle.

I led him over to a watering trough. He was gentle and minded—just did not move or nothing. I moved him to the trough, and as he was drinking, climbed up on his bareback. I headed out in the direction I wanted to go, and it was now getting light out.

Patruno led his horse out on toward the road and could see it was now busy with activity—German vehicles and troops scrambling about frantically. Patruno calmly led his horse on, waving at the Germans in the distance, and they waved back. He continued on through several fields and away from the Germans at "Turkeyville." Having discovered that Pouppeville had been already captured, Hugh Borden and his group met up with John Taylor at the command post in Cloville, near Saint-Lô. Borden was shocked to see Taylor, as he thought he had drowned after parachuting over the flooded waters outside of Houesville. They spent their evening swapping stories while setting out identification panels on the ground and popping orange smoke grenades in a nearby field set up for glider landings. At 2100 the gliders arrived, most landing or crashing out of view. Firefights could be heard in the distance, and none of the arriving troopers was ever seen to arrive at the location by Borden and the cluster of Fox Company men.

Back in Houesville, the townspeople had discovered the bodies of the two drowned Fox Company men. Eugène Enot, a young man living in Houesville, had watched the scattered planes passing over during the night, the parachutes drifting down from the sky, and the tracers of the German antiaircraft fire. From the safety of the darkness in town, he watched as the landing paratroopers pulled one of their own from the flooded waters nearby, only to abandon him.

In the morning Enot went along with a small group of townspeople to the Cul-de-Fer. There they found the bodies of Lieutenant Semon and Rebel Waters. They were not sure what to do, but knew that as Catholics, they could not leave the men behind. Enot and the others stripped the men of their parachutes and web gear, and carried them back into town. The bodies were placed in a small building, their town hall, and burial plans were made.

Gus Patruno rode his stolen white horse southeast from Turqueville to the distant sound of gunfire. The closer he rode, the louder the exchange of fire became. Patruno rounded a curve in the roadway and galloped his horse into a heated firefight between paratroopers and German soldiers holed up in a nearby house. Two machine guns ripped fire from the house into the hedges and ditches along the road where the Americans were taking cover. Patruno recognized the men were from the 506th when he spotted white spades painted on the sides of their helmets. As Patruno galloped through the firefight, he heard his sergeant, Joe Chappelle, yell to him "Gus, what are you doing?" Patruno halted his horse, looked down at Chappelle, and shrugged "I don't know." As bullets snapped past the horse-mounted trooper in the roadway, Chappelle yelled to Patruno, "Hey Gus, there's a war going on!"

Patruno dismounted his horse in an adjoining field. He ran up to Chappelle, and the group moved from the ditches to attack the farmhouse. The two machine guns continued to fire at the paratroopers, who in turn tried to suppress the fire to allow men to move in on the house. Patruno fired sixteen times at the house—two full clips from his rifle—and then discovered he had a malfunction.

"I had a ruptured casing in my rifle. The extractor pulled the back of a shell casing off, leaving most of the casing behind in the chamber. The last round fed into the broken casing, jamming the rifle. I had no way to fix it. I was down to hand grenades and a knife when Chappelle handed me a German submachine gun, a Schmeisser that he had planned to keep as a souvenir."

Patruno was given five loaded magazines for the German weapon, and the assault on the farmhouse continued. As they neared the house, the firing stopped from inside. Patruno pitched a hand grenade into the living room, and after it detonated the men rushed inside. The Germans had fled, leaving behind only a motorcycle, which had been destroyed by Patruno's grenade. But they found champagne in the basement of the house. Patruno took three bottles, keeping one for himself and giving one to Chappelle. He also gave one to Lt. "Moose" Heyliger, who had led them in the assault.

Having already arrived in Pouppeville earlier in the day, Sgt. Russ Schwenk headed off with a small group in an attempt to locate the remainder of Fox Company. Several men who had accompanied Schwenk to Pouppeville stayed behind, waiting to meet up with their unit's officers and other missing men. Schwenk and his group moved along using the ditches, shadows of the hedgerows, and the tall summer grass for concealment. They soon discovered that their highly coveted jumpsuits were too khaki-colored for the lush green of Normandy. The only green on their uniforms that matched their surroundings, were their new olive-drab cartridge belts and the dark burlap they had strung through the netting of their helmets.

Along with Schwenk were George Lovell, Joe Flick, Jim O'Hara, Ed Brennan, and Alan Summers. They were accompanied by a dozen or so men from several different units. As the sunlight began to fade, the men moved into the tiny village of Brucheville, southwest of Pouppeville. The name looked like "Brushville" to the Americans, and the title stuck, as they had no idea how Brucheville was actually pronounced in French.

Unknown to Schwenk and his gang, a small group of German troops occupied several of the homes in Brucheville. As they came upon the village, a shot rang out, and within seconds a heavy firefight broke out. The men began to fire into the homes, attempting to pin the Germans down, while others rushed the windows and tossed hand grenades inside. When enemy fire prevented the paratroopers from rushing one home in the village, Flick and Lovell moved around it in an attempt to sneak up behind the defending Germans. In the dimming light Flick made out the silhouette of a soldier moving behind the home in their direction. They were only ten feet apart when Flick realized the advancing soldier was a German and the German realized Flick was an American. Both raised their rifles to fire. Flick was a moment faster and snap-shot the German dead.

Flick then fired three rockets from his bazooka into the back of the home, and the men out front followed up with grenades. When the house fell silent, the group moved back toward Pouppeville. While en route they came across their company commander, Capt. Thomas Mulvey.

Mulvey had spent the early morning hours at the aid station in Sainte-Mère-Église nursing a badly sprained ankle. He managed to get back on his feet with the assistance of a commandeered bicycle and headed off for his objective, accompanied by Lt. Andy Tuck. He was now in the process of rounding up his troops in and around Pouppeville for their next ordered objective.

For the troopers of Fox Company, there would be no rest. Already awake for over twenty-four hours, most were too excited to sleep anyway. A few minutes to sit down and drink some water from an almost empty canteen or a quick bite of a chocolate D-ration bar were the best they could hope for. Friends had been shot or drowned. Others were still missing. Many in the company had killed in combat, a testament to their training and skill. The day was finally ending, but another was beginning, with no real respite from the action.

CHAPTER 10

NORMANDY

At sunrise on 7 June, John Taylor watched in relief as a column of about three hundred paratroopers moved down the road to the command post. Many of the missing Fox Company men were in the group, almost a third of the company. Leading the troops was their commander, Capt. Thomas Mulvey, and Lt. Andy Tuck. The men were using several forms of transportation to assist in the march. They pulled handcarts for ammunition, and Bob Noody rode a German motorcycle with his bazooka and rockets filling its sidecar.

A short time later the company moved out, along with their sister companies D ("Dog") and E ("Easy"). They trailed the First Battalion of the 506th toward the small village of Vierville. As the men moved into it, they came under a heavy burst of enemy machine gun fire. With bullets snapping past them, the paratroopers took cover in the ditches and hedges along the road. Benjamin Stoney from Headquarters Company moved up to a split in the roadway, looking for the source of the fire. Fox Company's Pfc. George Yochum looked up from the ditch and yelled, "Watch yourself, Stoney! Keep your head down!" It was too late. The German machine gun position opened up again, and Stoney dropped to the roadway, mortally wounded.

John Taylor, who was moving up in the rear of Fox Company, described the action.

JOHN TAYLOR ● *Just as we moved into town, Sgt. Stoney was machine gunned down and torn up badly in the chest area. He was already dead and laying out in the street when I got there. At that point, so early in the action, his body would have just been moved over to the side of the road. It was not practical to do anything else. Later on burial squads would gather the dead.*

The men poured fire back at the Germans, shooting into the front of every house, every possible location someone could be hiding, and every blind spot. After thirty minutes of battle, the Germans in Vierville began to surrender. John Taylor looked for a water source for his long-empty canteen.

JOHN TAYLOR • *The only thought on my mind was getting something to drink. My canteen was empty. The water was not safe, but we had purifying tablets we used to prevent dysentery. In the center of town was an old church with a graveyard. Near that was a big house and surrounding buildings with a gate going in through a rock wall. I ran over there to see if I could find some water. As I crossed the road and started through the gate, a couple of American troopers double-timed some prisoners out of the gate heading back up the road.*

From somewhere in the group, I saw a grenade fall to the pavement right at my feet! It scared the living hell out of me! I can still remember seeing it hit the ground. I don't know if it fell from one of the prisoners, was thrown from somewhere, or whether it was dropped accidentally by one of our guys. I did, however, know it was live, because I heard the fuse pop.

I immediately yelled, "Live grenade!" and made a headlong dive behind the stone fence. I think everyone else did likewise. The grenade had about a five-second fuse, so no one was injured. I figured it must have been a concussion grenade rather than a fragmentation grenade, or we'd have had some people hurt.

Moments later another firefight broke out. A Fox Company man from upstairs in a building spotted some Germans in a gully behind it, and after a few shots were exchanged, a squad of Germans surrendered.

A heavy volume of fire could be heard off in the distance. The men moved out toward the battle and marched into the small village of Angoville-au-Plain.

JOHN TAYLOR • *I remember that small, rural village as being a depressing-looking place, with ancient stone houses and a central town square. I did not see any civilians around. There was no fighting there to speak of. The Germans apparently at this point were pulling back. We could hear more fighting over to our right, on the Sainte-Mère-Église road, and so we headed in that direction.*

Taylor was sent ahead on a scouting patrol, along with three members from his Second Squad, Second Platoon. Orders were given to observe and report. They moved out toward a nearby crossroad at the village of Beaumont.

Back in Angoville-au-Plain, the men of the company gathered around a dead German soldier in the middle of the village's only road. He was a large, handsome man, and his body almost spanned the width of the roadway. American paratrooper K-rations protruded from his uniform's pockets. One trooper remarked, "That guy must have had all the frauleins falling all over him," which was quickly countered with "Yeah, they'll have to do some tall falling to reach him now."

Taylor, Orel Lev, Tiger Cauvin, and Joe Trepelka moved up toward the crossroads to Beaumont hugging a hedgerow. They went into the yard of a nearby home, taking comfort in the fact that it was fenced by a brick-and-masonry wall. The protection they assumed they had was quickly shattered when mortar rounds began to explode around the home and yard. German small arms fire began to chew up the brick wall. Taylor moved out of the yard and spoke briefly with Major Foster from the First Battalion of the 506th. As Foster was advising Taylor of the situation, Col. William Turner rolled past seated on top of an American tank. Turner was the commander of the First Battalion of the 506th, and the tank was a welcome sight to Taylor.

Heavy small arms and artillery fire began to funnel into the crossroads and down the leading roadway. A short time later Colonel Turner was shot dead by a sniper as he commanded from the top the tank. Taylor moved out back toward Angoville-au-Plain, with the image of Turner slumped over the tank still fresh in his mind. Moving back with Taylor were Lev, Cauvin, and Trepelka, all having been wounded by the mortar fire.

Taylor returned and gave his report of the situation, while his fellow patrol mates were treated for their injuries.

The company was held in reserve, eventually moving after darkness to the fields just southwest of Angoville-au-Plain. They took a defensive position and dug foxholes for the night. Exhausted, many got their first bites of rations and their first few hours of sleep in days. Joe Flick managed to swipe two comforters from a nearby home to line his foxhole with, and E. B. Wallace and Victor Tamkun scrounged up some wine and passed the bottles around.

Medic Millard Moore and an E Company medic, Ed Pepping, had located a German vehicle to use as an ambulance and had been running wounded paratroopers to the church in town for treatment. Eventually Moore, his signature brass-knuckle knife on his hip, ended the night by heating up a small pot of stew made of issued rations and local supplies.

In the distance were the ever-present reports of small arms fire. Artillery shells began to drop in on the Fox Company position, and the men hunkered down in their holes to avoid the blasts and flying shrapnel. A patrol was summoned for reconnaissance to locate the harassing artillery. Bill True, Pat Casey, Sgt. Frank Griffin, Joe Flick, and Bill Olanie "volunteered" for the patrol. Like Taylor's prior mission, they were told to avoid contact—to observe and report only. At 1900 they headed west in the direction of Houesville.

After slowly moving through fields and over hedgerows for a few hours, lead scout True spotted three German soldiers in a field in front of him. He quickly raised his rifle, took aim, and squeezed off a shot, dropping a pistol-carrying German. The others in the patrol began to shoot as well, but the two other Germans managed to disappear into the now darkening foliage. The Americans continued on and came within a thousand yards of Houesville as darkness was falling.

Deciding it was too risky to keep advancing, fearful of both enemy and friendly fire in the dark, the group began to head back. They hugged the hedgerows, reversing their direction. Casey, who was leading the group, paused to peer over the next hedgerow that blocked their advance. A silhouette was in the field on the other side, moving toward him. Casey raised his rifle and let the unknown subject get closer. Griffin came up alongside him to see what was going on, and raised his Thompson in support. They allowed the subject to get within ten feet, at which time the subject was recognized as a German soldier. Spotting the two paratroopers, the German reached for a holstered pistol. Casey fired a shot, and Griffin let off a burst from his tommy gun. The German was illuminated by the paratroopers' muzzle blasts as the bullets tore into him. He fell to the ground, tried to get up while screaming, and then slumped into the grass, dead.

The patrol headed across the field toward a road visible in the distance. As the men approached it, they found a parachute-dropped equipment bundle in the high grass at its edge. Flick and Griffin went over to open the bundle while the other three covered them from the grass. True then noticed a black dog stepping into view on the road, walking slowly toward the group, then suddenly realized that trailing the dog were three Germans. He opened fire at the group with his M1 rifle, followed by Flick with a tommy gun burst from the hip. The Germans, and the dog, scattered off into the darkness. The men grabbed several cans of machine gun ammunition from the supply bundle and headed back to their company with their report.

A second patrol was sent out at 2000. It was led by Lt. Russell Hall from the Second Platoon and included Sgt. Charlie Jacobs, Pfc. Jack Dickerson, Pfc. Chelal "Pop" Clark, and Sgt. Charlie Reese. They brought along a walkie-talkie to stay in touch with their unit's leaders. After traveling to the small village of La Basse Addeville to their south, then east to the sound of gunfire, they turned on the radio to make a report. When powered up, the radio made a loud screeching noise that immediately brought mortar fire in on their location. Under enemy observation now, they were pursued by shelling as they fled through several fields.

The patrol finally managed to get out of the view of the German observers and ran back to the company. No one was injured, and the men settled down for a few hours of rest.

News of casualties, objectives taken, and the general confusion of the first days in Normandy began to trickle into the 506th's command post by way of messengers and radio communication. Information was logged into the regimental journals for personnel (S-1), intelligence (S-2), operations (S-3), and supply (S-4). One such note was made about two Fox Company casualties, Lt. Charles Semon and James "Rebel" Waters:

7 JUNE 1944, S-1 JOURNAL
2130—Received cards on Lt.Seamon and James F. Walters 14139019, who were both drowned near Houseville. Card as follows—Seamon Grid 35-91 sheet 6-E, Walters 32-91 sheet 6-3. Cards being turned over to Med.Det.

Another note was made about a patrol by the F/506th:

7 June 1944, S-2 Journal
2000—Lt Hall went as far south as Addeville and 500 yards east.
Heard en & friendly machine gun fire.

The morning of 8 June brought a few more hours of rest for the men of Company F who were assembled in Angoville-au-Plain. At 1215 they moved out in force, through Beaumont, then west, and headed toward Houesville. They arrived at 1530, and "Kidnap"—the code name for the 506th—made contact with "Kickoff"—the 502nd.

On the way back from Houesville, three more men joined up with the company, Marion Grodowski, Ralph Provenzano, and Raul Ochoa. The trio had wandered and hidden in the area east of town for two days, hiding from German patrols while nursing their jump injuries. A hailed reconnaissance jeep with the Fourth Infantry Division, in from Utah Beach, finally directed them back to their unit. After contact with the 502nd, the unit pulled back to Angoville-au-Plain.

Later in the evening the company got word to move out again, this time to a farm overlooking a lock on a canal south of La Basse Addeville. The location, La Barquette, had been fought for and occupied by members of the 501st Regiment. The locks were in a flat, marshy area about a thousand yards from Carentan, and Fox Company was to occupy the high ground to the north.

The company moved out in three long skirmish lines, with one platoon in front of the other. With the moonlight spilling out from behind clouds, the men passed though fields of dead German soldiers and livestock. The stench from the rotting bodies and carcasses hung in the air. Dead paratroopers were also passed by, many still in their parachutes after being killed during their jump. Adding to the already surreal landscape, passing breezes occasionally caught parachutes, causing them to momentarily billow up, like ghosts from out of the grass.

JOHN TAYLOR • *We moved down to the locks on the far side of the river just outside of Carentan in order to relieve some battle-weary troops. My platoon went across the locks and talked with some of the troops that we were replacing to find out what the situation was. We could see that the shelling had really torn things up around there. Our main objective was to guard the locks on the river from destruction by the Germans. We were told that the Germans had tried to swim down the river and blow these locks.*

The company settled in among the few small houses and barns around the locks. Manning Haney and Joe Hogenmiller set up a machine gun near the locks, overlooking the water. Haney had managed to locate another machine gun after having cut his away during his jump at Houesville. Several hours passed as the men listened to the shelling of Carentan.

At 0300 a burst of machine gun fire from the locks sprang the company into action. A few moments of confusion followed, as everyone tried to determine where the enemy was coming from, and who was firing. Dozens of eyes scanned the wide horizon, looking at every shadow and watching for movement. Nothing.

A few shouts from Haney calmed the men down. He had fired the machine gun into the water at what he thought was a German saboteur floating down the canal. It turned out to be only a large, drifting log. Although the gunfire ended for the night, so did the men's rest. Most were now too alert to get back to sleep.

The morning of 9 June was a clear one. A visitor arrived at La Barquette, a Navy forward observer. He was directed to a home on the south side of the locks. John Taylor climbed with him into the attic. After a few shingles were removed from the roof, the observer used a high-powered range-finding periscope to view the activity in and around Carentan. Germans were seen moving about the town, and a body could be seen about five hundred yards away, between the locks and Carentan. It appeared to move occasionally.

Taylor took medic Joe Droogan, Joe Watkins, and Bernard Tom to investigate. It was an injured paratrooper from the 502nd. The man had been lying in the marsh with a badly broken, and now severely swollen, leg since he jumped on the 6th. German soldiers had found the man days before and stripped him of his watch, ammunition, and rations, leaving him with only his rifle, one cartridge, and one cigarette. "I knew you guys would come along sometime," the trooper said, explaining why he did not take the offered option. He was carried back to the locks, and then evacuated by the medics.

The men spent the day cleaning weapons, eating rations, and sitting in foxholes while watching the artillery fall on Carentan. Harvey Morehead arrived in style, riding a tracked German motorcycle called a Kettenkrad. Riding on the back of the contraption was Bob Vogel and Linus Brown. They arrived in time to watch American aircraft drop bombs on Carentan, which was now billowing with smoke.

MARION GRODOWSKI • *I watched a P-47 fly over our position. He flew right up to the edge of Carentan and dropped a single bomb on the railroad. It looked like a bird dropping an egg. You could see parts of railroad track flip through the air. It was impressive!*

TOM ALLEY • *A P-47 flew past us and dropped a bomb on the tracks in Carentan. The tracks curled up, just like a pretzel!*

Breakfast the following morning was meager. The last of the rations were eaten, and small groups of men went out in search of supplies and rations. A young cow was rounded up in the afternoon by Charlie Jacobs, and the company decided that steak sounded good for dinner. The cow was led into a barn, and Jacobs and Ray Ballew did the butchering. The afternoon was relatively silent, with the exception of a few mortar rounds dropping in near the locks.

The Second Platoon's Matt Carlino decided to go over to the barn and obtain a hindquarter of meat for the men staying in the house at the locks. He had just shouldered the slab of beef when two German fighter planes flew over on their way to a strafing run.

BOB JANES • *Two German Me-109s flew past us towards Carentan. They were clipping along just over the tops of the hedges—looked to be about twenty feet off the ground. They were low enough for me to make out the faces and clothes of the pilots inside. One pilot even waved to me in passing.*

Thinking the planes were moving in on him, Carlino, made a break for the house from the open ground in front of the yard. He never stopped running—and never dropped the shouldered beef. He arrived to the farmhouse amid the cheers of the men of the Second Platoon.

10 JUNE 1944, S-2 JOURNAL
1800—White reports 5 mortar shells in Fox Co. position. Mortar

shells hit F co. position.
2005—2 ME 109's flying west over F Co.

10 JUNE 1944, S-3 JOURNAL
1800—F Co. received 5 rounds of artillery in their position (locks).

As darkness fell at the locks, the men began to cook up their fresh cuts of beef on a stove located inside the farmhouse. Squads rotated through the home to take turns watching their portions sizzle and spit in a "borrowed" skillet. After a quick browning, they returned to their foxholes outside to enjoy their steak dinners. At one point the meal was interrupted.

JOHN TAYLOR • *We started to cook our beef that night on the stove in that house. We had men on guard duty, with foxholes dug outside. Without warning, we heard an explosion that sounded as if the roof had caved in. A German plane (a Heinkel 3, I believe) had dropped one of its bombs about two hundred yards from the house. Of course it rattled the house, and we all hit the front door about the same time for those holes outside.*

However, the action was not over. An American antiaircraft unit shot the plane down as it passed over the area, and it crashed about a half mile away. It was quite a show for the steak-eating men of Fox 506th.

Dinner was capped off with a drink. Calvin Wright and William Neubert rode to the locks a short time later on Bob Noody's misappropriated German motorcycle, and in its sidecar was found a milk can of calvados, the local apple brandy. Most took a drink, except Linus Brown who did not drink alcohol, so E. B. Wallace drank Brown's ration plus any left over that the others could not, or would not, finish.

Don Replogle had joined up with the unit that afternoon as well and had a graphic image stuck in his mind. Before he rejoined his unit, Replogle had been fighting the entire time with the 82nd Airborne on the edge of Sainte-Mère-Église. At one point he was involved in a small fight where the troopers were taking occasional shots from Germans across a field.

They had about two dozen prisoners seated behind them in a ditch with their legs up on the road. A few men were guarding the prisoners, and American tanks and vehicles were rushing past the paratroopers and prisoners toward the town. Suddenly one of the tanks sped up and drove right along the edge of the ditch, running over the legs of the prisoners. Replogle doubted any of the prisoners survived the crushing injuries.

The warm evening turned into a chilly night, and the men shivered in their foxholes. No fires were allowed, as they could be spotted by the enemy. Most of the men had discarded their woolen long-johns and pants during the first few warm days in Normandy. They now were paying for it—a lesson learned the hard way.

The morning of the 11th contained a blessing for the troops: Rations arrived. Along with them came more cigarettes from the Army and candy bars and treats from the Red Cross. After munching down the rations and smoking a few cigarettes, the men spent the day covering dead German soldiers and animals up in shell holes, and even dumping a few dead Germans into the canal. But the smell of death still hung in the air around the locks and wafted into the area with every breeze.

That afternoon after a hot lunch, and with the sound of the shelling of Carentan in the distance, the men were told to prepare to move out for a night maneuver toward the town. Just as they had prepared for their night jump, the men secured loose equipment, making sure nothing rattled or clinked, and checked all their weapons and ammunition so that everything was clean and ready to use. After an inspection, the company moved out near dark along with the rest of the Second Battalion.

CHAPTER 11

CARENTAN

The men of the Second Battalion of the 506th moved out across the marshland toward Carentan. Along the way, the companies became separated several times, causing an accordion effect in what should have been a fluid but linear movement. At one point Yochum was sent out alone to find E Company. Formed up again, the battalion crossed a bridge to the north of town and passed over the railroad that ran west from town. While on the move, the men passed a dead German soldier.

TOM ALLEY ● *I saw this dead German. He had an American fighting knife stuck in his neck, right behind the ear. It was all the way to the hilt. I do not know if that is how he was killed, or if someone stuck that knife in later. But it was quite a shocking sight.*

Several hours past midnight, Fox Company managed to get settled in southwest of Carentan. They were allowed an hour's rest before preparing for their assault on the town. Somewhere along the route John Taylor and his First Squad had become separated, not only from the Second Platoon, but the entire company as well.

JOHN TAYLOR ● *They had moved out ahead of us, and our squad couldn't make contact and couldn't tell which way they had gone. We didn't have radios at the squad level. Radio contact was at the battalion and company levels, and walkie-talkies were used to communicate between platoons and platoon headquarters.*
We moved on anyway and came upon Captain Peters from the

Regimental Headquarters Company who was headed in our same direction. He had about eight or ten men with him and said we could just latch on to his group. So we did. We moved pretty cautiously that night, weaving in and out of backyards along the edge of Carentan. When we got close to the center of town, the captain decided he did not know where he was. I sure didn't know where I was.

Our first clue that we were kind of isolated in that place was the fact that we could hear Germans talking all around us. This convinced us we'd better pull back and try to hook up with the rest of our units. We carefully made our way back out to the hedge and found the whole company about daybreak. They had not even gone the way we did. They had instead flanked around to the right and come in that way.

When we caught up with them, they were right at the edge of town. As we moved along, I noticed that we had passed the same place where the captain and my group had already been that night. We almost reached downtown Carentan and didn't even realize it.

Taylor and his group were directed to the Fox Company position by Captain Peters, who then, along with his own men, disappeared into the hedgerows. Although Peters was supposedly killed in action on D-Day, there were multiple, credible sightings of him days later, such as Taylor's account. (This mystery and other fascinating stories can be read about in *Avenging Eagles: Forbidden Tales of the 101th Airborne Division in World War 2* by Mark Bando.)

When Taylor arrived he heard that the Second Platoon had a casualty a few minutes before.

BOB JANES • *It was beginning to get light, and we were moving up to the edge of town. I had been first scout for the Second Platoon. We were the right flank of the company. Chester Nakelski was second scout, right behind me. Our movement into every field involved throwing a grenade or two over the hedge before we crossed over or went in any openings. I was a little tired of being first scout, always being in the front, so I complained to Sergeant Jacobs that he should have Nakelski switch with me. He agreed and told Nakelski to take first scout, and I switched places with him.*

We went through a couple fields, and we came up on an outbuilding on our right. As we moved toward the building, a paratrooper stepped out from the backside of it and opened fire with a tommy gun on Nakelski. He dropped to the ground not ten feet in front of me. Sergeant Jacobs and I could see it was another American shooting, and Jacobs yelled, "Cease fire!" The other guy stopped shooting. Jacobs and I ran to Nakelski and tried to pull him up. The whole top of his head came off in his helmet.

Still reeling from the tragic death, Janes and Jacobs left their friend's body behind and headed into town. As they crossed an intersection, the company came under artillery fire. Several white phosphorus shells exploded over the Third Platoon, and Carl Pein, Gus Patruno, Joe Chappelle, and Angelo Peluso were hit by the burning shrapnel. After clearing the roadway they were treated by the company medics, and Peluso was evacuated.

Lieutenant Tuck then led the First Platoon into town on the left flank. At first the men were confused by the lack of shooting by the Germans, as they hugged each doorway, alley, and building corner for cover. The town was in terrible shape. Rubble and debris were everywhere. The men's confusion ended with a deluge of German mortar and machine gun fire toward Fox Company. They rushed for cover. Company runner George Yochum and radio-man Louis Burton tried to fit into an outhouse that was nothing more than a roofless square box, a foot above the ground and only a few feet high. The machine gun fire was zipping all around them, striking a nearby brick wall and showering the two with bits of plaster and stone. The men squeezed back out of the outhouse's door and ran to a doorway occupied by their company commander, Thomas Mulvey.

The men of Fox Company rushed from doorway to doorway, firing at upstairs windows and across the streets into shops and houses. When one man would reach a doorway, he would wait for another. On the arrival of a second man or third man, they would rush out and fight to their next position of cover. Whenever possible, the interior of the homes and businesses were checked for enemy troops. The close-quarters street fighting was slow and dangerous.

At one point, rifle fire from a building drew Captain Mulvey's attention. He sent Sgt. Huber Porter and Nick Cortese to flush out the shooter. The two men crept into the building and slowly moved upstairs, and when they had gone all the way up to the attic's door, Porter yelled, "Who's there?"

There was no answer, so Porter fired his tommy gun into the door, shattering it. A grenade quickly followed the burst, tossed in by Porter. An explosion was heard inside, and out through the door came an infuriated, but unhurt, Sgt. Gordon Mather. Mather had not heard Porter because he had been firing from the attic at a German sniper in another building.

Around 1100, the south end of Carentan was cleared of enemy troops, and by all appearances the Germans throughout the town had either been killed or fled. Fox Company met up with the 401st Glider Infantry Regiment in town, and the men were given a short time to rest. One could smell bread baking. Following his nose, he went to investigate.

BUD EDWARDS • *I was sitting there and suddenly smelled bread baking. I got up and found my way to a small shop. Some Frenchman was inside baking bread. I walked in and told him I wanted some bread. I didn't speak French, and this guy didn't speak English. So, I slapped one of my invasion notes down on the counter. The baker seemed to be staring at the two grenades I had on my suspenders. I think he really knew what I wanted and handed over a couple loaves of bread. I went back outside with the bread, and the shop was quickly filled with other guys from the outfit. I'm sure we cleaned him out. The bread was delicious.*

With a few hours for rest, the looting began. Men filtered into homes in search of food, wine, and liquor. Bob Janes and the rest of his squad appeared to strike the jackpot.

BOB JANES • *We went into this house and went down to the cellar looking for something to drink. We all managed to get some wine, and after taking a few slugs of the stuff we decided to check out the rest of the house. The people that had lived there must have been loaded, or Nazi collaborators. The place was full of liquor and food. The furniture was very nice— they even had a refrigerator. Lots of luxuries! In one bedroom there were six large bottles marked perfume. I smelled each one and picked the one marked "Cologne." I could not figure out what to do with it, but one of the guys told me the stuff was worth five bucks an ounce back in the States. So, I poured out the water from my canteen and filled it to the top with the cologne I had selected. I was the best smelling trooper in Normandy after that.*

After the improvised resupply, the company moved out from Carentan to the west at 1500. The men were told they were going to move out two miles from town and clear the area of any German snipers. They were tired and wanted rest but were assured they would be back in town by dark. They went back into a skirmish line formation and headed out.

They went over a thousand yards from Carentan, with the Second Platoon on the right and the First Platoon on the left. There was no sign of the enemy. As the First Platoon passed through an orchard, Lt. William Brooks went with his men to scout a hole in a hedgerow in front of their position. The company came to a halt. As Brooks neared the opening, machine gun fire tore into him from the opposite direction.

Brooks went down, wounded in the neck and chest. Medic Joe Droogan ran forward to the opening in the hedge and dragged the officer back to safety. Brooks was evacuated. The company was quickly running out of officers. Only three were left.

The Second Platoon did not fare any better. Using binoculars, John Taylor spotted German troops, clad in black, several fields ahead of their location.

CHARLIE JACOBS • *We were on a light cleanup action. After taking Carentan, the Second Squad was on the left, First Squad on the right. As we advanced, I never could contact the First Squad. We double-timed up a few hedgerows—still no First Squad. About the third or fourth hedgerow, we spotted a bunch of krauts, dug in a field. Lieutenant Hall joined us and decided to dump everything we had at them and withdraw. Everything came off okay on the line, but German mortars picked us up on the withdrawal.*

One hedgerow back, we counted heads. Somebody thought Lyman Dickey had been hit. Cpl. George Martin and I went back and found Dickey in a small trench cut in the side of the hedgerow. We withdrew carrying Lyman with us. We could feel that at any minute we would be shot by the Germans. Lyman did not appear to have any visible wounds. We felt a concussion grenade or the mortars killed him.

As darkness fell, the men were told to dig in where they were in the orchard. So much for being back in town by dark, they thought, as they chipped away at their foxholes. Rations, ammunition, and water were brought up to the company from Carentan. The men ate their rations in the dark and settled in for another night in the Normandy soil. One remembered an issue with orders he received that evening.

BOB JANES • *George Martin and I were sent out on the far right flank of the company. We were at the top of a rise in a large field, looking down a slope towards the German lines. The rise we were on sloped off to our left as well, and we found the soil to be too tough to dig into. Martin left to notify Lieutenant Hall. He was gone for what seemed like a very long time, and on his return he told me to fall back with the company.*

12 JUNE 1944, S-2 JOURNAL
0730—Fox Company White assisted C.P. personnel to beat off attack.

As it began to get light, the company prepared to move out. The Second Platoon was on the right flank, the Third on the left, and the First trailed behind. A small lane separated them from Dog Company, which was moving west as well, with a railroad line running parallel on their right flank. Easy Company was behind Dog Company, as reserve.

Moving out from foxholes and slit trenches, the men advanced to the first hedgerow. Joe Hogenmiller climbed over it and began to scout ahead of the company. The rest of the Second Platoon, fanned out in a skirmish line, began to move up to the same hedge. Then they saw the German tank.

BOB JANES • *I looked to my right, and at the roadway intersection was a German tank. I do not know if it had rubber on the tracks or had been creeping slowly or what, but it was just there, not fifty yards away. I never heard it approach.*

CHARLIE JACOBS • *I was on top of the hedgerow. We were preparing to attack when I heard a tank. I looked to the right forty yards or so and saw two German tanks coming fast! The tanks blasted away into hedgerows where our people were.*

MARION GRODOWSKI • *I was looking at Clyde Jeffers at that moment, who was leaning against a hedgerow. He sprang to his feet, looked over the hedgerow, and was met by a torrent of tracers. With the glow of the tracers about his head, it looked to me as if he was wearing a halo. Jeff ducked and, with that ever-present infectious smile on his face, quipped, "Damn it. A guy can get hurt around here." He was about to say something*

else when I heard a call for a bazooka or a grenade launcher. It seemed
a German tank was on the road heading for us.

The tank turned and fired at the troopers at almost point-blank range, knocking Matthew Carlino and Bill McNeese off the hedge they were attempting to climb over. They pulled themselves up from the ground in a daze. Blood streamed down Carlino's face, and McNeese's hands were bleeding. One finger was dangling.

Grodowski moved up to stop the tank with his rifle grenade. He had never fired one before. He shouldered his bolt-action rifle and aimed at the German tank only forty yards away.

MARION GRODOWSKI ● *I fired the first grenade off, and the rifle somersaulted over my shoulder, knocking me on my ass. I had missed. I swore, then stood up and fired a second grenade off from the hip. I missed again. Tommy Wolford ran over and told me he knew how to shoot the grenade and wanted a shot at knocking out the tank. I loaded the rifle and handed it over. I stepped back about ten feet. It was too late. The tank fired its gun, the shell found its mark and exploded next to us and knocked me back and down several feet. I rose to my feet and saw Tommy Wolford was dead. If it hadn't been for Wolford, I would be lying there on the ground dead."*

The company was in a panic. Captain Mulvey looked shocked to see the tanks and German troops swarming down the road toward them. He attempted to contact the battalion headquarters but was unable to get through. As a deluge of enemy fire poured into the line, the men ran for cover and crouched behind the closet hedgerow, attempting to fire back. Grodowski was again nearly hit by a blast from the tank. Lieutenant Hall, Pfc. Kenneth Hull, and Sgt. Charlie Jacobs from Second platoon were wounded in the blast.

MARION GRODOWSKI ● *Another shell exploded. Again I was pressed to the ground. Lying there I heard a gasping, fluttering sound like someone blowing on the edge of a sheet of paper. I looked up and saw Les Hegland rising to his feet and saw his throat slashed open. The wound was not too bloody, and his windpipe was flitting in and out of his throat with every breath he took.*

Grodowski was frustrated at his inability to help Hegland. He tried to keep a calm face and be reassuring as he directed Hegland back to the aid station. The situation was desperate. The company was being decimated. Hugh Borden sent the order down the line to move back. The men began to withdraw, not in a rush en masse, but in small groups, as if following any other order. Grodowski watched as the First Platoon's Johnny Supco went past him, his rubberized gas mask pouch on fire, dangling from his hip. He yelled to Supco about the fire, and Supco yelled something back, but Grodowski couldn't hear him.

Hugh Borden stood in the roadway and covered the company's withdrawal, firing from the hip with his tommy gun at a German armored vehicle as it rushed past toward the retreating men. It was a Marder—a tank destroyer with an open top—and the crew inside ducked down to avoid the spray of bullets fired by Borden as they passed.

With Willie Morris and Nick Cortese leading, the company moved back uphill to the next hedgerow, about a hundred yards behind them. The defensive line was jumbled, and with the Germans right behind them, they moved back again to the next hedge. What they did not realize was that in the confusion they had left an injured man behind, Hegland. After being pointed toward the aid station by Grodowski, he had moved back only a few yards and over to the road on their right flank, where he sat down next to a truck to rest. In pain and having difficulty breathing, he did not notice the company withdraw.

"Bazooka-men up front!" was the order as men jumped into slit trenches on both sides of the hedgerow. Rushing toward safety, Janes and Grodowski leapt into the slit trench against the hedge where there was only room for one. Janes squirmed on top of Grodowski as they tried to position themselves to face the oncoming Germans.

Bob Noody rushed forward hearing the order. The line was now a mix of men from different squads and platoons. Gus Patruno loaded Noody up with a bazooka rocket, and Noody headed out into the field to face an oncoming German tank. The tank fired, striking the hedgerow above Janes and Grodowski, wounding Janes in the knee. Janes was shocked to see blood pouring from his pant leg.

BOB JANES • *I was not sure what to do but did not think I could walk. My knee was tore up pretty bad. So crawling, I dragged myself out of the field and out towards the road. Once I got to the road, there was a jeep zooming up and down, picking up wounded men. Someone put me on the hood of the jeep, and we were driven into Carentan to a field hospital.*

The field was covered in knee-high grass, which offered no concealment for bazooka-man Noody. As the tank fired into the hedgerow, wounding more men, he fought back.

BOB NOODY ● *I was about a hundred yards from the tank. I placed the sight picture on the tank, as elevated as it would go, and fired off a shot. It hit on the left front of the tank, and I think it disabled the track.*

Noody reloaded the bazooka alone, as the tank turned toward him slightly and began to fire its machine gun in his direction. He kneeled and fired a second shot, this time hitting somewhere below the main tank gun. He kneeled as low as possible again and loaded a third time. Machine gun fire clipped his way in the grass.

BOB NOODY ● *I stood up and tried to move away from the fire. From out of nowhere a horse ran into view. It was chestnut brown, wide eyed, and running. It was terrified. I moved, using the horse as cover, keeping it between myself and the tank. I could hear the machine gun bullets striking the side of the horse. It turned around, and I moved with it. I could hear more fire striking the horse, the thump of the bullets striking its side. As the horse fell, I fired again. It was my last rocket. It struck the tank next to the main gun. A second later four Germans bailed out the backside of the tank and ran away from our lines. Everyone seemed to be shooting at them, but I never saw any of them go down. As I moved back I thought about the horse. It was sad it had been killed, but it had saved my life.*

The fight continued. German soldiers moved into the field along with two more tanks. A third tank crept up the road to their right flank, with enemy soldiers crawling up the ditch alongside it. The fight continued. German tank fire burst into the hedges and their tree tops, raining shrapnel down on the men below. The First Platoon's Dude Stone was struck by the fire, as well as Ken Steinke. Radio-man Doug Roth rushed to treat Stone, bandaging his leg. In a panic, Roth fumbled with a morphine syrette, by first trying to inject Stone with a capped needle. After a moment of composure, Roth managed to get the cap off the tip and inject Stone.

The company's "Mutt and Jeff," little Johnny Supco and lanky Don Davis, moved up behind a low hedge and began firing their machine gun at the swarm of advancing Germans. A few feet away, Tom Alley was on the company's right flank in a ditch where two hedgerows met, butting toward each other from across the roadway.

TOM ALLEY • *A German tank was coming up the road towards me from over a knoll, and German soldiers were crawling up the ditches on both sides of the road. I drew a bead on the first German in the ditch and fired. I saw him drop and knew I had hit him. The soldiers in the ditches stopped moving forward, and a moment later the tank fired back at me.*

The tank's return fire struck the trees just above the hedge. The blast knocked down both Supco and Davis in a shower of leaves and debris. Alley waited for them to get up but saw no movement. He rushed over to them and found that both had been killed by the concussion from the blast.

The Second Platoon had filled the gap in the middle of the company's defense. Manning Haney fired his machine gun trying to hold the line, but the Germans advanced, and their fire was intense. Tank fire exploded along the hedge, knocking Haney down and wounding others. Running out of rockets and rifle grenades, the company had no chance against the tanks— they were being decimated. After firing over twelve hundred rounds of machine gun ammunition, a tank finally wounded Kentucky Haney.

When Fox Company pulled back, it exposed the left flank of Dog Company, forcing it to withdraw and move back between Easy Company and Fox. The Fox Company line was actually bowed and veering 150 yards back toward Carentan. The flank to Easy and Dog Companies was still exposed, but Fox Company still took the brunt of the armored attack. They had a road now to their rear, with the battalion aid station on their far right flank, and were looking uphill at the Germans soldiers firing down on them. The German tanks drove in figure eights, moving up and down the line while firing on it.

Hugh Borden got on the radio and spoke with battalion commander Colonel Strayer. Strayer put Colonel Sink on the radio and Borden told him, "If you want any of your Second Battalion left, you had better get us some tank support!" Colonel Sink said that he would come up and check on the situation, and a short time later he and Colonel Chase arrived at the Fox Company position to assess the situation. Borden filled Sink in.

Colonel Chase moved along the line with Captain Mulvey. They came up on Dutch Ostrander crouched behind the hedge, armed with his rifle grenade. Peering over the hedge, they could see a German tank firing into their location, with its commander brazenly viewing the action partially atop the tank. Captain Mulvey asked Ostrander why he was not firing his grenades. "The tank is too far away sir, and I've only got a few rounds left," he responded. "Fire anyway. I'll get you more," Chase told him.

Ostrander lobbed a round at the tank. It bounced off the hull. Ostrander lobbed a second grenade. The grenade arched up, dropped down, and hit the tank commander, knocking him back inside the tank before exploding and disabling the tank. Captain Mulvey proudly slapped Ostrander on the back and declared, "That's one of my boys." Chase took off for more rifle grenades to be sent quickly to Ostrander. With the tank disabled, the German advance slowed. But then a German tank rumbled up the road on the right flank and began to fire into the small dwelling being used as the battalion aid station. The building was marked with a Red Cross flag. E. B. Wallace watched the action from a hedge a short distance away.

E. B. WALLACE • *I had been ordered back across the highway and was on a bazooka antitank position less than a hundred yards from the aid station. This German tank drove up to the aid station, and the tank commander peered into the building from atop his tank. An officer came out. I do not know if it was our chaplain or surgeon. Whoever he was, he faced off with this German tank commander, waving his finger "no, no, no" like he was scolding a child. The tank commander went back down into his tank, and it reversed straight back down the road from my view. We had a good laugh over that!*

The First Platoon's Sergeant Mather saw an American machine gun across the field from their location. Braving the enemy fire, he climbed over the hedge and ran into the field and retrieved the gun. It had no tripod. Once back behind the hedge, Mather fired the machine gun, with Bob Vogel assisting. The battle, now several hours long, continued.

The order came to move forward, and the men advanced toward the next hedgerow to their front. As the Fox Company line was stabilized, ammunition was brought forward and wounded men were evacuated, but enemy tank and artillery fire still pounded the Fox Company line. Pfc. George Yochum was struck by a piece of shrapnel in the boot, which knocked off its boot. He yelled for a medic. Joe Droogan rushed over and advised Yochum, "You don't need a medic—you need a shoemaker."

American tanks from the Second Armored Division arrived on the scene. Grodowski watched tentatively as a small Stuart tank battled it out with a German tank on their right flank road.

MARION GRODOWSKI • *I watched these two shoot back and forth at each other. The little American tank would rush up, fire, and reverse. The German tank would do the same. You could see the rounds flying over the top of each other. A short time later, the little tank backed up and held. His gun was really no match for the larger German tank. It became a standoff.*

Across the battlefield, amid the multicolored tracer rounds, exploding shells, and shouts of men, a figure appeared. An American paratrooper staggered from the German lines, a bandage held to his neck. It was Les Hegland.

When the Germans overran the company's position, they came upon Hegland, dazed, bloodied, and struggling for air. For some reason, he was not shot, he was not ignored, and he was not taken away as a prisoner. The 506th were up against the Seventeenth SS Panzergrenadier Division and paratroopers, and in their ranks was a medic who showed compassion for Hegland. His wound was dressed as well as possible, and in the lull of the battle he was pushed back toward his own lines. Hegland managed to make it back without further injury and was evacuated.

Larger American tanks, Shermans, rumbled into the fight. Several moved into Fox Company's line but because they drew heavy enemy fire, the men quickly moved away from them. There was only so much one could do, and the fire intensified as the tanks fired to push the Germans back. Ray Aebischer continued to work his machine gun at the German troops along the roadway ditches. Enemy fire returned. Aebischer and Conrad Ours were both hit and evacuated.

When one American tank drew fire, a shell burst nearby, wounding three more men. Clyde Jeffers, Jack Dickerson, and Waldron Bettelyoun were all hit by shrapnel. Bettelyoun was a Sioux Indian who had grown up in the Black Hills of South Dakota. The Normandy hedgerows were certainly far from his life on the Pine Ridge reservation. With a severely pierced helmet and shrapnel throughout his back and in both legs, he dropped unconscious in a bloody heap. The company had shriveled in numbers. Another man was hit in the Third Platoon, but this time it was by small arms fire.

ROY ZERBE ● *I was leaning over a hedgerow firing when a bullet struck me right in my Screaming Eagle patch. The bullet entered from the right side of the patch and lodged in my arm. I was later evacuated to a hospital and the bullet was removed. It was an American .45-caliber. I don't know where it came from, but I suspect it was a stray from one of the companies on our right.*

Late in the afternoon, with the paratroopers and tanks having subdued the German attack, the company moved off the line and back into Carentan, its position filled by another unit. "The Battle of Bloody Gulch" was over but at a terrible cost to Company F. Three men were dead, and twenty-two had been wounded and evacuated. Remaining in the ranks were over two dozen more who had minor shrapnel wounds and injuries that did not warrant evacuation and were treated in the field. They were nearing half strength and had only two officers left.

As the men filtered back into Carentan, several were sent back to retrieve their dead. Linus Brown, E. B. Wallace, Victor Tamkun, and Charlie Jacobs were given the task of loading their friends' bodies into trucks. Gus Patruno rushed out to find his pal, Tommy Wolford.

GUS PATRUNO ● *I found Tommy lying in the grass. He looked to me like he was just sleeping. I did not see any injuries on him, and he had a slight smile on his face. He looked very peaceful.*

Tom Alley followed the men out and walked the ditch that had been the company's right flank during the battle. Standing between the two abutting hedgerows, he looked down to the area where he had fired at the advancing Germans crawling up the ditch. Moving down the ditch, he came to the man he had killed. It was a German officer with a camouflaged smock. Alley removed his Luger pistol, holster, and belt, and returned to Carentan.

When he arrived he found many of the men were already asleep where they had sat down, exhausted from the sleepless days and adrenaline-pumped fighting. Others were busy drowning their graphic memories in looted booze.

CHAPTER 12

WINDING DOWN

W hen Fox Company came back into Carentan, the men saw a peculiar sight under the shade of a tree. It was Merlin Shennum, who had not been seen or heard from since he jumped into Normandy. Shennum had been on his own adventure without the company.

MERLIN SHENNUM ● *I arrived in Carentan after the battle just west of town. I had been rounded up with other members of the 101st who had been fighting with the 82nd Airborne, and we were trucked into town. I was out of water and quite thirsty. I saw a dead German soldier in the shade and found he had a canteen of water. I propped myself against his body and was drinking from the canteen when the company arrived back in town.*

Shennum had joined up with an officer from the 82nd Airborne near the railroad west of Sainte-Mère-Église during the night of D-Day. After ambushing a German motorcycle and sidecar, they walked down to the La Fière manor and joined up with other men from the 82nd there.

MERLIN SHENNUM ● *I went along on a patrol across the causeway. As we neared the far west side, a German machine gun opened fire on us. We all hit the dirt. Some guy in the 82nd was in front of me. He dropped to the ground and from a prone position fired his rifle back at the gun, striking one of the crew. He then rolled over and went back into his prone firing position and fired, killing the second gunner. He must have practiced the move, because it was textbook—like something from a training film or manual. I was impressed.*

Shennum and his party moved on and met up with another group of paratroopers near the church on the west side of the causeway. He decided to join up with them as they moved southward along the flooded marsh. It was not long before they again made contact with the enemy.

MERLIN SHENNUM • *We were heading south when a small German tank drove up behind us near the causeway. It began to fire at us, and we fled into the grass in the flooded fields. I do not think they could really see us well, but the firing continued toward us. We headed back across the flooded field toward the manor. At one point we came to a wide area and had to use some cut up parachute cord to help as a safety line to get some of the guys across the deep areas of the marsh. We came out just south of the manor near a steep hill, and who was standing there to greet us but General [James M.] Gavin from the 82nd Airborne. He told us to get behind the manor and to dry out our clothes, and clean our weapons.*

Shennum and the others stripped off their uniforms, wrung them out, and let them dry on the manor's fences. After cleaning weapons, Shennum was sent south along with a group of soldiers to the town of Chef-du-Pont. He remained with the soldiers there in reserve, stealing cheese from a nearby factory. He would finish his fighting in Normandy with the 507th Parachute Regiment of the 82nd Airborne, before being trucked into Carentan to re-join his unit.

13 JUNE 1944, S-2 JOURNAL
1230—2 Mark 4 tanks at 395840. 1340—Knocked out three Mark III tanks—other two forced to withdraw.

13 JUNE 1944, S-3 JOURNAL
Two Mark 4 tanks reported at 095890. 1345—2nd Bn. Reports three Mark III tanks and two others forced to withdraw. 1630— Tanks still combing our front, doing considerable damage and greatly relieving the pressure.

The company remained in town to rest. Houses were occupied, and the men experienced their first few hours of sleep in Normandy. A few of them managed watch a movie, *Moonlight in Vermont,* that was shown in a cigarette smoke-filled garage next to the destroyed railroad tracks in town. Most of the audience was lost in thought.

The company spent the next few days on patrol in Carentan before being moved back out to the lines outside of town. With cool nights, wind, and plenty of rain, the men huddled in soggy foxholes along the hedgerows. Patrols were sent out to probe for the enemy. Bottles of wine and calvados were drunk, and enemy shelling continued to keep the men on edge.

19 JUNE 1944, S-2 JOURNAL
1850—White reports a 150 located in a quarry at Meautis. 2300—Artillery fire rept. landing in Fox Co. area—reported by outposts.

On 24 June, the First Platoon's Bud Edwards managed to pen a quick letter home to his family in Madera, in the central California farm country:

June 21, 1944
Dear Mother and Dad,
I just received three letters from you. They were June 2nd, 4th, and seventh. I have received all your mail but never got the package. I imagine I will get that when I get back to England. So you didn't sleep at all when you heard something really big was coming off. Well I didn't sleep for the first few couple days there either, but I have caught up on it for now and I hope that you have done the same.

I know that since I have been here in France either God has been looking after me or you have been doing a lot for praying for me. When you are in a fox hole and shells start busting around you, you do an awful lot of thinking and praying. When we get out of here I believe there will be a lot of fellows who change quite a bit.

I received your birthday card with the money order but I haven't been able to cash it yet. Thanks a lot. Tell my friends hello for me.

With all my love,
Bud

26 JUNE 1944, S-2 JOURNAL
0130—260145—Mortar fire by patrol. Kidnap White 2 364813.
0145—Tree burning in Fox Company area. Drawing fire. 0230-260223 small arms. LMG on Fox Co. 260232—Easy Co. 1500—

3 Germans (?) opposite F Co. in ditch. Near main highway. 3 soldiers unarmed—asked for bread.

26 JUNE 1944, S-3 JOURNAL
1645—Meeting of Reg. Staff and Bn C.O.'s. We are to be relieved
by the 83rd Division and 330 Inf. Each Bn to supply officer guides
to move their units in. There will only be moderate patrolling tonight due to move. Patrols to only go out 200 to 300 yards. This
move should be completed by 10 o'clock tomorrow.

27 JUNE 1944, S-3 JOURNAL
Col. McLendon and his staff arrived to coordinate relief of our unit
by theirs. Col. Chase went to St. Sauvier La Vinciente to look over
our new area.

The surviving men of Company F collected their gear and moved off
the line. Filthy, wet, and tired, they marched back with rifles slung to await
truck transportation to Cherbourg. One trooper recalled a humorous incident during the withdrawal.

JOHN TAYLOR • *We finally got word that we were going to be relieved.
We started being pulled out a platoon at a time. The 83rd Infantry came to
relieve our platoon. By then we were seasoned veterans. They, on the other
hand, had not yet had their first taste of combat. For meanness and a good
laugh, Ralph Robbins of our platoon got right beside some of the new guys
and fired his rifle. He didn't even unsling it—he just reached back and
flipped the safety off and fired! Every single one of them hit the ditch. Of
course, we had a big laugh over that.*

Lt. Andy Tuck (known to his family as "Ed" for his middle name of
Edward) scribbled a letter home to his mother once the company left the
front lines of Carentan:

June 28, 1944
Dearest Mom,
This is Sunday and a beautiful one at that. Chaplain Maloney (a jumper
from Rochester, NY) is coming around this afternoon to give Holy

Communion. He has certainly done a fine job on this operation and has the respect and admiration of all the unit.

We're all a lot more tired than we ever thought we could get, having little sleep since we started before D-day. The first seventy two hours I lived on D rations (chocolate bars), then K & now 10-in-one which is swell. The morale of the troops is very high. "Jerrie" doesn't like us one bit. They call us the "Big Pocket Devils" who don't take prisoners. I only hope that we can get a little rest now and we'll be roarin' to go again.

I'm in the best of health and hope that all at home is well. Sure do like to get mail even when it gets stacked up.

Best Love, Ed

Company F was trucked just southeast of Cherbourg and camped alongside a vacant German bunker complex. The bunkers and pillboxes were searched for food and souvenirs. Gordon Mather located a large bag of Vichy francs, suspected to be German payroll. As the currency was believed to be worthless under Allied occupation, it was used for kindling and toilet paper. German rations were mixed in with the American ones, and a cow, just as outside of Carentan, was butchered for the mess.

JOHN TAYLOR • *Back near camp, we found a cow that had some shrapnel in the leg, and we drove it a couple miles to our area to butcher. That afternoon before dark we had this beef hanging in the tree, and all of us had a little fire going, cooking our steaks. I had a beautiful one-inch-thick piece that was sizzling along real good. I couldn't wait to bite into that thing. I then heard someone behind me say "Sergeant, that's a fine looking piece of beef," and I remember saying, "You're just not. . . ." I didn't finish the sentence because I saw the guy behind me was Colonel Chase, the regimental executive officer.*

With him was a French farmer and a French paratrooper in uniform. This farmer was talking up a storm, chattering right at me. The colonel sent for our platoon leader, Hugh "Blackjack" Borden. The farmer told the colonel that we had killed two of his cows. Now, we had killed a cow, but it didn't belong to this farmer, and we sure hadn't killed two of them! That farmer had just seen us kill that cow and figured out it was a good swindle for himself.

Anyhow, Colonel Chase told Captain Mulvey to have $120 delivered to

*the regimental command post by 0900 the next morning to pay the farmer
for his cows. We each had invasion francs. I forgot what a franc was worth,
but we had another plan. We got Gordon Mather to finance this operation,
and Captain Mulvey sent it over. We still got a little meat, and that took care
of that.*

An officer in the regular Army arrived in camp the next day searching
for his brother, Chester Nakelski. No one had planned for his arrival, and
it became very apparent to the brother after questioning a few men that
something was wrong. With no real story prepared about Nakelski's friendly-
fire death outside of Carentan, the men of the Second Platoon struggled to
explain what had happened. The brother left, distraught and confused.

Swimming occupied the company for a time the next day with a trip
down to the ocean. Although the water was cold, the men were able to rinse
off as they swam in the surf. The sun was out, and within a short time their
dirty bodies went from black to white then a bright red. Bob Noody had
spent a few hours floating around naked and managed to severely burn his
rear end. He could not sit for several days after the swimming trip. Most of
the men left the beach red as lobsters.

An award ceremony was conducted the following day by General
Bradley. John Taylor participated in the color guard along with Sgt. Mercer
of Easy Company. They sweated out the ceremony in full class A uniforms.

JOHN TAYLOR • *At this ceremony I recall that Lt. Dick Winters from
E Company received the Distinguished Service Cross. Dick had gathered
up some other troops shortly after landing and knocked out four artillery
positions overlooking Utah Beach. Winters was a good example to his men:
He didn't drink or smoke, and he trained his soldiers right. He was tough
and used the force of his personality to inspire his men. He was the finest
soldier I ever knew.*

The men of the battalion filtered through Cherbourg after the ceremony. A house of prostitution was located, and a line soon formed around
the building. Some headed off for food and drinks. Tom Alley headed to a
shoe shop.

TOM ALLEY • *I went to the shop and had the guy make me a holster for the Luger that I had obtained outside of Carentan. I had an equipment hook that we used to hang our gear from our web belts. The leather holster I had made was top-draw, with a safety snap that held the pistol in the holster. Several inches of extra leather were above the holster and fastened to the hook for my belt. This allowed for the holster to hang low off my belt. I wore the pistol in combat and for the rest of my time in the Army.*

A trip to Utah Beach near Pouppeville was the next destination for the men of Fox Company. They obtained 10-in-1 rations from supply dumps. These could feed one man for ten days or ten men with one meal and were a welcome addition to their mess—the men had a feast with the new supplies. After spending a day on the beach, the company loaded up on an LST (Landing Ship, Tank). Company F won a coin toss and took over the bunks. Canned chicken was served in the mess hall, freshwater showers were taken, and after drifting out with the tide, the ship headed off across the channel to Southampton. Trains brought the men back to their huts in Aldbourne. Their Normandy Campaign was over.

CHAPTER 13

BACK IN ALDBOURNE

O n arrival back in Aldbourne, the survivors of the Normandy Campaign were issued furloughs for seven days. Those who had come out with no injuries or only minor ones scrambled to get packed and dressed up for travel across England. Bill True had shaved for inspection just prior to the company moving into Carentan, but had left a goatee, arguing it made for good camouflage. Once back in England, he left it on and headed off for London with Johnny Jackson, waiting to shave it off after his return from the furlough.

Other members of the First Platoon, such as Tom Alley, E. B. Wallace, Otto May, and Linus Brown, took trains up to Edinburgh, Scotland, for a much-needed vacation. The Second Platoon's John Taylor, Marion Grodowski, Manning Haney, and Ralph Robbins went to London. They managed to get hotel rooms on the edge of Russell Square. Other than being blasted from their beds one morning by a V-2 rocket's impact, their furlough was uneventful and was filled with the usual drinking and girl chasing. One soldier spent his time in the city taking in the sites.

RAUL OCHOA ● *I tried to keep my mind occupied, to keep my mind on good thoughts, and avoid the bad memories. I was really treated well by the locals. They were excited to see us back from the invasion and really gave me first-class treatment.*

The Third Platoon's Merlin Shennum headed off to London with Alan Summers.

MERLIN SHENNUM ● *We were just grateful to be back. So many guys were wounded, and we had lost a lot of friends. We got the most out of that week furlough and never slowed down.*

Drastic changes occurred in Company F behind the scenes while the men were off on furlough. Angry over the company's falling back outside of Carentan, the battalion's leaders dropped the hammer hard for discipline. Willie Morris, a career soldier and company first sergeant, was demoted to private and transferred to I Company of the Third Battalion. The move had been in the works before the men had even left Normandy. Captain Mulvey, who had been with the men from their start, lost his command and was moved to the regimental headquarters.

MARION GRODOWSKI ● *I could not believe what had happened to Willie Morris. He was a good senior sergeant, a career Army soldier. He was hard but fair. For him to get demoted of all his stripes and to be transferred out was wrong. It was a typical Army double standard.*

JOHN TAYLOR ● *I could not believe what had happened to Morris and Mulvey. If we had not fallen back outside of Carentan, we would have ceased to exist as a company. We would have all been killed or wounded, and the enemy would have broken through. You cannot defend against tanks and infantry with rifles, with grass as your only protection.*

With Captain Mulvey leaving at the end of July, new leaders came in to fill the gaps of those killed, wounded, or transferred. Frank McFadden took over as company commander, and Lt. William Hudelson came over from Easy Company to replace the severely wounded Lt. William Brooks. Lt. Freeling Colt had been killed by a sniper on D-Day as he stepped out from a field just outside of Baudienville. He left behind a wife and two young children in Hazelton, Pennsylvania. Colt was replaced by a new officer, Herbert Eggie, who had big boots to fill.

MERLIN SHENNUM ● *Lieutenant Colt was the best there ever was. He was great in his lectures, he was great in drill, and he was complete in the details of our training. He was a real down-to-earth guy. We had lost a good man in Normandy.*

As new Officers came in, and Captain Mulvey went out, the men returned from furlough to find those not seriously wounded, like Bob Janes and Roy Zerbe, returning from the hospital. A large group of replacements came in as well, trying to fill the boots of over a dozen killed and three dozen wounded in Normandy.

The unit's training began immediately, there being a rush to bring the replacements up to speed with the veterans. The lessons learned in the hedgerows of Normandy had to be drilled into the new men by those who had been there. This was a painful but necessary task. The Normandy veterans had to teach the new members what had caused the death of their close friends and what may have kept themselves alive. The pain of losing a friend also kept the replacements at a distance from those who had already been in action.

MARION GRODOWSKI • *We tried to give the new guys the low-down on how it went in Normandy. They listened to us and took it to heart. Our futures depended on it.*

RAUL OCHOA • *We tried to teach these new replacements everything we knew, everything we had learned. We tried to help them out and take them under our wings for training.*

The replacements felt a lack of acceptance by the company, not unlike those who had joined the unit back in the States and had not been "Toccoa Men." But the replacements looked up to the Normandy veterans and understood their admission to the unit would not be easy.

JOHN HIMELRICK • *We replacements were a breed apart. We were not accepted right away. It was not meant to be derogatory. But we newcomers were not allowed into that group. They (the combat veterans) had a camaraderie made in combat.*

With the first sergeant being demoted and transferred, the company leadership looked for a new senior noncommissioned officer. Pathfinder Charlie Malley got the job.

JOHN TAYLOR • *Charlie Malley was certainly one of the more colorful characters I got to know during the war. He had gotten into some trouble prior to Normandy. At that time he was platoon leader for the Second Platoon. He was a pretty high-tempered fellow. One night Charlie slugged an officer in town. He received a summary court-martial and was reduced in rank to private first class. The only reason Malley didn't get a general court-martial, I'm sure, was because of the variety and strength of his capabilities as an officer.*

At this time, Willie Morris had been transferred out of the company as first sergeant, and we needed a replacement. The noncommissioned officers got together and asked the company commander to make Malley the first sergeant of the company.

Malley had not fought in Normandy, his Pathfinder plane having ditched in the English Channel the night before the D-Day operation. His water landing did not go without the occasional joke by the men of the company, who frequently commented about Pathfinders being trained as frogmen or cold-water swimmers. Although Malley had a short fuse, he also had a good sense of humor and took all the ribbing and joking in stride.

With all the weapons training, night field problems, and map and compass instruction, the men were still allowed short passes for weekend trips to Swindon and London. Bob Janes and Manning Haney went to the latter. Haney managed to find himself a girlfriend in the city, and the two men also obtained tattoos while on pass. Haney had the word "Lucky" tattooed on his arm, as a symbol of his lucky landing on the railroad tracks outside of Houesville, and not having the misfortune of drowning in the Cul-de-Fer. Janes had his wife's name Nadene tattooed on his arm, placed on a ribbon between two birds. Both men were quietly unsure of their survival of the war.

Others carried on the company's tradition of rowdiness and trouble-making, with Charlie Jacobs managing to get himself arrested in London for "drunk and disorderly" and Horace Vick for "insubordination to an officer." Others tried to improve their training and avoided the passes. Orel Lev headed off for a brief training with Jerry Farley at the Pathfinder School, while the others from his Second Platoon were being tattooed or arrested in London.

New uniforms were issued, as well as weapons. The men would no longer be wearing their prized paratrooper jumpsuits in combat. Instead they would wear the same new jackets and pants as the regular infantry, the only difference being cargo pockets sewn onto the thighs of their pants. Regular combat boots were issued as well, with the company being advised to wear them in combat. The issue of regular Army uniforms and boots was supposed to help with logistics in combat.

With a bulk-up in staffing, a third rifle squad was added to each platoon, giving each platoon a total of four squads, one being a mortar squad. Marion Grodowski, refusing to use another bolt-action rifle and grenade launcher combo again, picked up a Thompson submachine gun.

MARION GRODOWSKI • *I was able to obtain a new Thompson. It was a model 1928 with a ventilated barrel and a Cutts compensator. Since I was from Chicago and grew up in the same neighborhood as Al Capone, I felt it was only appropriate. With a magazine pouch on the back of my belt with five magazines inside and a few extra magazines in my pack, I was ready to go.*

Bob Janes managed to find the time to write home to his parents, relating the news of the company, a promotion, and his marriage:

England
August 25, 1944

Dearest Mother & Dad

Received your wonderful letter last evening Mom, and was happy to hear from you again and find things going so well there in God's Country. Seems like letter writing is a special privilege around here anymore because we are working night and day. They finally ran out of things for us to do this evening and gave us the night off, first time this week.

I was thinking of going to the dull old town this evening but didn't have any schillings, so I am spending the night in the sack. Spent most of the evening up to now sewing a couple of stripes on my new blouse. Maybe I will get to London this payday and have those pictures made I have been talking about all winter. After two years now I have something to show for my effort. A Corporal rating may not mean much in some outfits, but in the paratroops it means a hell of a lot to me after what I have put out. One thing about being a non-com is that I don't have to do any KP, stand on guard duty, and we also have a non-com club here that has a good supply of cognac and beer, which comes in very handy when I get down in the dumps.

Mom, what you said about Nadene meeting some other guy and falling for him and because we got married so young, and shouldn't judge her too harshly if it happened.

I understand what you mean but when I read that and started thinking about it I went to pieces inside for a while. If that should happen, well there just wouldn't be anything left to live and fight for, but if it did happen I want to know about it before I get home because I couldn't stand to come home and find everything my life stands for shot to hell.

The way you said that left me with the feeling that maybe something could be wrong.

I guess I told you that our Division, the 101st received the Presidential Citation for the job we did on the invasion. I believe the paratroops are finally receiving a little recognition now. I'll bet you thought I had made another jump when you read about the invasion of the south coast of France, and to tell you the truth, I'm surprised I wasn't.

Well folks I have seventeen jumps to my credit now and can now wear a star on my wings for the combat jump. Another combat jump would take a lot more guts than the first one because now I know what to expect. Oh well, why worry till the time to climb into the plane, there is plenty of time to smoke and sweat it out up there.

Write often and I will try to do the same. Don't worry about me as I am feeling fine and getting fatter every day.

Goodnite, All my love, Bob

Please send some t-shirts, shorts (jockey type) and some candy, gum, after shaving cream, face lotion, bar soap, powder, single edge razor blades, and a tooth brush.

After being alerted for two combat jumps in August that were cancelled, the company had an awards ceremony on 7 September. Colonel Sink pinned Purple Hearts on all those who had been wounded. Three days later the company was back in the marshaling area, alerted for another combat jump. This one would not be cancelled. They were going to Holland.

CHAPTER 14

HOLLAND

For the Normandy invasion, the men of Fox 506th had been trucked over a hundred miles. For the invasion of the Netherlands, the men were trucked to Membury Airfield, only five miles from Aldbourne. Once again they were housed in tents and kept in an enclosed, secure area. Briefings began with maps, aerial photographs, and planned objectives.

The plan was for the company to help seize the Wilhelmina Canal Bridge north of the city of Eindhoven. British armored forces were to rush up from the south, move through Eindhoven and continue up through Nijmegen and into Arnhem, crossing the Waal River and the Lower Rhine. The lower bridges and highway were to be held by the 101st Airborne, the Nijmegen sector bridges and highway by the 82nd Airborne, and Arnhem by the British First Airborne. It was known as Operation Market Garden.

The day of the move to Membury Airfield, Lieutenant Tuck wrote a letter to his mother after receiving the news of his sister's wedding:

Mom Darling,
I suppose that only now are you shaking the last of the rice from your hair and normalcy has again come to 80 Chatsworth. I felt very close on that day of family joy and appreciate so very heartily your kind thoughts of me during the bustle of things. It feels rather a nick out of my life, missing that "once in a lifetime" occasion but with your blow by blow description it was closer than one could imagine.

We're enjoying a lovely St. Martin's summer just now—and all the world seems to slumber. I'll be so glad when I can tell you all has happened—but in our business security is of paramount pertinence.

Enclosed is a snapshot of Staff Sgt. "Black Jack" Borden, who conducted himself in exemplary fashion throughout the various engagements. He once held a town with only seven men for better than a score of hours. (An ex-bootlegger)

I don't know that I've mentioned it before—but I'm now Company F's Second-In-Command (Executive Officer). The troops look fine in spite of many discrepancies.

That campaigning in France is fast joining the ranks of episodes past.

Best love and prayers for you all, Ed

A few officers had come and gone in the past two months: 2nd Lt. Moore, 2nd Lt. Fleming, and 1st Lt. Perkins were only in the company long enough for it to be noted in the company morning report. Replacement 2nd Lt. Robert Perdue joined the Second Platoon. 1st Lt. Rhodes returned from being wounded to the First Platoon and was joined by 2nd Lt. Edward Thomas, also a replacement joined up with the First Platoon. And 1st Lt. Ray Schmitz (formerly of E Company) took over the Third Platoon with replacement 1st Lt. Herbert Eggie. The leaders of F Company in September 1944:

COMMANDING OFFICER: 1st Lt. Frank McFadden
EXECUTIVE OFFICER: 1st Lt. Andrew Tuck

1st Platoon	SSgt. Gordon Mather, Sgt. Alvin Wilson
1st Lt. Thomas Rhodes	Sgt. Vince Occhipinti, Sgt. Robert Vogel
2nd Lt. Edward Thomas	Sgt. Otto May
2nd Platoon	SSgt. Hugh Borden, Sgt. John Taylor
1st Lt. Russell Hall	Sgt. Charlie Jacobs, Sgt. George Martin
2nd Lt. Robert Perdue	Sgt. Frank Griffin
3rd Platoon	SSgt. Huber Porter, Sgt. Russ Schwenk
1st Lt. Ray Schmitz	Sgt. Charlie Reese, Sgt. Roy Zerbe
1st Lt. Herbert Eggie	Sgt. Joe Chappelle

Medics Millard Moore, Bill Baird, Phillip Thompson, and Mark Dusich joined the unit in the marshaling area. Joe Droogan was already with the unit. He, Moore, and Baird were veterans of Normandy and loaded all the medics up with medical supplies. With their combat experience, they were preparing for the worst.

SSgt. Don Replogle was promoted to second lieutenant and transferred to I Company in the Third Battalion of the 506th. Sgt. Vince Occhipinti was back in the unit for the jump, having recovered from two badly sprained ankles in the night jump into Normandy. 1st Lt. William Hudelson was attached to the unit as well, assigned to the First Platoon.

The men prepared for their jump, which would take place early on Sunday, the 17th of September. As they made last-minute adjustments to their parachutes and secured their gear, a gunshot rang out from the area of First Platoon.

VINCE OCCHIPINTI ● *One of the members of F Company who shall remain nameless made the jump into Normandy with us. He was preparing for this Holland jump—or so we thought. This fellow had been in the service for almost two years and was a veteran on the use of a weapon. Somehow while he was dismantling his rifle to insert it into the carry pack, the weapon fired. He had just missed his foot, and the ricochet could have hit someone else. Fortunately it did not.*

His first lieutenant, Rhodes, came over and asked him what the trouble was. He replied, "I didn't know the gun was loaded." When he started to dismantle it, it went off. The lieutenant believed him and left. A moment later, the gun went off again. Now there is no way that can happen. This bullet, too, just missed his foot. The lieutenant came over again and yanked the rifle away from him, dumped it in the case, and asked if he forgot how to to handle his rifle.

BILL TRUE ● *One of the members of our platoon had been badly shaken up in Normandy. He had found his best friend killed, hanging from a tree in Sainte-Mère-Église. You could tell the days leading up to our Holland jump that he was stressed. He was visibly stressed. He is the one who had the rifle discharge as we prepared for the jump. But he still loaded up with the rest of us.*

Over in the Second Platoon, the men decided to jump without the rifle cases. The veterans of Normandy schooled the replacements on the necessity of having a rifle ready to go the moment you landed. They advised the new men to jump with weapons slung over the left shoulder or shoved behind their reserve parachutes, which were snapped across their front. Bob Janes planned to jump with a Thompson in hand, with its double sling wrapped around his wrist.

On 17 September at 1035, the men of Fox 506th took off into a blue sky and sunshine in their usual mode of olive drab transport, C-47s. The planes were piloted by members of the 82nd Squadron of the 436th Troop Carrier Group. While flying away from England, John Taylor stood in the door of his transport and watched the famous white cliffs of Dover fade away. Because it was daytime and they were being escorted by fighter planes,

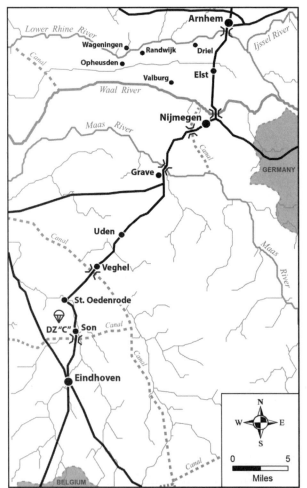

OPERATION
MARKET
GARDEN

the men of Fox 506th were relatively relaxed on the flight to Holland. In a cloud of swirling cigarette smoke, they spent their time trying to take in the views from the open door and side windows.

At 1300 the planes neared their drop zone, "C," and the order came to "stand up and hook up." Enemy antiaircraft fire began to sporadically burst in the air, and an occasional tracer round zipped past. The men stood in their aircraft preparing for the green light and command to go. In the plane carrying the First Platoon's First Squad, the troubled jumper who had discharged his rifle at the airfield decided he was done with fighting in the 506th.

VINCE OCCHIPINTI • *The red light was on. We were all standing, hooked up and ready. Suddenly, he unhooked his static line and sat down. Two of his buddies told him to get up, it was time to go. He would not look at anybody. He also would not move from his spot or speak to anybody. Nobody gave a damn because a person's state of mind is certainly not something you can monkey with. The line all of a sudden started moving closer to the door. The green—the signal to go—came on and everybody jumped except the trooper. He went back to England with the plane.*

Over in one of the Third Platoon's planes, antiaircraft fire claimed its first casualty of the company.

ART PETERSON • *I was just sitting there when I was hit by shrapnel flying through bottom of the plane. It came right up through the seat and hit me in the bottom of my left thigh. It felt as though someone had stabbed me with a hot poker and caused me to jump up.*

Sgt. Russ Schwenk told me to stay in the plane and not to jump. So I remained behind when the men jumped over the drop zone. A few moments later the crew chief of the plane came back and told me to jump, as the plane was going down. So I jumped. Once I landed on the ground, I managed to find my unit and sergeant. He asked why I had jumped when he told me to stay in the plane. I told him the plane was shot down! So he had a medic tag me for evacuation, and I left the drop zone for a field hospital.

MARION GRODOWSKI • *You might say the jump was a snap. We encountered some antiaircraft fire—not too much. The planes held their formation, eased back on the throttle. We jumped, and it was an easy landing for me. I managed to get out of my harness, and I looked up, and about thirty to forty feet from me a guy came down. His chute never opened—just a streamer. Hit the ground with a thud. I never went over to check on him. We had our orders to get off the drop zone and get to the assembly area.*

Dropping parachutes and life vests, the men quickly assembled on the drop zone. With the Dutch Resistance directing traffic off the drop zone, the company left behind the bloodied Art Peterson, as well as Sgt. Bill Neubert from the company headquarters who had broken his arm in the landing. The company headed south for the Wilhelmina Canal Bridge, trailing a string of other companies from the Second Battalion. Along the roadside, Dutch citizens handed out treats and drinks for the liberating Americans.

Just as the bridge came into view for the men of Company F, it was blown up by the Germans. Taking cover along the road between Zon and Eindhoven, they watched as debris rained down on their sister companies from the smoke cloud now pluming over the canal. A nearby church was suspected of containing German troops, so Fox Company was detailed to clear them out. They found the church and surrounding area deserted.

The bridge was destroyed. However, its supports still protruded from the water. Always adapting to problems, the paratroopers threw together a makeshift footbridge. That afternoon the company inched its way over the canal, and after several hours made it to the other side. The men moved a few miles closer to Eindhoven, then dug foxholes in the fields adjacent to the road. They spent the night battling only the rain and prepared to assault the Germans in the city the next morning.

At 0600 the regiment moved out toward Eindhoven, with the Second Battalion trailing the Third. When heavy artillery fire halted the advance, the Second Battalion moved to the left flank and attempted another route into town. Fox 506th was tasked with moving into the city and knocking out the artillery pieces holding up the Third Battalion. Lt. Russell Hall's Second Platoon would take the lead. After meeting with Capt. Charles Shettle, the battalion's executive officer, the platoon headed off with Dutchman Bert Pulles as its guide.

They headed north on Kloosterdreef and stopped briefly on Runstraat.

Pulles explained that they were just south of the guns, which were at the top of a triangular shaped block, with Runstraat at the base, Kloosterdreef on their right heading north, and Woenselsestraat on their left, heading north.

The Second Squad, with Lieutenant Perdue and Sergeant Janes, moved off to its left and headed north on Woenselsestraat toward the guns. The First Squad, with Lieutenant Hall and Sergeant Taylor, moved to the right, heading back onto Kloosterdreef. The Third Squad and the mortar squad held back on the corners of the base of the triangular block, on Runstraat.

The area contained homes and small businesses. Sneaking up on the guns undetected would be a tricky maneuver. The men moved into backyards, using gates and hoping fences to move to the top of the block. For the moment they had the element of surprise.

While in the backyard of a home on Kloosterdreef, Taylor noticed a woman across the street in the upstairs of a home, waving three fingers and pointing down the roadway. It was Pulles's fiancée, Coby. Three German soldiers walked past their position heading toward the gun position. Hall, Taylor, and Sergeant Borden jumped out from behind a gate and quickly captured the three startled men. They were moved back under the guard of the Third Platoon. Merlin Shennum helped search the prisoners before they were herded to the rear.

MERLIN SHENNUM ● *I had this one German soldier spread-eagle against a wall while I searched him. I went through his pockets and in one pulled out a handful of condoms. I asked what they were in German, and the soldier replied, "Das ist fur frigging." We both had a laugh over that.*

The men moved forward and were now just under a hundred yards from the gun position. As Taylor and replacement Bob Sherwood went into the street, they spotted the gun position—an 88mm. Just then a half dozen Germans began moving toward the gun. Taylor shouldered his rifle, took aim, and fired off all eight rounds. Two Germans dropped. But then the gun began to rotate toward Taylor and Sherwood.

Taylor's rifle failed to eject his clip, so he moved behind a porch stair to clear it. Sherwood launched a rifle grenade at the gun. The grenade arched up and struck close to the gun, but with the crew not injured from the blast, it still rotated and pointed at their position. Sherwood took cover behind

Taylor, now in the process of reloading. The German gun fired, striking the building above the duo's heads, raining debris down all around them. They moved behind the building for more cover.

Sgt. Frank Griffin carried his mortar tube and plate into the street across from Taylor. He quickly sat down and straddled the tube between his knees. Then, without using the sight, he launched two shells at the gun position. As the shells arched down the street, a German officer ran toward the gun. Taylor, back in action, fired at him and wounded him in the leg as the first mortar shell exploded near the gun. The officer dropped, then ran north up the street. The second shell, a direct hit, destroyed the gun.

Over on Woenselsestraat, the Second Squad began to exchange fire with the Germans around a second gun position that was just north of the first. Both guns were trapped. While Janes blasted away with his tommy gun, replacement Homer Smith fired two rifle grenades. The second was a direct hit on the gun. It was out of action.

The Second Squad's Cpl. George Martin set up his machine gun and began to exchange fire with a German machine gun down the street near the second gun position. An incoming bullet struck the jacket of Martin's gun, throwing a piece of shrapnel into his eye. Medics evacuated him, and the injury sent him home to the States.

The platoon advanced forward on Woenselsestraat with Taylor and Sherwood watching the wounded German officer stumble into a building near the second gun position. Sherwood lunched another rifle grenade and watched as it followed the officer right into the building before exploding. The second gun began to fire down at the men of the Second Squad, with three rounds exploding in nearby houses. Replacement Pvt. Clarence Shrout, now at the top corner of the block, fired magazine after magazine from his tommy gun onto the gun position. Homer Smith launched three rifle grenades at the gun as well, with no direct hits. The Germans, knowing they were doomed, destroyed their gun breach and attempted to flee.

The men of the Second Platoon swarmed their position, with Hugh Borden leading a group toward the east, near the next street, Kaakstraat. Germans fled in front of them into a beet field. The Americans responded with a volley of fire at those who attempted to flee, rounding up the bulk that was wise enough to surrender. In the building where Sherwood had launched his rifle grenade, the wounded officer was located, along with nine others, all injured by the grenade.

MARION GRODOWSKI ● *I saw a bloodied German NCO nearby. What caught my eye was he was reaching for a rosary he had dropped. Being a fellow Catholic, I could not help but feel for the guy. I went over, picked up the rosary, and placed it in his hands. I then called for a medic, and someone ran over to treat him.*

The Third Platoon moved up and took positions north of the location, covering the intersection of Hamsterstraat at Woenselsestraat. The men were right across from Borden during his skirmish and immediately began to exchange fire with Germans up the street. The company fired and maneuvered up the street in a deadly form of leap frog while pushing the Germans back. A Third Platoon veteran of Normandy, Pvt. Delmar Newhouse, fell wounded to rifle fire, but the attack moved forward.

As the platoon advanced, Marion Grodowski saw a figure cross the street about a hundred yards ahead of him. Wearing a uniform and an oddly shaped helmet, and carrying a rifle, he was no paratrooper. So Grodowski tried to stop the man, suspecting he was a German.

MARION GRODOWSKI ● *I yelled, "Halt!" to this guy, and he ignored me. I yelled a second time. He just waved at me, like a motion to go away. I raised my Thompson as he began to climb into the window of a home. I squeezed off a few shots, and he spun out of the window and fell onto the ground below. When we got up to him, I could see his uniform was not German. It turned out he was a Dutchman, a Resistance fighter. I was devastated. But why didn't he stop?*

The Third Platoon saw a group of German soldiers run into a nearby lumberyard. Gus Patruno and a few others raced to flank them.

GUS PATRUNO ● *We ran around behind the yard to where a big storage barn was filled with lumber. Five Germans ran out the back, and I was waiting for them. It was a machine gun crew, and they surrendered. I led them to the office of the business and dumped off their weapons and equipment. One of the Germans, a sergeant, spoke English. He told me he had been wounded five times while fighting on the Eastern Front. He was in the Netherlands to recover. I took his pistol and medals, and their watches.*

As Patruno had run to cut off the fleeing Germans, Grodowski and the men of the Second Platoon were still out in the street. A machine gunner opened up on the Germans as they trailed into the lumberyard. Grodowski yelled for the firing to stop.

MARION GRODOWSKI ● *I yelled, "Cease fire!" and the Germans dropped to avoid the incoming burst of fire. They were out of my sight. I had picked up a lot of German growing up in South Chicago. So, in my best German I yelled "German soldiers! I am an American paratrooper! Come out and bring your wounded!" It worked. A few moments later a German officer appeared with about nine other men. Most were wounded."*

The firing was over, and the men of Fox Company had only two wounded. And through their efforts, the Germans had lost two gun positions that had been holding up the advance of the entire operation in Holland. Additionally, the Germans had lost thirteen killed and forty-one wounded. Second Platoon would later receive a commendation for its action in Eindhoven.

With the fighting over, the company linked up by 1330 with men from the Third Battalion of the 506th, as well as a scout section of the British armored advance. The officers and sergeants spent the next few hours trying to round up men from the outfit who had been pulled into homes and restaurants by the grateful Dutch population. It was a trying task, as the town had erupted in celebration. As the company tried to push along through the streets, it was surrounded by the cheering Dutch. Apples and pears were handed to the men, as well as glasses of beer and milk. It was wonderful, but they had to move on. The fighting in the Netherlands had just begun.

CHAPTER 15

ON THE MOVE AND BLACK FRIDAY

L eaving the wild afternoon celebration in the center of Eindhoven, the men of Fox 506th headed off to the south with orders to move to the outskirts of town. They stopped to rest at St. George's Church and watched the locals.

JOHN TAYLOR • *We moved over into another part of Eindhoven and occupied some houses near a large church. Eindhoven was a nice-looking city. It had hardly been damaged. We had a chance to scrounge around the area for a while, and it was then I saw Dutch collaborators for the first time. These were the people who had cozied up to the Germans during the years of the occupation.*

I remember watching some of the Dutch go in a house across the street there, a big house, and they rounded up several women and men and clipped their hair off. It was obvious that the anti-German Dutch knew exactly who these traitors were because the minute the Germans were gone, they went to get them. They paraded the short-haired collaborators through the streets and jeered at them. I don't know what else happened to them after that.

Taken into the Dutch homes, the men of the company washed up, ate, and managed to get a few hours' sleep. When the company moved out to the east during the night, several of the men were left behind accidentally, having missed the order. They had to head off on their own to catch up.

By the morning of the 19th, the company was in Geldrop, a small town just southeast of Eindhoven. Fours scouts from the Third Platoon were sent out to the north to look for German patrols—Merlin Shennum, accompanied Roy Zerbe, Carl Pein, and Rody Byrnes. They traveled light, carrying only weapons, ammunition, and a set of binoculars.

MERLIN SHENNUM • *We patrolled through town and came up on a bar that had a German soldier posted outside. As we approached he ran inside, and we went after him. He along with a few other Germans ran out the back door into the countryside. They had left behind a couple plates of food and some beer. While two of us guarded the outside, the other two went in and drank the beer and played a round of pool. The patrol ended when we were met by a group of Dutch citizens, who celebrated our arrival. We stopped, and they took some pictures with us, and that was the end of the patrol.*

The company then moved toward the east end of town into Mierlo and attempted to hold a bridge at that location. The men were met with German machine gun fire and forced to take cover under and around the bridge. It soon began to get dark, and before they could mount an attack, they were pulled back away from the bridge and toward Eindhoven. Trucks were to meet them halfway to Eindhoven, to move them rapidly back into the city. As they marched back in the moonlight, German bombers passed overhead.

MARION GRODOWSKI • *I remember the planes going overhead. It was as we were nearing our truck transport. There was some moon out, and we were all silhouetted on the road. Why they did not bomb us I am not sure. Perhaps they had orders otherwise. Perhaps they thought we were their own troops. The planes continued on and bombed Eindhoven. They really hit it hard.*

Unknown at the time, four members of the Second Platoon had been left behind at the bridge, not hearing the order to move back: Bernard Tom, Paul Peterson, Joe Trepelka, and a slightly wounded Nick Darah. They were quickly sheltered by the Dutch, who spent the next few days smuggling them back to their unit.

The next day Company F was on the move constantly, eventually traveling on British tanks north toward Nuenen, where a heavy fight was under way. Before they could engage, the men were back in an area between Geldrop and Eindhoven called Tongelre. They spent most of the day waiting there in a defense, before being informed they were to move out in the morning to Uden.

The next morning they climbed aboard trucks and headed off to the north to Uden. On the way there they were stopped on the main highway in the small town of Veghel. What initially looked like a scenic tour of the town suddenly turned deadly when the convoy came under enemy artillery fire. The Germans had launched an attack from the southeast, attempting to cut off the highway supply north. Once again Company F, just as in Normandy, faced German infantry, tanks, and armored vehicles.

The trucks were stopped and the Third Platoon was ordered to attack the incoming enemy forces. The Second Platoon trailed behind and passed small houses along the elevated roadway where British trucks were scattered about and burning. The First Platoon went to clear a section of homes.

HERBERT EGGIE ● *I was very tense but had little fear. In fact, though tense I had a deep inner calm. I recall the feeling very well. I had not then had enough combat experience to feel much fear. I did not know what violent, close combat could accomplish in the way of destruction of human life. I was soon to know.*

We moved fast. We moved towards the open highway, hugging close to the houses that lined the road leading to the edge of town. We came to the last house and paused for a moment. I saw that a ditch running by the highway side commenced about twenty-five feet from where we stood.

I gave the order, and three of us ran at a low crouch for the ditch and jumped in. Still crouching I proceeded up the ditch, the others followed closely. I had gone but a few feet when machine gun bullets began crackling over my head. At the same time I came to the end of that part of the ditch, which was crossed by a dirt road leading to a field to the right. I saw that I had to cross this open and unprotected spot to get where the ditch began. I hesitated.

The machine gun bullets were crackling right over the spot. I didn't want to cross that piece of ground just then. I looked behind me. The ditch was beginning to fill up as more and more men of the platoon jumped in. I knew then I had to get out and move ahead. There was no way to stop the men from coming in. I knew that we could not crowd up. It would be murder if a mortar shell landed in among us.

Then I saw Lieutenant Schmitz come into the ditch. I yelled to him to hold the men up a minute until we could get across. I remember Lieutenant

Schmitz's face as he moved up to where I was. It was white, tense, and grim. I jumped out of the ditch and ran swiftly to the right to a hedgerow into which I flung myself. I began to crawl quickly in to a right-flank position with the other two men. After going several yards I peered out into the open field to my front.

A German tank broke through the trees across the field from the men of the Third Platoon. It rushed toward the road, firing its main gun several times. Two more tanks emerged trailing the first. Merlin Shennum was among the men in the ditch when his pal Carl Pein had crawled past, trailing Lieutenant Schmitz. He joked with Shennum, saying, "Don't worry Merlin—only the good die young," and continued up the ditch.

A round from the advancing German tank struck a British truck stopped on the roadway above the troopers. It was full of ammunition, and the impact caused a huge and deafening explosion. Those in the ditch below tried to move back away from the burning truck and stay low in the ditch to avoid the enemy machine gun fire. But two men were not moving in the ditch: Schmitz and Pein. Shennum and Russ Schwenk tried to move Carl and the lieutenant, but their bodies were limp. Both were dead from the explosion of the ammunition truck.

The leading German tank moved on to the road and began to roll past the men of the Third Platoon, hunkered down in the ditches right below.

RUSS SCHWENK ● *I couldn't believe my eyes. Here come three tanks rolling down the road toward us, all guns blazing—shells exploding off the road, smaller turret guns swinging and firing continuously. This was not a good place to be. We had some cover, as the roadside ditches were perhaps one to two feet deep.*

MERLIN SHENNUM ● *I was down in the ditch and watched that tank slowly go past. You could see every bolt and lug on the thing, it was that close. I then remembered that back in the States in training they told us you could shove a piece of wood or your rifle stock in the bogey wheels of a German tank to stop it. As that tank went by I thought for a second to shove my rifle stock first into the tank wheels as it passed. Then I realized whoever thought that idea up was completely crazy and had probably never really tried it in real life. I stayed put!*

With the Third Platoon in the ditches alongside the tanks, the Second Platoon began to take the receiving end of the tank fire coming down the roadway. A British soldier from the truck convoy ran down into the ditch to avoid the fire and collided with John Taylor. The two slipped around in the mud momentarily, then found themselves attached in a tangle of their web gear. After several seconds of readjustment, they managed to get free and move apart.

Pfc. Don Harms took the initiative to stop the advance of the tanks. He saw an unoccupied jeep nearby with a 57mm antitank gun attached to its hitch. He ran from the ditch to the jeep and made a quick U-turn on the road. The gun crew materialized and went into action. Harms and the crew quickly set up the gun and rushed ammo to it from the jeep. With Harms assisting, the crew fired several times but missed. The lead tank was now only a hundred yards away. Finally a round sent it spinning off the road into a field. When its occupants attempted to flee, members of the Third Platoon cut them down.

The tank was knocked out, but the damage it had left behind was felt hard in the Second Platoon. During the duel, a tank round had skipped off the roadway, striking an empty 57mm shell before it continued down the road. The casing flew into the ditch, striking replacement Eugene Skelton in the face. Skelton was knocked out from the impact, and his face bloodied. Several men initially thought he had been killed.

Tank fire into the roadway and machine gun fire into the ditch hit several men. Hugh Borden took a bullet through his arm, Marion Grodowski had shrapnel tear through his calf, and Raul Ochoa took shrapnel through the shoulder. Ralph Robbins had a portion of his boot heel blown off, taking part of his foot with it. He was pulled from the ditch by Harms and Tiger Cauvin. Taylor found Joe Watkins riddled with shrapnel. He died in his arms.

MARION GRODOWSKI ● *I took a hit to my calf—a large entry and exit wound. I crawled away down the ditch as the tank took a direct hit. When I got to where I thought I was safe, I tried to bandage my wounds. It was so muddy, and there was so much blood, I made quite a mess of it, dressing the wound. A British medic came into the ditch and used his bandages. He did a very good job. While he was at work I saw a jeep go by with Ralph Robbins hanging over the hood. It looked to me like part of his heel was gone. I was loaded up in a jeep. I was then transferred to an ambulance and evacuated to a field hospital. Once there I was treated by a British doctor. He looked at my dog tags and saw I was Polish. He then spoke to me during my treatment in perfect Polish. A few seconds later I passed out.*

As the tank was hit on the roadway, Lieutenant Hall with the Second Platoon moved his men off to the exposed left flank. The wounded were left behind in the ditch to be evacuated. The second tank moved into an open field to flank the antitank gun and was immediately hit by several rockets from a passing British Typhoon. The third tank, still on the roadway, turned back to the woods for concealment after the Third Platoon's Armand Beauchamp dropped a mortar round right onto the top of its turret. Jerry Farley followed it up with a bazooka round. The attack was over.

The day had laid a heavy toll on the men of Company F. They had three men killed: Schmitz, Watkins, and Pein. The Second Platoon had seven men wounded: Skelton, Robbins, Borden, Sharp, Cauvin, Grodowski, and Ochoa. The Third Platoon's Charlie Reese had a gunshot wound to the lung, and mortar-man Marvin Crawford was wounded as well. The First Platoon, not even in the fighting with the bulk of the company, had one wounded, Bill Clemens. In addition, one of its lieutenants, who had been attached to the unit for Holland, was found hiding in a cellar in Veghel. He was evacuated as well, for battle fatigue.

As night fell on Veghel, the men dug in to wait for another attack. Rain began to fall, the night was as black as ink, and the squeaks and clanks of enemy armor could be heard moving around off in the trees. Men were told to fall back one at a time near the company command post for chow. A jeep had been set up with cans of rations stacked on its hood. Each man was told to select two cans and fall back to his foxhole. It was too dark to see the cans well.

BOB NOODY • *I went back and grabbed two cans off the hood of the jeep. When I got back to my foxhole, I found that one large can contained only butter. So I sat there in the dark and the rain, and ate an entire can of butter for dinner. When you are hungry you will eat anything, and the butter was not too bad.*

Lieutenant Hall went to the company command post and requested more reinforcements for his left flank, which he suspected was exposed, as no contact had been made there with the 327th Glider Infantry Regiment. He sent Lieutenant Perdue to attempt to link up with the 327th, and Perdue asked for a volunteer to accompany him on the patrol. When no one answered, Bob Janes stepped up.

BOB JANES • *The lieutenant and I walked down this road for what seemed to be several miles. It was very spooky, and I was tired. I expected we would run into Germans at any moment, but I could not smell any. You could smell the Germans by their tobacco and leather. For some reason a cow decided to follow us, so the lieutenant took out his pistol and hit the thing in the head to get it to leave us alone. We never did find the other Airborne unit, and seemed to walk for hours. I managed to get back into my foxhole just as it was getting light. I really wanted to get some rest.*

As Janes tried to settle in for a nap on 23 September, he was approached by his squad leader, Charlie Jacobs. The two of them needed to move up to a nearby barn to scout for a location for the platoon to move. The rest of the squad waited for orders across the road, taking shelter in a ditch lined with trees. The two cautiously went inside and moved up to look out the windows on the opposite side of the barn. Just then a German artillery barrage screamed in.

BOB JANES • *Jacobs and I jumped into a concrete trough for protection, and shells exploded all around the barn. When the shelling stopped, we got out and looked out the window. German soldiers, less than twenty-five yards away, were running toward our location. Right behind them was a bunch of German armor—three half-tracks and a tank. Jacobs and I fired a burst out the window and ran to the back of the barn. Jacobs was taller than me and had no problem going out a window. I struggled to get out, and just as I cleared it, a German grenade went off inside the barn. Jacobs took off down the road toward the rest of the platoon like he was running in a hundred-yard dash. The Germans were firing at him, and I saw him get hit in the hand. He did not stop running until he reached our guys.*

Janes was waiting against the barn and could hear German soldiers yelling. They were on both the left and right sides of the building rushing forward and firing down the road. Seconds from being discovered, Janes decided to make a break for it. He sprinted to the closest ditch from the barn and jumped in, just as several German troops ran out from the side of the barn firing.

BOB JANES • *I landed in the ditch, and a German soldier jumped in not five feet behind me. He was looking further up the ditch, and I guess did not know I was that close to him. With his rifle right at my butt, he looked down and saw me as I rolled over. I fired off my Thompson. Only two rounds fired, and the gun jammed. I had not cleaned it since I had been in Holland. Both rounds hit the German in the chest, and he went down in the ditch. I began to crawl back toward the platoon.*

I came up on Joe Trepelka, and he had been wounded. I looked back and saw the German I had shot was crawling away out of the ditch. I took Trepelka's rifle and finished him off. At first Trepelka would not move, so after some encouragement I got him crawling back to our machine gun position. Carlino and McNeese were there and neither was firing; they told me the machine gun had jammed. I took Carlino's rifle and began to fire. Germans were climbing toward us from over a fence next to the barn. As one would come over the top I would fire, and down they went one after another. As I fired my last round, a German tank pulled on the road from behind the barn and began to fire.

Directly in the line of fire, Janes moved across the road into the other ditch, with McNeese, Carlino, and the rest of the squad trailing. A split-second decision was made. With tank cannon fire exploding in the trees around them, and machine gun tracer fire snapping down the road, Trepelka would be left behind. He would not move anymore on his own, and with the enemy closing in, someone would have to come back for him later.

JOHN TAYLOR • *By the light of day it was clear to us we didn't have very good positions. We had set up during the night and hadn't been able to see the lay of the land. This left us in an open area, and Lieutenant Hall, Haney, and I were behind the rise in this unprotected spot. We had been trying to move the machine gun to cover that area when the half-tracks came out into the field. I noticed Lieutenant Hall was sort of up on his knees and all of a sudden, that half-track opened up. It caught him on the left side of his body and spun him around like a top. I hollered at him, "Was it bad?" and he said he thought he was all right and could make it back to a ditch where he would have some cover and could get some aid. He started crawling back across the open spot.*

BOB JANES • *By then most of the platoon had pulled back and were crawling down a shallow ditch. It was hardly enough to keep your butt out of the horizon. I looked back towards the barn and saw this large trooper running across the field. We saw him fall, and I remember someone saying that it was Lieutenant Hall. I remember he did not move after falling. There was no attempt to get him as the small arms fire was clipping the grass in every direction.*

The Second Platoon moved back while taking the brunt of the enemy attack, crawling down a ditch to the previous night's positions. Over the sound of explosions from the mortar rounds and the snapping of small arms fire, the paratroopers paused when they heard the voice of President Franklin D. Roosevelt: "I hate war, Eleanor hates war, and even my dog hates war! I hate war!" It was actually mimic Gaston "Rebel" Adams. The men found it impossible not to chuckle for a moment but began to crawl again.

One man in the Second Platoon remained behind to cover the withdrawal, Pfc. Orel Lev. One of the smallest men in stature in the outfit but the most aggressive, Lev took the initiative to protect the others as they moved back. He went into the upstairs of the house being used as their command post. With a high-ground view of the swarming German infantry and armor, Lev went on the attack. He fired a bazooka at a passing German half-track. The rocket slammed into the crew compartment, instantly killing the four men inside. The Germans then directed small arms fire at the house.

With bullets passing through the walls and roof, Lev peered out with his rifle. His attention was drawn to a Mark IV tank. Standing in the turret was a German soldier, talking on a radio and waving his arms, directing the attack. Ignoring the incoming fire, Lev took aim, fired, and killed the commander. He then ran back to radio-in the coordinates for an artillery strike. The shells soon dropped on the battlefield, slowing the attack. The remaining Germans fell back.

A barn down the road was being used as the temporary aid station. Tom

Alley was there with the battalion doctor, Jackson Neavles. Yesterday's hero, Don Harms, was brought in severely wounded.

TOM ALLEY • *I was in the barn helping out Doc Neavles when they brought in Don Harms. Don had been hit in the leg by machine gun fire. His thigh was a mess, with lots of blood and splintered bone in a gaping wound. The doc had me putting pressure on the wound while he tried to treat him, but Don passed away moments later.*

With the attack stopped, Company F moved back up to retake the lost ground, supported by British tanks. Medic Phillip Thompson ran to the downed Lieutenant Hall. Hall was dead, peppered with shrapnel. He had been killed instantly by the mortar round that struck next to him.

Thompson removed Hall's .45 pistol and holster, and reported back to Lieutenant Eggie. Lieutenant Perdue had been hit in the knee early in the attack and was being treated, so Lt. Edward Thomas was moved over to take charge of the leaderless Second Platoon.

Black Friday was over but at a terrible loss for the company. Six men had been killed and seventeen wounded. The German attack on the Second Platoon had killed one officer and wounded another. Joe Trepelka was located where he had been left in the ditch, killed by the American artillery fire that had helped stop the attack. Don Harms was dead, Charlie Jacobs shot through the hand. Joe Hogenmiller and Frank Griffin had been wounded as well but were rescued from a field by Merlin Shennum and Bob Noody. Bazooka-man Jerry Farley had been hit, as well as the Third Platoon's Ray Aebischer, Charlie Rivenbark, and replacement Hubert Smith. With six dead and seventeen wounded, the operation in Holland was turning out to be more deadly than Normandy.

HERBERT EGGIE • *No one will ever know what it was that made Lieutenant Hall decide to cross that open field. He could have easily taken to the ditch like the rest of us. He was an excellent soldier and a fine leader. Knowing Lieutenant Hall, I can only say that it was sheer contempt for danger, mixed perhaps with a little bravado. This led him to the decision which cost him his life.*

The company officers, during a lull in the operation, remembered Lieutenant Hall in the staging area remarking that he felt he would not get out of this operation alive. He had said as we sat around in the tent that he had a premonition he was going to be killed. We had all laughed at him and told him not to worry. If his time was up he would get it, and if it wasn't he would not get it. I do not know whether fate enters into it or whether the date of one's death is fixed by some power at his birth.

Early in the afternoon the company moved out along the highway toward the town of Uden. A resupply effort caught their attention as C-47 transports flew overhead to the north, many pulling gliders. After moving onto a side road, the Second Platoon was sent out into an orchard, where an antenna from a German half-track was spotted poking out above the trees. John Taylor led the platoon into a ditch as they closed in on the half-track.

JOHN TAYLOR • *The ditch we were walking in was about waist high, with bushes and vines. I saw something move in the vines and poked my rifle down in them. All of a sudden, a German officer rose up right in front of me! In fact, when he stood up, he touched my rifle, and I was eyeball to eyeball with him. He was hollering, "Kamerade! Kamerade! Kamerade!" and was really scared. He didn't know how close he came to getting it, because I was already squeezing the trigger when he rose up. I just grabbed him and yelled and shoved him up on the road. I didn't even get a chance to search him. I could've gotten a good Luger and a good watch off that guy if I'd had time.*

Anyhow, I had to go back and get closer to the half-track before I could really see him. The half-track spotted us and took off like a scared ape. That simplified our job.

The German officer was led out to the roadway where the bulk of the company remained. The officer glared at the paratroopers in a condescending way, and according to Bob Noody, "looked down on us like we were a lower form of life." After he was stripped of his pistol and belongings, he was sent down between the two columns of paratroopers. The look on his face quickly angered a few. As he passed the men, they punched and kicked him. By the time he had reached the rear of the company and was being led off to the battalion headquarters, he had been beaten badly. The look on his bloody face had disappeared.

The company moved back onto the main highway and finally was allowed some rest on the 24th. Food and ammunition was brought to the men in an orchard where they had plopped down for the day.

John Taylor led the company back down the highway toward Veghel during the early morning hours of the next day. The Germans had cut the highway again, so the company was sent to support the British troops fighting to the south.

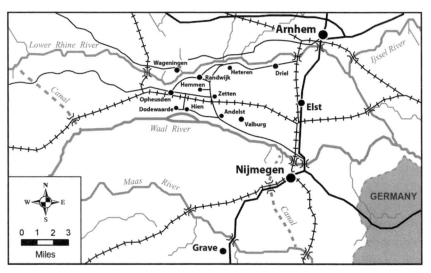

THE ISLAND

JOHN TAYLOR • *About the middle of the afternoon, we were moving along a road parallel to the main highway when a big firefight broke out at our left front. I was given another patrol assignment. It seemed like I would always get the patrol assignments. This one was the standard "Get over there and see what is going on."*

There were only four of us for this particular patrol. We had to scoot across real open terrain and got some small arms fire as we proceeded. We finally got over to a big, deep ditch and ran into a full company of British troops. They were lined up and down a big drainage ditch. There was a large concrete culvert in the roadway nearby. Apparently the British troops had started through this culvert for several hundred yards until the ditch curved. There at the curve was a German machine gunner who had wounded four of five men so far.

I spoke to the British officer in charge, and he wanted to know if our patrol could go over there and check out the gun for them. Well, I hadn't survived this long by being so stupid, so I just said no, I wasn't going up there. I then pointed out to him that one of his British tanks was sitting over by a tree about three hundred yards away and suggested he use that to knock out the machine gunner. This was done.

Our mission down south accomplished, we hitched a ride on a truck back to the column and went with them on to Uden. We went back to that same orchard and finally did get a few days' rest.

On 2 October, Fox Company moved through the 82nd Airborne territory at Nijmegen to an area called "the Island." It was a mass of land, ringed by dikes between the Lower Rhine and Waal Rivers. It was to be their home for some time. Trucks rushed them over the bridge across the Waal while under artillery fire, and the men were soon bivouacked in the town of Zetten. There they rested and prepared for their next fight.

CHAPTER 16

GUS AND POP

W hen Company F moved out of Eindhoven, two men stayed behind—Pfc. Gus Patruno and Pfc. Chelal "Pop" Clark. The best of friends, Patruno was the respectable rebel in combat, and at thirty-two years of age Clark was one of the oldest men in the unit. When British tanks rolled in to town, the duo decided they were going to be the first two men from the 101st Airborne into Berlin. And they planned to be at the spearhead of the planned rush across the Rhine.

The two climbed on the back of a passing tank covered with British soldiers. They rode along all clinging to the tank like a family of opossums on their mother. They quickly became frustrated with the progress.

GUS PATRUNO ● *Every few miles up the highway, a German sniper would pick a guy off of a tank. The whole column would stop. Everyone would take cover. This happened numerous times, and several men were shot off our tank as well. I could not understand why they were stopping. I went up to a British officer and asked him about all the delays, and he told me they were "evaluating the situation." Well, when we finally got close to Nijmegen, they stopped for tea. We finally had it and decided to go ahead on our own.*

In the middle of the afternoon, the two men walked alone ahead of the column and right into the city of Nijmegen. There they managed to locate an 82nd Airborne platoon engaged in street fighting, and were quickly absorbed into the unit. They fell in with Lt. W. R. "Rusty" Hays of Fox Company of the 505th. British tanks assisted as the paratroopers moved up the streets on the left flank toward the prized Nijmegen Bridge.

With Hunner Park in their path, Patruno and Clark paused with the other men next to a department store. Patruno was admiring the merchandise through the plate-glass window when an explosion rocked the building. The glass shattered out and into the paratroopers. Both Patruno and Clark were untouched except for a deafening ringing in their ears. Another trooper was not as fortunate and was blown to the street, bleeding profusely. While he was treated, the group moved forward.

Patruno moved up and quickly came under sniper fire from an upstairs window across the street. He took cover behind some debris and returned fire, pinning the German down with several shots from his M1. He looked over after hearing another shot into the upstairs window and saw it was from a young Dutch boy in his Boy Scout uniform, shooting a bolt-action rifle. Patruno finished off his loaded rounds into the sniper's location, then reloaded. He handed the rifle over to the scout and told him to fire and not to stop. As the boy fired at the window, Patruno ran across the street and threw a grenade up to where the sniper had been. He then returned, collected his rifle, and told the boy to go home, afraid that if he continued with the paratroopers, he would be killed.

The platoon fought its way up to the edge of the park. Patruno walked into a building that he suspected had been some sort of German command post, as the room had damaged radio equipment and maps strewn about. He admired a canvas map of Nijmegen and quickly pocketed it. A heavy firefight soon developed in Hunner Park, with the Germans holding the position to deny access to the bridge. The Germans managed to force the men back with a hail of fire in what appeared to Patruno to be numerous machine gun positions. The Americans took cover in the homes that skirted the park.

During the night Patruno and Clark took shelter, along with several other Fox 505th men, inside a home's low, walled yard. The Germans attacked with an armored car.

GUS PATRUNO • *The Germans came up to our position with an armored car with a machine gun on it. It was firing into our house and trying to hit us behind the wall. There was a little guy there from the 505th. He was really short but big on courage—he had nerves of steel. He jumped up and tossed a grenade over the wall at the armored car. He did that several times—toss the grenade, crouch down. I handed him a Gammon grenade I*

*got from a British tanker on my ride up there. He took it and tossed it over
onto the side of the armored car. There was a huge explosion, and the
armored car blew up.*

With the danger from the German attack over, Patruno contacted Lieutenant Hays to obtain a message slip confirming that he and Clark had been fighting with the 505th. Patruno had realized that he and Pop were not going to make it to Berlin anytime soon and would need a note when returning to their own company. Lieutenant Hays's note to their company's commanding officer said that Clark and Patruno "participated in some rather hot, night street fighting and did very well." Thus, although Patruno and Clark were known for going off to fight their own personal wars, they were never listed as AWOL or MIA. Everyone back in Fox 506th expected them to eventually show themselves and have a bunch of stories to go along with their pockets full of German souvenirs.

The following morning the attack on the park continued. Patruno and Clark were on the move again with Fox 505th as they fought in close quarters and pushed the Germans back to the bridge. British tanks once again supported in the assault, firing at the retreating Germans and blasting the stubborn ones determined to hold the ground. Patruno and Clark moved down to a road next to the bridge.

GUS PATRUNO • *We were right down by the river when a sniper fired
at me. I could feel the bullet go past. I suspected he was on the bridge or at
the other side, so I took cover behind a burned-out German vehicle. I moved
up and looked over the hood to see if I could spot the sniper when he hit me
from off the hood. It felt as though I had been slugged in the face. I spun to
the ground, got up, and walked over to a medic for treatment.*

Patruno had been shot in the cheek, the bullet lodging in the back of his throat. With a badly swollen and bloodied face, he was evacuated out of Nijmegen. His war was over. Clark would be left behind, only to rejoin Company F as it passed though Nijmegen heading over the bridge onto the Island. They were probably the only men in the 101st who took part in the combat and liberation of both the 101st's objective of Eindhoven and the 82nd's objective of Nijmegen. The note regarding Patruno's injury reads as follows:

MESSAGE
TO C.O. Co "F" 506

Pvts Clark, Patruno were with
my platoon night of 19th & 20th
at which time they participated
in some rather hot, night street
fighting and did very well.

Platn Ldr 3rd Plat Co "F"   W.R.Hays, 1st Lt.

CHAPTER 17

THE ISLAND

While the other members of Fox Company waited in reserve at the north end of Zetten, the 506th set up its headquarters in the town. The remaining two rifle companies of the Second Battalion were strung out along a dike about two miles north of Zetten, around the tiny village of Randwijk. The Germans occupied the high ground north of the dike, just across the Lower Rhine River. It was not long before the two sides clashed.

In the early morning hours of 5 October, Company E made contact with an enemy patrol on its right flank along the dike. Fox Company was alerted to prepare to move up to assist, and by 0800 they had a platoon back on the line, helping its sister company at a crossroads just east of Randwijk. And by 1900, after Company E had routed a large enemy force back to the Rhine, all of Fox Company was up along the dike.

Company F soon took over the American position on the dike, with the Second Platoon on the western flank in Randwijk, the First Platoon at the crossroads to the east of town, and the Third Platoon in between them. The company command post was to be moved up into Randwijk. Each platoon left a squad in reserve behind the dike, and a listening post was placed in the no-man's-land in front of each platoon, between the dike and the river. At the crossroads there were a few farmhouses, a windmill, and a large orchard filling the fields behind the farm. Those not on the southern slope of the dike tried to dig in between the trees of the orchard.

It did not take long for the enemy activity to start up again. A German shepherd dog was spotted on the northern slope of the dike at Randwijk. Knowing an enemy patrol had to be nearby, the listening post was pulled

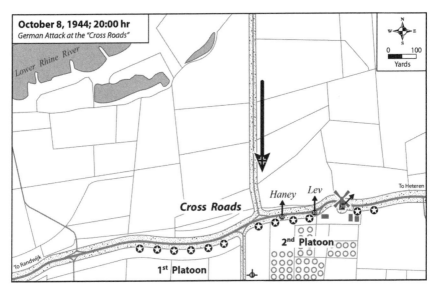

THE CROSSROADS IN HOLLAND

in, and everyone tensed for an attack. A report came in that a German patrol may have been in the area of the farmhouses just south of Randwijk, so Sgt. John Taylor led a group of men from the Second Platoon to check it out. No one was found, and the men returned early the next morning, tired and hungry. There had been little rest or food for the past twenty-four hours for everyone in the company.

The Germans had the high ground across the river, above the Americans by several hundred feet. It was almost impossible for the paratroopers to move anywhere along the dike without drawing enemy fire. When the men decided to dig better foxholes behind the dike and in the orchard, they received an immediate response: a series of artillery rounds and rockets falling on their line. Those in the open had little chance to escape unharmed. The Third Platoon's Sgt. Russ Schwenk, Lt. Thomas Rhodes, and Lt. Andy Tuck were all hit by shrapnel. Merlin Shennum removed Lieutenant Tuck's binoculars as the men were evacuated, knowing the prized possession would serve no purpose in an aid station or medical tent.

At the same time, Bill True had been sent out on the company's right flank to make contact with the 501st Parachute Infantry Regiment. He brought along replacement and Ohio native Pvt. James Shears. They traveled almost a thousand yards along the dike before they made contact with the 501st. The front line was spread terribly thin. True and Shears headed back, but they were now under observation. A lone mortar round fluttered in a few feet behind them, dropping Shears and slightly wounding True. True crawled over to Shears, giving him a shot of morphine and applying a field dressing. True went back for help and quickly returned with a medic. Shears was carried from the battlefield to the company command post but died a short time later.

The activity continued. German soldiers could be seen at the edge of the river across from the Third Platoon position. Men in the Second Squad, on the edge of the dike, began to fire at them. From his mortar position, Roy Zerbe could see Otto MacKay and others from his squad lined up taking shots at the Germans. Believing the range was too far for small arms, Zerbe complained to Lieutenant Eggie that the firing was doing nothing but giving their position away and requested it be stopped. Eggie disagreed, and the random shooting continued all afternoon.

That evening, Merlin Shennum was placed on the listening post in front of the Third Platoon lines on the dike. Soon after dark he spotted a German patrol moving through some trees to his left, toward the dike and the Third Platoon position. Shennum called back on his field phone to alert the men that trouble was on the way. At the same time, Armand Beauchamp and Roy Zerbe were on top on the dike.

ROY ZERBE ● *Beauchamp and I were lying on the roadway on top of the dike, looking off toward the river and the German position. We heard the distinctive thump of a mortar round being fired and decided it was time to get off the dike and get into a foxhole. As we ran down the backside of the dike, there was a brilliant flash, and I felt as though someone had punched me in the face. I fell into a foxhole, and although dazed I could tell something was wrong with my face and I had been hit.*

As Beauchamp and Zerbe ran down the back side of the dike, a German mortar round exploded next to them. Beauchamp absorbed the bulk of the blast. Lieutenant Eggie looked up from his foxhole after the explosion, only to be struck by a portion of Beauchamp's fragmented head as it rolled down the embankment. Eggie moved over to Zerbe's foxhole trying to shake the image of the body parts from his mind. But once in the hole, he was frozen by the sight of Zerbe. His entire jaw had been blown off. Zerbe was fumbling around trying to stop the blood from the mess of his face.

Johnny Metropolis came to the rescue and dropped into the hole. He spoke softly to Zerbe and began placing bandages around his neck and the front of his face. His actions helped stem the bleeding and calmed not only Zerbe but the lieutenant as well. Zerbe was sure that Metropolis's quick action had saved his life.

Meanwhile the German assault was not over. Mortar fire rained in on the dike, forcing the men into their foxholes. A German patrol rushed over the dike after throwing hand grenades and firing into the foxholes. The position they chose to rush was MacKay's, the same area where all the rifle fire had come from earlier in the day. MacKay, Eldridge Gaston, and replacement William Sievers were pulled from their holes and rushed off by the Germans as prisoners. A wounded Courtney Kelley was initially pulled away as well but was abandoned after he was found to have a severe gunshot wound to the groin.

Zerbe was taken to the safety of a nearby ditch, where he waited to be evacuated. His dirty uniform and the pocket Bible he carried were soaked with blood, his head and face wrapped in an assortment of field dressings. Numb from a shot of morphine, Zerbe tried to remain calm and by early morning was rushed away for treatment.

The men were shocked over the dead, wounded, and three men captured by the enemy. Many wondered about the fate of Gaston, MacKay, and Sievers. Everything had happened so fast: four "Toccoa men," Normandy veterans, gone from the platoon in a matter of seconds. For the replacements to the company, if they had not had it before, a wake-up call about their future had just dropped on them like a ton of bricks. The veterans took it all in stride, several spending the remainder of the morning crawling around in the grass looking for Beauchamp's expensive watch. It was never located.

UNIT JOURNAL (S-3)
0055 hour—Platoon of "F" repulsed breakthrough.

Later that morning the men of the Third Platoon were pulled off the line. The Second Platoon came in and took the right flank of the position, with the First Platoon on the left. A few heavy weapons were brought in to help with the defense of the area. An 81mm mortar was positioned in a brushy area behind the apple orchard. Tom Alley and Charlie Malley moved back to man it. A .50-caliber machine gun was also dropped off with the Second Platoon. Manning Haney went to work on the gun, making sure it would be ready for use on the dike and that a supply of ammunition would be close by.

Haney moved the .50-caliber machine gun to the middle of the roadway at the top of the dike. It was the only location to allow the maximum amount of coverage and elevation to defend their location. Two more machine guns, .30-calibers, were placed in front of the Second Platoon's front on the dike—one in front of a windmill near the farmhouses and one between Haney and the windmill.

Orel Lev, Bernard Tom, and Ken Hull took up the middle gun position. Haney asked Matt Carlino to keep ammunition nearby and had replacement Clarence Shrout remain with him as his assistant gunner.

Lev was disappointed about being moved to the front, as the night before he had been able to sneak over the dike with his bow and arrow, looking to hunt down German sentries. Although he came back empty handed, he was sure he could eventually, and silently, spoil some German soldier's night.

At 2030 the Germans made another attack on the Fox Company line. They desperately wanted the crossroads back in their hands and sent a platoon against the Second Platoon's front. Enemy mortar shells fell along the roadway at the top of the dike and throughout the platoon's lines. Men hunkered down in their foxholes and waited for the push over the top of the dike. Those who could, pitched grenades up and over the embankment, hoping to catch the Germans as they moved up into the company's blind spot.

Manning Haney had an excellent field of view of the advancing German troops. His .50-caliber machine gun chugged away as the Germans tried to advance up the ditches from the river. The other two machine gun positions used interlocking fire in an attempt to stop the attack. Haney's fire was so accurate that the assault ended almost as quickly as it began. The Germans withdrew, leaving their dead and wounded littering the ditches in front of the Fox Company's position.

As it became light, Haney and Shrout moved their gun back to the edge of the dike and dropped into foxholes. Haney removed his helmet and put on his favorite head cover, his raccoon cap with the letters "KY" in beads sewn on the front. The Kentucky native drifted off into a nap, weary from his night of fighting. Others smoked and ate rations while they cleaned up. The mud and grime from foxhole living was beginning to take a toll on the men and their weapons. They splashed water from their helmets to clean hands and faces, and oiled rifles and machine guns. They were fighting the moist claylike soil of Holland as much as they were fighting the Germans.

Bob Janes decided to do some souvenir hunting. He took a bold risk in sliding over the dike in broad daylight and down to the German dead. He crawled up to a soldier whom he suspected was an officer and quickly searched him. A photograph was retrieved from his pocket. It was of the soldier and his bride on their wedding day. Janes slipped the picture into his own pocket and removed a cased binocular from the dead man's belt. He slipped back over the dike disappointed that he was unable to find a pistol.

The next evening, Haney and Shrout dragged their gun onto the roadway at the top of the dike. Haney kept his coonskin cap on under his helmet, the striped tail poking out the back and down his neck. Lev, Hull, and Tom moved back into their foxhole to the east of Haney and prepared their .30-caliber machine gun for what was expected to be another fight on the dike.

John Taylor checked along the line and made sure all of the men in the platoon had ammunition and grenades, and were aware of their areas of responsibility along the front that evening.

Darkness fell, and the line became silent. Only the wind could be heard blowing over the dike from the river. The men tried their best to stay alert. Their senses peaked for anything that would warn them of an attack—the smell of leather, a squeak of a rifle sling, the snap of a firearm's safety. At 2000 it all came in one violent burst of color and sound.

Rifle fire snapped over the top of the dike, mortars began to flutter into the Second Platoon's line, and machine gun fire stitched its way back and forth along the roadway. Haney opened up, but immediately his weapon malfunctioned. He quickly went to work on a headspace problem as others opened fire along the front. The enemy fire began to be directed toward the gun manned by Lev, Hull, and Tom. They fired back, and the enemy responded with a mortar round directly on the top of their position. The shell's fragments tore into the three men, killing them instantly.

Lieutenant Thomas had contacted artillery support earlier that night to place two locations in front of his lines on record using map-grid coordinates. They were common areas for the Germans to attack from and were prearranged for fire by call signs. As the Germans began their attack, Thomas called for artillery support. Yet when a barrage fell on the dike, causing American casualties, Thomas suspected it was coming from his own artillery, not the Germans'. He tried to call off the fire but found the communications for the Second Platoon had been knocked out in the barrage.

JOHN TAYLOR ● *Our first impression was that our own artillery shells had fallen short and killed those men, but with no radio it was impossible to tell the artillery guys to recalculate their ranges. The only radio nearby was in the hands of the First Platoon on our left, and Lt. Thomas told me to go use it to tell the artillery what happened.*

Haney got his weapon back in action and began to fire on the advancing Germans. Immediately the bulk of the enemy fire switched from across the front of the dike toward Haney's position. Haney kept firing, Shrout kept feeding their weapon, and Carlino waited perched at the edge of the dike with more ammunition for the duo.

JOHN TAYLOR ● *I quickly headed toward the First Platoon and was down behind the dike about thirty yards from Manning Haney. He was on top of the dike along with Shrout, firing at the German positions. All of a sudden the place that Haney was defending just exploded. Bob Sherwood and I ran up to their position, and they were dead. I thought at the time that the artillery had again misfired on our own guys, and I was heartsick at the loss.*

As I raced over to the First Platoon for the radio to stop the artillery, I got shot at by platoon sentry [Vincent] Kiesnowski, who had not heard me say the password. Fortunately he missed.

Taylor got to the First Platoon radio and called for the artillery to cease firing, but was informed that they had not yet fired any rounds. He rushed back to the Second Platoon position where he told this to Lieutenant Thomas. As the firing died down and the German attack again faltered, the men of the Second Platoon began to absorb the details of the past few hours.

Bob Janes had been running to the company command post for more grenades when the shells fell on the dike. When he arrived back to his foxhole on the side of the dike, he found an unexploded German mortar shell a few inches from the opening. The men began to realize that they never heard any scream or whistle of artillery before the explosions. Mortar shells made only a faint fluttering sound, giving almost no warning before impact. They soon realized that their comrades had been killed by accurate German mortar fire and not friendly artillery fire.

Regardless of how the men had been killed, the survivors were still devastated by the loss. Hull, Lev, and Haney had been with the unit since Toccoa. Tom joined the unit after jump school. Shrout was new to the unit but was well liked and respected. He had proven himself in Eindhoven and on the dike as a reliable soldier. For his two nights of brave battle on the dike with the .50-caliber machine gun, Haney would be awarded the Distinguished Service Cross.

Early that morning Taylor took one last look at his best friend Haney up on the dike. His helmet askew and raccoon cap perched on his head, Haney was slumped over Shrout, as though the two were just sleeping. Next to them was the .50-caliber machine gun, mangled from the mortar shell's deadly impact.

The 501st moved into the Fox Company lines a short time later. The men were finally going to move into reserve. They picked up and marched south out of the orchard.

GEORGE YOCHUM • *We had withdrawn about a mile from our former position when a jeep stopped alongside our column. We were told to halt. Our first sergeant (Malley) said he needed two volunteers. "Yochum and Rasmussen, front and center! I want you both to go with the driver of this jeep, and he will tell you what to do."*

A small trailer was being pulled by the jeep, and in the trailer were canvas stretchers. We got in the jeep and asked, "Where are we going?" He replied, "Back to the front to retrieve some bodies and then deliver them to Graves Registration." The driver took us back to the area we had just left. He stopped at the Second Platoon's former position. The driver parked the jeep at the bottom of the dike. He said, "I'll stay with the jeep. The bodies are at the top of the dike."

We took a stretcher out of the trailer. The driver said, "Be careful. The krauts can see you up there." Rasmussen and I climbed up the side of the dike until we reached the bodies. They must have been close together when the shell hit. There were five bodies. We knew all of these men. Death was instantaneous, thank God for that.

Yochum and Rasmussen carefully placed each man on the stretcher and brought him back down the embankment to the waiting jeep. With Hull, Tom, and Lev, it was a particularly gruesome scene. Yochum saw a dismembered arm in the roadway near the bodies and placed it on top of the appropriate soldier. By the time the two were finished with the job, they were shocked to the point of speechlessness.

After placing the dead men inside mattress covers and laying them in the trailer, Rasmussen and Yochum were driven back to their unit. The company had a history of recovering most of its casualties and seeing that they were taken to Graves Registration and properly identified. But this time the task pushed both men to their limits.

––––––––

The Second Battalion of the 506th swapped places with the 501st and moved eastward down the dike to near Driel. The Second Platoon was pulled from the reserve before a moment's rest and sent off for division guard duty. Lieutenant Thomas arranged for the men of his platoon to be fed, but they were awake for another twenty-four hours providing security at the division headquarters. The following afternoon the remaining twenty-six men of the Second Platoon were driven back up to join the company and meet its new commander.

At 1600 the trucks dropped the Second Platoon men off in an orchard with the remainder of the company. They were all informed that they were to fall out for inspection. The men had just spent four days straight with no rest while being in nearly continual combat. They were filthy from foxhole living and had had no change of clothing or showers in almost a month. Yet their new leader, Capt. James Nye, chose this time to inspect his new unit.

JOHN TAYLOR ● *Well, of course none of us were prepared for inspection. He reamed us out pretty good. He particularly told me that I had two men that needed a haircut real, real bad. He wanted me to get those men's hair cut before I went to sleep that night and ordered me to report to him when I had the task done.*

Getting the hair cut for a couple men was not a big problem. George Lovell over in First Platoon had a pair of clippers, and in a little while I got the two men's hair clipped. But Captain Nye's little inspection performance didn't sit good with me. It didn't sit good with Lieutenant Thomas, and it didn't sit good with the men. In his initial meeting with the guys under his new command, this company commander should have made some effort to find out what they'd been through the last few days and not had them stand for inspection or chewed them out about anything.

On top of that, he had to tell me to report back to him to get the simple job of getting the men's hair cut rather than trust me, as a sergeant, to get it done on my own.

Well, I had a mean streak show up in me at that point. I had the men's hair cut by around seven that night. Rather than report back about this then, I waited until about 1:00 a.m. I then woke up the good company commander and informed him that I had been able to just now get these men's hair cut and I was reporting that it had been taken care of. This, of course, didn't sit too good with him, but I didn't care. I had done everything exactly as ordered, except I did it on my own schedule. And that took care of that.

CHAPTER 18

PATROLS

The men settled into their new location along the dike. The weather was poor. Between the occasional hours of sunshine, Fox Company lived with piercing cold winds, icy showers, and a relentless blanket of mist and fog. The foxholes were soggy, their clothes soiled and damp, and the men were filthy. The only bright spot in living on the Island was mail, cigarettes, and hot chow—all of which was in short supply. Bob Janes wrote about life on the Island in a letter to his parents:

October 19, 1944

Dearest Mom & Dad

Haven't heard from the old spread for quite a while now but know everything is going alright. I imagine you have been reading about the First Airborne Army operations in Holland. We have been right in the spearhead and going strong for over a month now. We have met everything the kraut has to offer this trip and still whipped the hell out of them. If they keep us here in Holland much longer they will have to issue us ice skates instead of parachutes. Did I tell you my platoon was cited for gallantry in action for a certain piece of action we were in? Besides that it looks like we are going to get the oak leaf cluster for our Presidential citation that we received for the Normandy operation. If this keeps up I will have more stripes on my blouse than a zebra. Two overseas stripes, wound stripe, Purple Heart, ETO ribbon, etc. To hell with that stuff give me that ticket to the good old USA. Please don't worry about me. Maybe I will be able to write more often and please do the same. Tell everyone hello.

Your son, Bob

Rations on the Island were usually British. Many men, like Tom Alley grew to enjoy the tea that complimented the Allied rations. Others quickly grew tired of the canned ox tails and corned beef that seemed to dominate the food stock. So they decided it would be in the best interest of everyone to supplement the meat supply.

Orders had been given that no cattle were to be butchered unless they had been accidentally killed by enemy artillery fire. The order was issued to prevent the paratroopers from shooting cattle and the complaints from the locals that soon followed.

But several members of the company decided to do some cattle rustling anyway. After being given permission to look for dead livestock, they would head off in jeeps, driving around the Island until they spotted a live cow. It would mysteriously drop dead on their arrival. The cow would be brought back to the company, lugged into a nearby residence, and butchered. News of the meat would soon circulate around the company, and everyone would come by to take a share, leaving barely enough to feed the rustlers themselves. The routine continued whenever possible, usually by members of the Third Platoon, who were notorious for their ability to locate cattle killed by a single ".30-caliber artillery shell." Morale briefly improved.

Word came in late one evening that a large stock of cigarettes and candy bars awaited their retrieval from battalion headquarters. Bob Noody was sent off to bring them to the excited members of the company. Noody made his way through a mile-long maze of canals, dikes, and dense vegetation to headquarters. Finding no boxes to carry the items, he filled every pocket with candy bars. Cartons of smokes were stacked to arm's length and eye level.

Noody retraced his steps along a well-used path, but in the darkness he disappeared into a canal. Noody was shocked as he fell into the murky water over his head. He tried to save the supplies as he splashed over to the bank and pulled himself out of the canal. He returned to the company with only a few soggy cartons of cigarettes and some waterlogged candy bars. Noody was drenched, the supplies were lost, and the men were quite upset.

Being wet all the time, many men of the company began to have foot problems. SSgt. Vince Occhipinti solved his by obtaining a pair of the local wooden shoes. They allowed his feet to dry out, as well as his boots, and were actually very light and comfortable. It was not uncommon to see Occhipinti out running or repairing phone lines clad in a wool cap, wool sweater, combat pants, and his beloved wooden shoes. He may have looked comical, but when his feet dried out and healed quickly, he had the last laugh.

———————

For several nights in a row in late October, German rockets screamed across the Lower Rhine and fell into the paratroopers' position. Colonel Sink decided to send a patrol over the river to locate and, if possible, destroy the rocket launchers. The rockets were fired from a mobile multitube rocket launcher called a Nebelwerfer, and although they were not extremely accurate, their shriek was terrifying. They were known as "screaming meemies" to the men of Company F, and their harassment kept everyone on edge.

A ten-man patrol was assembled, made up of five men from Fox Company and five from the regimental S-2 section, one of whom was an officer. Both the officer and an enlisted man from the regimental section spoke fluent German. Three other men were assigned from headquarters as boat operators. Sgt. Alvin "Blackie" Wilson headed up the F Company men, which included West Virginia native John Himelrick, who had been "volunteered" for the patrol. Wilson handed out Gammon grenades to use on the rocket launcher if it was located.

Colonel Sink gave the group a pep talk before they headed out. Three collapsible canvas boats made by the British were used for the river crossing. The patrol silently crossed the river near the town of Wageningen, tying off the boats next to power-line supports. The three men in the boat detail remained at the riverbank, while the other men headed out toward the town.

The patrol moved single file with the German-speaking officer and enlisted man heading the column. They passed over a low dike near the river a short distance to the west of the Wolfswaard Ferry building and continued up to the high-sloped dike at the edge of the town. A fire burned off in the distance from an artillery strike, and the glow illuminated the top and opposite side of the dike from the patrol. The men spread out along the shadows of the dike slope as the front of the column decided their next move.

Screaming rocket fire and blinding flashes of light jolted the patrol. The screaming meemie had begun firing from directly over their position. With the German side of the dike illuminated, and no chance of quietly destroying the gun, the patrol decided to mark the location on a map and head back across the river to report their findings. They slithered back down the dike and into the darkness toward the river.

JOHN HIMELRICK ● *On the way back, as we approached the primary dike—the low dike down by the river—those in front of the column suddenly passed the word back to stop and get down, and to hit the ground. And I could hear some conversation, and I could hear German being spoken, and just in a moment after that there was a burst of fire. And the word then came down to head for the boats, and we did in a pretty good pace. The information I received at the time was that a German outpost had moved in after we had crossed that dike on the way up. The men in the outpost had been killed. Two men in the patrol were wounded, one through the hip, and Blackie Wilson had been wounded slightly in the foot.*

We managed to reach the boats, and the boat detail had the boats at the edge of the water ready to go. Of course we piled in anyplace we could find. We started across the river only to find ourselves going in circles. If you have ever seen three or four people trying to row a boat without any coordination you will understand what I am talking about. It took us a while to get coordinated out there in front of God and everybody. We actually crossed the river with no fire on us. There were flares while we were in the river, but everyone returned. Colonel Sink was there waiting for us as promised and had a hot drink for us.

At the time the men found no humor in the return crossing, but afterward the account of circling around in the river produced some laughs. All joking aside, no one from the patrol hoped to repeat the problem crossing. The coordinates of the rocket launcher's location were passed on for an immediate artillery strike. All things considered, the Wageningen river patrol was a success.

Early November saw the men of Company F along the dike between the towns of Driel and Heteren. The Second Platoon was given the task of running a patrol over the embankment at the damaged Arnhem railroad bridge near Driel. Lieutenant Thomas and SSgt. John Taylor would lead twenty other men on the prisoner snatch assault. The group included a medic, as well as Clyde Jeffers, radio-man Dutch Ostrander, Charles Shaeffer, Gaston Adams, Ralph Provenzano, Bob Janes, Bill McNeese, Bob Sherwood, Tommy Psar, Homer Smith, Calvin Wright, Bill Olanie, Whitey Swafford, Pat Casey, Walter Puskar, Roy Stokes, Warren Bell, Sylvester Bright, and the Third Platoon's Ray Ballew.

Helmets were left behind, faces were blackened, and several of the men

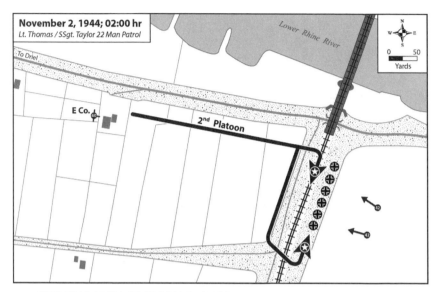

November 2, 1944; 02:00 hr
Lt. Thomas / SSgt. Taylor 22 Man Patrol

Lower Rhine River

To Driel

E Co.

2nd Platoon

THE EMBANKMENT NEAR DRIEL

swapped rifles for Thompson submachine guns. They also brought along two Browning Automatic Rifles, and Psar went as a rifle grenadier. Most carried concussion grenades instead of the usual fragmentation type, wanting to avoid close-quarter self-inflicted or friendly fire injuries. On 2 November at 0200, the group passed through an E Company mortar position and headed east into the darkness toward the railroad embankment.

The men crawled forward single-file with the dike to their left. When they reached the first irrigation ditch, they spread out into a skirmish line, passing through the ditch while trying to keep their weapons clear of the water and mud. After crawling through the muddy fields and dragging themselves over several water-filled ditches, the men were soon soaked. The temperature was near freezing.

They reached the final ditch and a small roadway below the railroad embankment. Taylor and Janes briefly discussed the possibility of mines in some recently plowed soil in front of their position. Deciding there was nothing to do but move through the terrain, the group split into two sections and began up the mist-covered embankment. Janes led one group in a skirmish line up the embankment as Taylor and Thomas took the other up the right flank.

Then a concussion grenade flew over the embankment from the German side of the railroad track and exploded. The Fox Company men let out a yell and charged up and over the tracks and down into the German positions.

JOHN TAYLOR • *I know that when I got to the top of the railroad, which had a double track on top, a flare went off from one side of the German positions about fifty yards away. I could see several enemy soldiers in this position out there. As I started down the German side of the railroad, my feet went out from under me, and I slid all the way down to the bottom and landed next to Clyde Jeffers, who had the phone and was on my left. We turned, a burst of fire came from a hole dug back in the railroad embankment there, and Jeffers said he was hit in the arm. I asked if he could make it back. He said yes and started back.*

Lieutenant Thomas threw a grenade into the hole where the fire that wounded Jeffers had come from. Taylor followed up with a burst of fire from his submachine gun. He then went into an adjacent hole and felt a body, and pulled a German soldier out. Thomas took the prisoner and headed over the embankment with him.

At the top of the embankment, just under the skyline and tracks, Janes and half of the patrol fired from above the foxholes toward two machine gun positions. The German gunners were raking the top of the embankment and railroad tracks with fire, causing the tracks to blink like Christmas lights from the ricochets. Smith opened up with his BAR and quickly silenced one gun position. The second German machine gun turned its fire on Smith, causing Provenzano to be struck in the hip. A moment later, still clutching his BAR, Smith slumped down next to him, dead. The paratroopers on the embankment continued to trade fire with the German machine gunner, with muzzle flashes aiming at muzzle flashes.

Psar rose up from his prone position and took aim at a machine gun with his rifle grenade. He fired the grenade off the end of his rifle and watched as it exploded directly on the gun. The gun fell silent. He quickly reloaded and fired off a second shot at the position. Down at the bottom of the embankment, the men were busy throwing grenades into every foxhole and dugout they could locate. When a parachute flare fired into the air from inside a hole, the revealed position was quickly dispatched with grenades and gunfire.

Taylor threw a grenade into another dugout and followed it with another burst of fire. A quick search in the hole located three dead Germans and one live one. He too was quickly removed from the hole and pushed up the embankment as a prisoner. Taylor then discovered he had a jammed weapon, with a live cartridge fed into a broken casing in the chamber. Deciding the havoc they had wreaked on the German position was enough, he blew his whistle to signal a withdrawal. The men quickly climbed up and over the embankment, dragging the dead "Smitty" Smith down the slope.

Once they were down at the bottom of the embankment, enemy mortar fire began to drop in on their location. But their attention was drawn to a splashing sound, and found Dutch Ostrander struggling in the ditch in front of them. A mortar shell fragment had knocked him into the water, blown the radio set off his back, and wounded him in the ribs. He was quickly fished out, minus the radio. Leaving Smith's body behind, the men sprinted over the ditches and fields that they had patiently crawled through earlier in the night. They slipped and slid covered in mud, helping the wounded. They were illuminated by the blasts and exploding shells as they went, but no men fell to the fire.

Once back in the relative safety of the Easy Company lines, Taylor did a head count and realized they had another man missing, Tommy Psar. Fueled with anger and adrenaline, Taylor headed back to the embankment followed by Whitey Swafford, Walter Puskar, and Pat Casey.

A small amount of machine gun and mortar fire harassed them as they approached the railroad. They found Psar dead at the top of the embankment, wounded in the neck. They dragged him down the hill, and Taylor tried to carry him back but fell in the process. A stretcher was hastily rigged using two rifles and a jacket, and Psar was brought back to the American lines.

A jeep rushed off the wounded Ostrander, Jeffers, Provenzano, and Ballew for treatment, and an attached trailer carried Psar's body. Intelligence officer Lt. Lewis Nixon drove a freezing Taylor and Thomas back to the battalion headquarters where they were given cups of coffee and blankets. A change of clothes soon followed, and they were debriefed on the entire incident. Two prisoners had been captured, and eighteen foxholes knocked out. For their actions Taylor and Thomas would be awarded the Silver Star.

2 NOVEMBER 1944, S-1 JOURNAL
0200 Patrol was sent out that contacted enemy. One radio lost when it was shot off the carriers back and fell into six feet of water. Two prisoners were captured and we lost two men.

2 NOVEMBER 1944, S-2 JOURNAL
0414 White Patrol is back. Took two prisoners of war one PW from 41st FT Battalion, First Company. One man a Pvt. One Pfc. Acting non-commissioned. Two of ours killed and four wounded.

2 NOVEMBER 1944, S-3 JOURNAL
0230 Twenty two man patrol from "F" Co leaves to cross dike in front of "E" Co. sector. 0300 Patrol across the dike returns six casualties; two killed, four slightly wounded. Captured two prisoners.

Homer Smith's body was not recovered from the embankment until the summer of 1954. His remains were found in a shallow grave during construction work and were returned to the United States.

The Second Platoon went back on the line with the remainder of the company on a four-hundred-yard front near Driel. A few days later they moved to Valburg for a much-needed rest. Bob Janes found the time to pen another letter home to his parents:

Dearest Mom & Dad
Well folks this is your son broadcasting from Holland once again. I have not had any letters from you folks for quite a while but received one from Marge the other day and she said everyone is okay. I am feeling fine. They just can't get old Janes down as much as they try. Life is no bed of roses here. Mud is deep, rains everyday, the nights are long and cold, and the wind, well now I know why they have so many windmills in Holland.

Outside of these weather elements as long as I have my share of stew, a cup of coffee, fags and a dry hole to sleep in, I believe old man luck is going to cheat hell out of the devil for this trooper. I received the package of underwear and socks, and also the can of candy. I don't think I was ever at a place [where] things like that were more appreciated. Thanks a million and God bless both of you. Now please don't worry about me because I have been taking care of myself and it shouldn't be too long before we are all together.

All my Love, Bob

While things were quiet, Captain Nye had a brilliant idea. 1st Sgt. Malley located a washing machine in an abandoned house and brought it to the company headquarters. By platoon, the men were pulled back and all uniforms were washed, wrung out by a hand wringer, and then put back on—wet. This was done in the middle of the night at nearly freezing temperatures. The decision did not set well with anyone in the company except its commanding officer.

Thanksgiving 1944 was spent in Valburg. A holiday meal was prepared for the men of Company F. It was perhaps without all the trimmings they were used to at home, but they still managed to have their turkey, potatoes, and gravy. Colonel Strayer and some of the other battalion brass joined them. They were all thankful, not only for the meal but also for surviving life on the Island.

A few days later the men were ferried by boat over the Waal River and off of the Island. They were taken by truck to Nijmegen where they were dropped off at a YMCA-type facility with most of its roof missing, a casualty of the earlier battle for the city.

Hot showers cleaned off almost two months' worth of dirt, blood, and grime. A heated indoor swimming pool waited for the men after the showers. With no swimming trunks, the men accepted a towel from a female Dutch employee and jumped into the pool naked. Now down to the strength of a reinforced platoon, the entire company had no problem fitting into the pool.

That afternoon after their showers and swim, the men put back on their dirty clothes and boarded trucks headed southward down the blackened Hell's Highway. Their seventy-three days on the line was over. Their next destination was France.

CHAPTER 19

QUAIL HUNTING

The company was trucked into Mourmelon-le-Grand, located a short distance from Reims. It was a French military base that had been vacated by the Germans, and in addition to its garrison, it now contained an artificial steel runway and airfield. The buildings were battered stucco and sat alongside the remnants of the battlefield trenches of the First World War. But the location seemed like a paradise compared to the soggy foxholes of Holland.

On arrival the men were treated to another Thanksgiving meal, this time with all the trimmings. They were thrilled to finally be able to get some hot chow, to bathe, and to get some rest in hastily built bunk beds. Those who had been wounded in Normandy and Holland and were able to return to the unit were waiting for their mates when they arrived at Mourmelon. They swapped stories and filled each other in on who would be going home wounded and who was lost forever from the company roster.

The First Platoon's Bud Edwards wrote home on 5 December about the new accommodations and food:

Dear Mother & Dad
I have been here in France for a couple of days. We had a big Thanksgiving Day dinner before we left Holland and we also had a big turkey dinner here. This place that we are at has foxholes beat a million ways. Since I have been here I have been in the town once and that is all I care to go. Only place I want to go now is Paris. I believe that one time you told me that I would be sorry that I never took advantage of [the] French that I was taking. Well I am sorry and I do mean sorry.

I am now a private again as you can see. It is beginning to look like I like to change my rating when I go into combat. I don't like to get in a rut. We will see what happens next time although I hope there isn't a next time.

I got my first package today from you which included the sun tan shirt and pipe. That pipe was in rough condition. The stem was loose. I sure appreciate this stationary. I wish you would tell that sister of mine to read the paper once in a while. She wrote to me and asked [me] to look up her boyfriends relatives outside of Amsterdam. That would take quite a bit of doing. I don't believe the Germans would like it at all . . .

I am enclosing a 40.00 money order which you can put in the bank for me. I am going to hit the hay now.

Love, Bud

Whether it was the food itself or the drastic change to their diet, the company quickly fell ill to "the green apple shuffle." Men spent the next day battling stomach cramps and diarrhea.

MARION GRODOWSKI ● *They had a very interesting latrine system at Mourmelon. The toilets were nothing more than holes in the corner of a tile floor. Tiles colored like a footprint were alongside the hole for your feet to rest on. You had to be very careful squatting in the latrine to assure you did not get your pants or suspenders wet. When we were sick, it was quite a challenge to use the latrine and not make a mess of yourself or the floor.*

With the stomach illness behind them, the men were issued forty-eight-hour passes to Paris. One man in the First Platoon, Pfc. William Clemens, won a lottery drawing for a thirty-day furlough back in the United States. Only two were issued in the entire 506th. Although Clemens was offered a thousand dollars in cash for the furlough, he did not budge.

Although Reims was a short distance away, it was also the Allied head-quarters. By sending the bulk of the men to Paris, it decreased the possibility of problems with unruly paratroopers and high-ranking rear-echelon brass. Wool uniforms were brought out, and shirts and pants were creased to a crisp edge using bars of soap. Coveted jump boots were donned instead of combat boots and polished to an admired high gloss. Passes in hand, and condoms in pockets, the men headed off by train to Paris.

Once there, they wasted no time in obtaining alcohol and seeing the tourist sites. Marion Grodowski tried his best to tag along and keep an eye on platoon mates John Taylor, Bob Janes, and Joe Hogenmiller but was lured from the group early in the afternoon.

MARION GRODOWSKI • *Paris was out of this world. I really wanted to go and see all the sights with the boys. But Paris was filled with beautiful women. I was partial to blondes and redheads. I was walking down the street when a redhead went past me. I made an about-face and went after her. I ended up spending my time in Paris with my new female companion, minding our own business. The boys in the platoon called the search for women "quail hunting." Other than drinking or the sights, what else was there to do?*

Quail hunting was not limited to the men of the Second Platoon. Bugler Bob Noody and the Third Platoon's Merlin Shennum paired up to take in all the action Paris had to offer in forty-eight hours. They quickly headed toward Pigalle (which the men called "Pig Alley"), an area known for prostitution, nude cabaret shows, and a thriving black market. Along the way they managed to meet two sisters who agreed to accompany them for the evening. They took in a burlesque show, had a good dinner, and managed to run into friends of Noody from basic training. When the two men tired of their selected female company, they just swapped dates with each other. It was an exhausting two days.

The men over in the First Platoon also managed to take in all that Paris had to offer. After being billeted at a Red Cross facility, they headed out on the town. Dates, dinners, and women of negotiable virtue filled the schedule for most on day one. Day two included Notre Dame, the Eiffel Tower, and the Champs-Élysées, with drinks and meals chocked between the sights. They even managed a game of ping-pong before going home. They were the kings of time management in Paris.

JOHN TAYLOR • *One night we went to a place where there were a lot of ladies from the Women's Army Corps. By coincidence we ran into Lieutenant Hall's girlfriend who was a WAC officer. We came face to face with this young lady, and she remembered me and Grodowski. Lieutenant Hall had previously introduced us to her in London. I really didn't know what to say because I didn't know whether she knew that Lieutenant Hall had been killed. It turns out she did not know, so we spent one evening there with her talking, poor thing. Our forty-eight hours in Paris went by fast, and we had to get back.*

Lieutenant Tuck wrote a letter home about his experience in Paris, 14 December:

My Own Mom,

Returned last night from a "forty-eight" in Paris, your beloved Paris, and lady, I can see why it is. Never in my life have I seen a more wonderful place. Quite expensive, but well worth it's cost. (Not as expensive as London, however.)

Arrived in the city at about 11:30 and had lunch & a few drinks at the Grand Hotel. (Very nice!) Then, forthwith, on a tour of the city. I saw all the places that I've heard so much about. Went to the Folies Bergeres that night and was very disappointed. (Very little real talent manifested!) On then to "Pig Alley" (Pigale sp?) and the Latin Quarter.

Had a good hot shower the next morning and went to place an order for a guide. Went shopping with her, the things that were at all worth while were criminally expensive. Took the guide, who turned out to be a very "chic" gal to lunch and to a show at the Hotel Olympia. In the late afternoon I had some pictures taken (not too expensive, I was pleasantly surprised!) They will [be] sent to me in four weeks.

Just before dinner I went to a "snazzy" little café and imbibed quite freely in cognac. Result mild paralysis. In the process I met a very beautiful model who spoke about three words of English, but was a real lexicon with the hands and eye. Depending on my "extensive" knowledge of language and a steady flow of champagne, we got on famously. Had dinner at a French Officers Mess and went to the Lido Club. (A very slick "lay-out")

I am going back to Paris in the spring. Just don't know which year. We'll go together, Wei?

Goodnight 'Mon Cheri.'

Lovingly, Eddie

The men understandably "blew off steam" in Paris. In Normandy the First Platoon had taken the brunt of the losses in combat. In Holland that unfortunate circumstance fell on the men of the Second Platoon, which left the Island with only a dozen men. The Third Platoon always seemed to fall a close second in both campaigns in terms of being battered by attrition in combat—and three of its members were now prisoners of war.

Replacements began to arrive over the next few days. They seemed to be very young and in poor shape compared to the original men billeted in England before D-Day. Joining the unit were George Glover, Arthur Kerlin, Claude Kitzmiller, Joseph LeBalbo, Ralph Massey, David Noonan, Clyde Philpot, Donald Rinehart, Robert Rodinger, Stanley Tommey, and Harry Wilking. 2nd Lt. Bob Cooke joined the unit along with 2nd Lt. Ben Stapelfeld. They would be assigned to help the depleted Second and First Platoons.

A week of physical training and drill filled the time for the men of Fox Company. The replacements had a difficult time keeping up with the veterans but tried their best to blend in and do their part. Another batch of replacement privates soon followed: Charles Burger, Werner Kordon, Donald Lawrence, Cyril Pederson, John Peterson, Lloyd Robinson, Walter Romero, Theodore Ulrich, Ewell Westmoreland, and Durward Wooley. Privates Maurice Zelik, Salvadore Ceniceros, Glenn Jones, and Antonio Casucci trickled in over the next few days as well. 2nd Lt. William Robertson, a Montana native and former Chicago Cardinals football player, joined the company as Lieutenant Thomas was transferred up to Second Battalion headquarters.

The company's equipment was turned in for an upgrade as well. Weapons, ammunition, web gear, and tools were dropped off for cleaning, repair, or complete replacement. With supply sergeant Ed Brennan in the hospital with ulcers, Len Hicks took over in supply and tried in vain to obtain new boots, clothing, and winter clothing for the men. Hicks dropped off the damaged weapons, clothing, and equipment with the regimental supply section, hoping new supplies would be delivered back to him in the next few days.

For Company F, 16 December 1944 was begun by washing combat uniforms in gasoline, then wringing them out to dry—a kind of dry cleaning that managed to get out most of the dirt, grease, and blood stains. Then word began to trickle into the camp that the Germans had broken through the American lines. The Second Platoon's Hugh Borden tossed his combat pants down on the ground and stated, "We might as well forget about it, fellas, because we're fixin' to move out!"

Bud Edwards scratched out a letter to his parents the next day:

Dear Mother & Dad

I hope you have received that card by now. Did you get that money order which I sent sometime ago? The trip which we took to Paris was very nice but we didn't have enough time there. I didn't get to see any of the sights. One thing I was able to do though was to get to the P.X. there and get some of the things I needed. I got your package with the scarf, soap, socks, and candy in it. Thank you very much. The mail here hasn't been coming in very regularly.

France is alright but it sure is hard to get around when you can't speak their language. One time there in Paris I will bet I was all over that town on the subway before I got where I wanted to go. . . .

It sure is cold here and I sure hope it doesn't snow. When it is cold like this it is hard to do anything. I sure feel sorry for those boys up front and I'm sure glad I am not up there. Well until next time.

Love, Bud

Just after midnight on the 18th, acting supply sergeant Hicks was called to the orderly room to meet with Captain Nye. After discovering that the men were short on supplies and their damaged gear had been dropped off with regimental supply, Nye ordered Hicks to retrieve the items he had dropped off. He took a truck and quickly returned with boxes and bags of torn web gear, battered rifles, and tattered clothes.

SSgt. Vince Occhipinti and Pfc. George Lovell were the only two men in the First Platoon who had kept their entrenching tools. All the others had been turned in for repair or replacement. Only a delay into Mourmelon, due to a trip to the hospital, had kept their equipment from being turned in. Theirs would be the only entrenching tools in the First Platoon when it headed off to combat the German breakthrough.

Hicks redistributed the weapons, clothing, and web gear that had been dropped off at supply. Occhipinti scrounged up ammunition for the company. Bandoliers of rifle ammunition were handed out, and Occhipinti located stick magazines and dirty ammunition for men like himself who were carrying Thompson submachine guns. A mix match of grenades was located as well and was randomly handed out in the platoons.

By late afternoon on 18 December, the men had climbed onto open tractor-trailer cattle trucks and were off to the battle in Belgium. The night chill cut into the men standing in the truck beds. They huddled together under snow flurries and rotated around the coldest spots on the trailer as the trucks lumbered along through the rolling hills and valleys.

It took almost ten hours to travel the hundred or so miles to their destination. At 0300 the trucks pulled into a large tree-lined field, and the men, stiff from the cold and travel, dismounted. They heard a voice yelling off in the distance: "No one knows what the situation is! The enemy can be anywhere! Keep all-around protection, and move out slowly and carefully! Welcome to Bastogne!"

CHAPTER 20

BASTOGNE

—————————————————————————————

T he Company formed up and moved out on the road toward the
city of Bastogne. Artillery fire thumped off in the distance, lighting up the overcast skies above them. Machine gun fire crackled off to the
east, indicating that someone was involved in heavy fighting outside of
town. As they marched forward the men passed troops leaving the area,
going in the opposite direction away from the fighting.

TOM ALLEY ● *There were troops coming down the road toward us.*
We tried to communicate with them to find out what was going on, but
we could not get much sense out of them. We started taking items from
them, ammunition, weapons, and their entrenching tools.

The column of paratroopers moved on toward Bastogne. The closer
they got to town, the louder the artillery and machine gun fire. The group
advanced and picked up their speed. Sergeants had to run up and down the
line and motivate the replacements, who seemed to have a hard time keeping up with the Company's new jogging pace.

After a short pause, the men moved through town from the southwest
to the northeast. The city center was a place of confusion, with troops and
vehicles going in every direction. Len Hicks and Ed Bishop were told to
remain behind and see what supplies they could locate for the Company.
The rest of the men headed out into the fog and were held up again just
outside of town at a crossroads.

TOM ALLEY ● *It was daylight and we were out on a road moving fast.*
We were told to drop our overcoats and bedrolls, as we would not need them

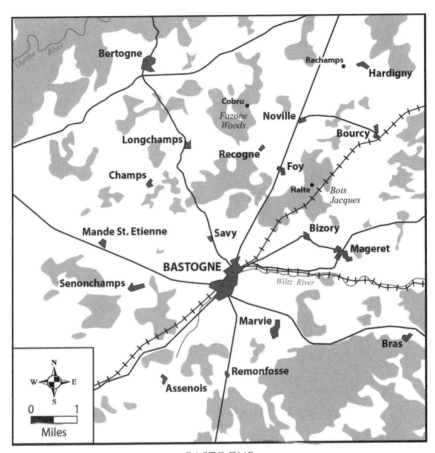

BASTOGNE

for combat. We were told we could come back and get them later. My mother worked for the Lance Packing Company in Charlotte, which made peanut butter and marshmallow snacks. My pockets were filled with snacks that I had just received in a Christmas package from home. I left behind a lot of the snacks in my jacket, expecting to return to it later.

The Company moved off a short distance into the nearby woods and began to dig in. They would be held in reserve for the battle sounding in the distance. The swirling fog and bitter cold began to wrap around them as they settled into foxholes. Most wished they had kept their overcoats and bedrolls. A few men snuck back to find the piles of wool, hoping to find their jacket or something to eat.

There were very few rations left with the men by the time they arrived in Bastogne, having only been issued one K-Ration before they trucked out of Mourmelon. Merlin Shennum was fortunate enough to have received a Christmas package of fudge from a girlfriend while in France. He quickly fished the treats from his pockets and shared it with others in the platoon. It was cold, and it was hard, but the creamy chocolate tasted fantastic.

Others in the First Platoon spent the night eating peanut butter crackers and orange-flavored marshmallow circus peanuts. The pickings were slim, but everyone seemed to get at least a piece of someone else's shared Christmas candy or treats.

The following morning the men stiffly climbed from their foxholes and moved out toward the northeast. Low fog hugged the ground, limiting their view to only a hundred yards. The men strained to peer through the lifting fog and mist to watch for Germans they were told could be anywhere.

JOHN TAYLOR • *A lot of action was taking place over to our right which was then occupied by the 501st Regiment. The next morning our regiment, the 506th, started moving in that direction. As we crossed a railroad, we started drawing a lot of artillery fire. Around noon we moved off to the side of the road to our right into some woods and held up there. We put an outpost to our rear and to our right. We were in an area that had a gap in our lines and the 501st and the 506th were trying to tie up together to bridge this gap.*

VINCE OCCHIPINTI • *The information given to us at the time was that there were half a dozen to a dozen Germans in the area. The action started at about 5:30 p.m. Dec. 20, just as it started to get dark. Although the entire area would be covered with snow over the next several days, that night the fields were bare; there was no moon. The entire area was dark. You could not see anything. The temperature was in the low-30s. Because I carried a Thompson, which doesn't shoot far, but shoots fast, I moved into the area where the scouts or the squad leader for the first squad would be leading the way.*

The men of the First Platoon moved forward, with Sgt. Gordon Mather following close behind scout Pfc. George Lovell. The men in the platoon tried to stay close and keep each other in sight, as they would otherwise disappear in the dense forest and low light. The silence of the woods was shattered by a violent burst of German machine gun fire ripping into the First Platoon. The men dropped to the ground as the gun blazed away. Tracer fire sliced through the darkness of the trees and whipped back and forth at knee level. Men hugged every inch of the ground trying to avoid the rapid incoming fire.

The firing briefly stopped. Sergeant Mather propped himself up and began to yell back instructions the men. With many green replacements in the Company, commands were essential as the new men lacked any combat experience. The German gun fired again from the darkness only fifty yards away and Mather dropped to the forest floor with bullets to the face and shoulder. The men began to dig in as the darkness swallowed them up in the trees. After a few insults in English about the United States and President Roosevelt, the Germans vanished from their ambush position.

The men were shocked. Sergeant Gordon Mather was dead. Scout Pfc. George Lovell had been badly wounded in the legs and torso and would not survive the removal from the forest, another casualty of the ambush. At the rear of the platoon, Pfc. Edward Jacques had been struck by the enemy fire as well and was quickly treated and rushed off to an Aid Station. For the new replacements, seeing a respected 'Toccoa' man and duel campaign combat veteran like Sergeant Mather killed, they were struck with a sudden realization of their own mortality. Perhaps no one would make it home alive, a reality the veterans already had accepted, and the replacements now quickly had to face. If it could happen to Mather, one of the best men in the outfit, it could happen to anyone.

As the woods soaked in the darkness, the men spent the evening using what small amount of entrenching tools they had to dig slit trenches and foxholes. Everything available was used to breach the cold soil—shovels, picks, hand axes, helmets, and even knives and hands. Men were sent out in front of the lines to post up in two-man observation posts. They would rotate the position every few hours. Instructions were given to go straight out to the OP's and straight back from the OP's to avoid being shot as an enemy infiltrator. The situation around Bastogne had still not stabilized and the Germans could be anywhere.

Over in the Second Platoon, two men received their instructions and were sent out to the observation post. During the night it began to snow. Cpl. Joe Hogenmiller headed out to relieve the men at the OP, paired up with a new transfer from Regimental HQ, Pvt. Salvadore Ceniceros. Back on the line another replacement, Pvt. Luke 'Ira' Atkins waited for their return and watched the forest for movement. Atkins, a native of Harlan County Kentucky was recognized back in France for his expert ability to shoot the M-1 rifle. He was a 'crack shot' who never seemed to miss.

Several hours passed, and it began to get light. Two men were sent out to relieve Hogenmiller and Ceniceros. Hogenmiller, as instructed, came straight as an arrow back to the lines, followed by Ceniceros. Ceniceros, though, used the trees for cover as he scurried back to the lines, rushing from one location of cover to the next. A lone shot rang out in the lines, its echo crackling off into the mist-covered forest. SSgt. John Taylor knew immediately who had fired—Atkins—and without looking knew the fatal result. Atkins did not miss. Hogenmiller and Taylor went out into the snow and retrieved Ceniceros. His death was a tragic result of his failure to follow instructions.

JOHN TAYLOR ● *Right after this mishap, Fox Company joined up with Able Company at around 8:00 that morning and we attacked a unit of Germans coming at us on our side of the railroad. We caught them dead right there. We killed about eighty of them and captured a bunch more. The rest took off back across the railroad to their lines.*

The 506th then succeeded in joining up with the 501st and set up for the night with this railroad station house and surrounding area as our outpost. We had people in the railroad station house and we had a good field of fire to protect our lines.

21 DECEMBER 1944, G-3 JOURNAL
(101ST DIVISION HQ)
506—0935 . . . Attack (Inf-Tk) hitting F Co at 581611. Holding.

While the men dug in and camouflaged new positions, a small patrol was sent out to look for suspected German tracked vehicles that could be heard idling behind the lines. South Carolina native Pfc. E. B. Wallace led the way, as they disappeared into the forest now shrouded in mist and dusted with snow. After crossing through the woods they found themselves walking up on a small group of dead and dying American paratroopers from B Company 506th.

Lieutenant Stapelfeld drew a map of the action in his diary on December 21:

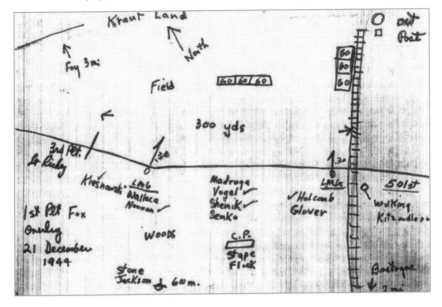

E. B. WALLACE ● *We walked up on what I suspected was another patrol. I do not know if these guys had been hit by artillery or ambushed. But there were several dead, and one wounded trooper. I spoke with him and asked him his name. It was John Robert Osborne. Turned out he was from Charlotte, just like me.*

As we were talking I discovered that I knew his father before the war, we had worked at the same job. We talked a little about his father and Charlotte. I went off on my assigned mission, and went to get him on the way back, but he was dead.

Wallace and the patrol returned and took up their posts with the First Platoon in their newly camouflaged foxholes and firing positions. The cold weather had made a turn for the worse; the temperature dropped and snow began to fall. Everything went white and the men, without any real winter clothes, struggled to stay warm and dry.

Out in front of the First Platoon, two pistol wearing German soldiers were observed slowly moving toward the lines. Pfc. Bill True and Sgt. Otto May watched the two men approach. Instead of wearing helmets, the two had only soft caps on their heads, known to the men of Company F as "Kommen Zee Here" caps, frequently worn during surrender. May kept SSgt. Occhipinti informed of the soldier's progress by field phone. When they came within a handful of yards from their foxhole, True ordered the duo over with the few German surrender words he had memorized. The pistol belts and prized P-38 handguns were quickly removed and the two were marched back to the CP to await transportation to the Battalion HQ.

Over near the Second Platoon position a canteen cup was steaming at the bottom of a foxhole. The last few packets of instant coffee had been pooled and with the help of a small can of fuel, a much-desired 'Cup of Joe' had been brewed. Several men stood around and passed the cup from man to man, allowing each to get a sip of the hot drink. When the cup reached Cpl. Bob Noody the handle came dislodged from its mount, and the cup dumped over into the snow. Icy glares were cast, profanity was spewed, and the apologetic Noody was left holding the askew empty cup as the others walked away.

Len Hicks and Ed Bishop trucked up to the Company lines after spending the past few days scrounging supplies in Bastogne. They managed to find a large supply of small burlap sacks in a storage building, possibly left behind by a US Army mess unit that fled the town on the paratrooper's arrival. Hicks had used burlap to wrap his boots while hunting rabbits in the snow back in the United States. He considered the find of gunny sacks to be a potential saver of both life, and limb. The bags were quickly handed out to the men of the Company, four to six per man along with balls of twine to secure the burlap to their boots. After leaving the remaining bags with the Battalion Headquarters, Hicks and Bishop trucked back into Bastogne for another scrounging mission. Below overcast skies the fighting at the snow covered Halte Station continued.

JOHN TAYLOR ● *We held this position against German attack for several days. Here's how the Germans tried to take the station house. First they would drop heavy mortar fire on top of the house, then they would move the mortar fire back behind the house and try to rush it from the front. We caught on to their strategy quickly and were prepared.*

In the first place, this stone station house was strongly built. We knew that when the mortar fire moved to the back of the house, we could expect the Germans to storm the front. Our machine gunners in the woods were

ready for them. The Germans got to the front door and around the back,
but they never got inside, and never did capture it. They lost quite a few men
trying, however.

During the night Bob Noody was sent out along the edge of the roadway that ran through the Fox Company position to check on the men at
their observation posts. Noody crept along in the trees at the roadway's edge,
and stopped to speak with two men in a foxhole. Up ahead a lone German
could be seen standing in the roadway. He was tall, with massive shoulders.
Surprised, Noody took aim at the massive silhouette in the darkness, and
fired off a shot from his M-1. The German dropped.

Noody moved up cautiously to check the dead man for paperwork, and
was surprised when he got up to the dead soldier to discover he was not a
soldier at all. It was not even a human being. Mistaking a distant horse's
rear silhouette for a man in the darkness, Noody had shot a stray horse in
the back of the head. The men in the OP's were not happy, as their location
had been compromised. Noody apologized and moved out.

The morning of December 23rd greeted the men in Bastogne with a
break in the weather. The dull gray overcast burned off to crisp blue skies,
and the surrounded 101st Airborne Division prepared for a resupply from
C-47s. With everyone low on ammunition, and lacking food, excitement
ran through the Company with the prospect of some hot chow and supplies.

Second Platoon Sergeant John Taylor and the Operations Sergeant, Tom
Alley, went out to mark the company position with orange colored panels.
The rest of the men donned chartreuse identification scarves over their
shoulders, left over issue from the operation in Holland. The scarves were
worn to mark the Company lines, in the hope they would serve not only as
a boundary marker for the overhead American aircraft, but also prevent air
to ground friendly fire incidents.

Hicks and Bishop arrived in their truck back to the Fox Company position. They had found a large stack of filled US Army duffle bags back in
town. Just like the burlap bags, they were also suspected of being abandoned
by a US Army unit that had fled Bastogne. Hicks and Bishop had sorted
through the misappropriated bags finding enough supplies for every man
in the Company to be given several new articles of clothing to wear.

Sleeping bags, cotton knit thermal underwear, wool socks, shirts, and
pants, blanket lined tanker overalls and jackets. The duffle bags even con-

tained some mess kits and canteen cups. The sleeping bags were made to pull over parkas, with holes cut for arms and the head. They may have been the worst looking Company in the 506th, but they were able to battle the cold with the new clothing. Those not lucky enough for a parka donned the extra wool clothing. Thanks to Hicks and Bishop, Christmas came early for Company F.

The re-supply was underway and the men watched as C-47s braved the enemy fire to drop bundles of supplies off in the distance toward Bastogne. American Fighter-Bombers, P-47s, buzzed the edge of the American lines looking for German armor targets to attack. One plane accidentally dropped a bomb short into the Fox Company lines. It whistled into their position and exploded, but there were no injuries. The crater was put to use after another failed attack on their position, and the numerous fresh and frozen dead German soldiers that littered their position were massed into the bomb crater.

Not everyone was happy to see the dead get buried in the crater. Merlin Shennum had been putting the dead to work while out on the Third Platoon's observation post. He used a frozen corpse as a snow covered sandbag in front of his foxhole. A second dead German was propped up in front of his hole at night, allowing Shennum to catnap knowing his scarecrow, complete with USGI helmet, would be attacked by infiltrating Germans before he would.

Even with the re-supply, few supplies initially trickled out to the men in Fox Company. Beans were found in a storage building near the railroad station, and a soup was quickly started to feed the men. On Christmas Day bread was brought in from town, along with a small supply of K rations. Morale improved when the men were given a Christmas letter from their division commander, General Anthony McAuliffe. It explained that the Germans had demanded the 101st surrender, and his response to them was 'Nuts!'

That night the men were treated to a slice of bread, a boxed K ration, and a steaming hot cup of bean soup. Over in the Second Platoon, two injured men shared the same frozen foxhole, Marion Grodowski and Bob Janes. Grodowski had been wounded in Veghel, and returned early from the hospital to the unit in Mourmelon. His leg had not healed and the wound was now badly infected. Janes injured his knee during physical training in Mourmelon. Shrapnel from Carentan was cutting up the muscles on his kneecap, forcing the leg straight and stiff as a board. He was informed he was to go back to the hospital for treatment, but unfortunately it was after they had left for Bastogne.

The eating procedure for the men was that either food was delivered to them on the line, or one man was to go back to the Company Command Post to pick up the chow for both himself and his foxhole buddy. For some reason, both Grodowski and Janes left their position during the evening chow call and headed back to the CP. As they waited in line the men heard the drone of aircraft and watched as German aircraft passed over their position. A single bomb dropped from one of the planes into the trees, and the men dropped to the ground for cover.

The lone bomb exploded in the Second Platoon position, and the men rushed over to see if anyone was hurt. To their relief there were no injuries. But to their surprise, the bomb had landed right in the vacated foxhole belonging to Grodowski and Janes!

The aerial re-supply continued as American forces fought their way into the surrounded paratroopers in Bastogne. Len Hicks watched in admiration as formations of slow moving cargo planes flew over their position and dropped parachute bundles of supplies into their lines on December 27th.

LEN HICKS ● *The pilots that flew supplies were our heroes. They had real problems. I saw one plane hit and begin to burn, losing altitude. Out came the crew chief, shortly after him came the co-pilot. The plane was coming almost directly at our supply camp and getting lower all the time. We were watching and offering a prayer all the time for him. We saw him [the pilot] come out of the escape window, slide back along that burning aluminum then his parachute opened, and he could not have landed much closer to us, or anymore softly. I asked "why did you wait so long?" "I was absolutely terrified of jumping!" The plane plunged into the snow across the roadway. We took him to the aid station. He was burned in the arms.*

After the plane crash, Hicks and Ed Bishop continued their scrounging in Bastogne for supplies. Hicks located enough materials to make pancakes, and maple flavored tablets that were used to make syrup. Several hundred small pancakes were made and quickly delivered to the Fox Company position, complete with syrup coating.

Enough batter material was appropriated to feed the men pancakes for several days. That, along with one meal of spaghetti kept the men content, and Hicks and Bishop proud.

With the siege over by December 27th, the men who were wounded and waiting in Bastogne, as well as those injured on the line, were evacuated. Lt . John Thomson, Whitey Swafford, James Rasmus, Alan Summers, 'Rebel' Adams, Billy Holcomb, Tom Brayton, William Murphy, and Walter Puskar had all been wounded in the several days of fighting for the station house. Several were evacuated out of Bastogne. Four men were wounded in the Halte Station from a grenade blast on December 28th. Jack Dickerson, Johnny Metropolis, Angelo Peluso, and Bob Noody were all injured by the shrapnel and shipped off for treatment. One man would lose his leg.

Water was constantly brought out to the men by Hicks and Bishop. In addition to the canteens, which froze, the men stored water in the empty cardboard 60mm mortar tubes. It would not take long for the water to freeze inside the containers, and the men would thaw them out and melt the ice on a small squad stove. When one stovetop container began to emit a strange smell, Delmar 'Red' Newhouse investigated. Taking the lid off he peered into the tube and was shocked to see a live 60mm mortar shell inside. He carefully hugged the container, walked it away from the other men and buried it in the snow. Another disaster avoided.

On December 31st the men were advised that overshoes (goulashes) had arrived for distribution within the Company. A large pile of the oversized, rubberized boots was dumped at the Command Post. Men filed back to obtain a pair of the new boots, with the hope it would keep the warmth in, and wet snow out. As a line formed at the boot pile a German shell screamed into the lines and exploded near the Command Post. Bud Edwards and Pat Casey were both struck by shrapnel. Edwards's ribs were broken and a lung collapsed from the hot metal shard that pierced his prone torso. Two medics arrived and loaded Bud onto a litter, hustling him off to a jeep for evacuation. Bud managed a slight wave and called out "so long fellas' as he was shuffled away for treatment.

JOHN TAYLOR • *We eventually moved back a few hundred yards away from our position by the railroad station house and another company took our place there. On December 26th, the siege of Bastogne had been broken through on the south by American troops. On New Year's Eve night, we were told to pick out a target and fire away with crew-served weapons. We fired our 60mm mortars and our machine guns. The next morning, January 1, 1945, we began to attack German positions at our front.*

The snow was about two feet deep and the winter situation was truly terrible. We had all the clothes on that you could possibly wear, we had goulashes, and we had some feed sacks that we tied around our feet, but the cold was still unbearable. A lot of men were getting frozen feet and we had lost a bunch of new people because of this. As we started towards our area of attack, our movement through the woods was difficult. The limbs of the trees were low to the ground and were loaded with snow.

With the defense of Bastogne over, Fox Company would now go on the offensive. They moved out through the Bois Jacques (Jacks Woods) and spent the day on a sweep through the forest toward the town of Foy. The fighting in Bastogne was far from over.

CHAPTER 21

FOY

The men made their slow push through the snow into the Bois Jacques. The tree branches dumped snow on the troopers, dusting their necks with icy powder, soaking their clothes as they crept forward. With no enemy contact they dug in before it was dark. Henry Beck and Art Peterson decided to do a little scrounging in a farmhouse they could see across an open field near their position. A chicken had been spotted wandering around outside the structure.

ART PETERSON ● *Beck and I crossed this big open field in the snow toward the building and no one fired at us. We had spotted a chicken. And where there are chickens, there are eggs. We took along a gunny sack and after some effort Beck managed to catch the chicken. I also located about 4 to 6 eggs. On the way back to our lines the Germans opened up on us with an 88 shell, an airburst. Both of us were knocked to the ground. I looked over and Beck was lying in the snow with his guts spilled out. I tried to help him push them back in. I took the gunny sack to cover his stomach, and put my pistol belt around his waist to try to hold everything in. I was then able to drag him back for help. They (Germans) did not fire again.*

506TH AFTER-ACTION REPORT, 2 JANUARY 1945
0930 2nd Bn attacked through the Bois Jacques (P585612) to the Foy-Mageret Road., 1400 yards to the north. At 1530 the objective was taken. F Co in contact, A Co, E Co center, D Co on right . . .

The next day Len Hicks and Ed Bishop loaded a truck with cut timber to be used as foxhole covers and headed out toward the Fox Company position, now overlooking the town of Foy. Braving enemy artillery fire while driving cross country, they managed to navigate through the snow and uneven terrain, reaching the Second Battalion position before dark.

LEN HICKS ● *When we did finally find "F" Co. they were just on the brow of a hill overlooking a small town. We pulled up by the side of E Company and met with Colonel Sink. I jumped out and quickly asked for "F" Co. He [Sink] wanted to know what in the hell I was doing with that truck up there. I said "Sir, I have a load of logs for 'F' Co. and would appreciate their location." He said, "Dump them right here, 'E' Co. can use them." I said "Sir, F Co. is going to need them tonight." He told me where to find them and get a detail there and for us to get out of there with that truck.*

The logs were distributed and quickly put to use covering the foxholes the men had chipped out of the frozen ground. From their position among the trees, the men could see the small town of Foy just over a mile from their location across a large open field of snow. Darkness fell, swallowing the Company into the shadows cast by the snow covered trees and timber covered foxholes.

Men tried to stay warm in the bottom of their holes by tucking their hands in armpits, shuffling their feet, or if lucky enough, brewing a canteen cup of coffee with a 'Sterno' type can of fuel. The motley bulk of clothing they wore, and the terribly brisk conditions, prevented any routine of hygiene. Shaving was out and teeth were not brushed; it felt as if even their teeth were wearing dirty socks. Cardboard ration boxes or small ration cans were used as toilets. Once filled, they were thrown in front of the previous owner's foxhole, or shoved into the nearby snow. The only thing that prevented the men from despising each other was the fact that they all looked and smelled the same—terrible.

As darkness fell from overcast skies, the men of Fox Company made last minute preparations to their positions in the woods. Small logs were packed over foxholes, a ration was eaten, a cup of coffee brewed. Everyone's attention was drawn to a thunder rumbling off in the distance. Veterans of the campaign in Holland recognized the shriek of the Germans 'Screaming Meemie' rockets. As the roar of the rockets became louder, those outside quickly slid into their foxholes, and those already inside waited for the impact.

The rockets screamed into the lines, exploded in the trees, and turned up the snow and soil in blinding flashes of light as they impacted into the ground. The men braced themselves, fearful that the next blast may be on their foxhole. There was nowhere to run, and nothing to do but wait out the barrage, hoping your time was not up. As the rocket barrage ended, artillery shells followed, also exploding in the trees and above the ground. The deafening blows of the 'air bursts' slung hot metal shrapnel and pieces of jagged tree trunk down on the Fox Company position.

When the barrage finally ended, the men began to check for casualties. 1st Platoon had taken the bulk of the wounded. Sergeant Occhipinti had taken a large piece of shrapnel through his jump boot. Lt. Holland Oswald, Sgt. Otto May, and Pfc. E. B. Wallace were hit as well. All of the men were evacuated, with members of the unit assisting or carrying them behind the lines to an awaiting medic's jeep.

The next evening the men trudged off the line and into reserve west of the Noville-Bastogne Highway. The weather conditions and poor clothing continued to cause casualties in the Company. On arrival to their reserve position, nine enlisted men left for the hospital with frozen feet, festering wounds, or pneumonia. Those not able to come off the line tried to get a few days of rest and chow in the new reserve position in the woods north of Savy, southwest of Foy.

While in reserve the men were able to clean up a bit, read mail, or perhaps write a note home. Rumors trickled in with supplies and complaints went out with the suppliers. Word came in that two former Fox Company men had been killed around the New Year. Sgt. Willie Morris had been killed by friendly fire from a P-47 strafing too close to the American lines on December 30th. The men grumbled and bitched about the loss.

Morris was a career soldier and original member of the 501st Parachute Infantry Battalion, one of the first paratroopers in the Army. He had been demoted and transferred after the Company withdrawal outside Carentan. Everyone thought the punishment was unfair. The men wondered what his fate would have been if he could have remained with them in Company F. 1st Lt. Carl MacDowell had been killed on the 31st of December. Len Hicks was especially distraught over his death, as the two considered each other a good friend. The news of the loss of both men troubled everyone and morale suffered.

The morning of January 9th the men prepared for an attack in the Fazone woods north of their position. Broken clouds closed into a thick soupy overcast sky as the men made their push into the woods at 1100. As they pushed ahead, German artillery fell into the woods to greet them. The farther the men went into the woods, the heavier the raining barrage of German artillery.

Sergeants kept their men moving forward through blinding flashes of light, deafening explosions, and billowing clouds of black smoke. During the advance, Sergeant John Taylor found Company Commander Jim Nye hunched over and cowering in a foxhole. The Company moved on without him, relying on the motivational leadership of the platoon leaders and NCOs.

The intensity of the shelling increased, falling like rain through the trees. Men dropped with the blasts, then rushed back on their feet covered with dirt and tree debris. Several men went down and remained down with shrapnel wounds. Pfc. Johnny Jackson fell with metal in his back. Privates Ted Ulrich, Horace Vick, Ken Mottern, Nick Mika, and Joseph LeBalbo were also hit in the barrage. Private Art Peterson also came off the line with shrapnel in his thigh, trailed by a wounded 'Pop' Clark.

Those not coming off the line wounded, or helping those who were, took refuge from the shelling in old foxholes, shell holes, and under fallen trees. The barrage ended and the woods were cleared to their required edge position by late afternoon. Fox Company came off the line the next day and moved back to their reserve position for a few more days to re-supply with good rations and to get some rest. The Company then moved into a defensive perimeter in Foy on the afternoon of January 13th.

JOHN TAYLOR • *We moved on to a place called Foy, Belgium and set up the Platoon Headquarters in a house on the far side of the town. When we arrived, E Company pulled out and H and I Company stayed. These companies had very few men left. We had set up communications with the Company Command Post which was located back on the edge of town where we started from. That night we didn't get any food [delivered] because we were expecting a counterattack. I was discussing plans for a patrol with Lt. [John C.] Williams from the Third Platoon when heavy fifty-caliber machine gun fire started coming down the street that fronted the Platoon Headquarters house.*

Sergeant Taylor ran down the hallway to the back of the home and looked outside. A German tank flanked by soldiers was moving toward their location and only thirty yards away. Taylor ran back to the front of the house and alerted Lt. Williams. There was a small group of men in the cellar of the home, and Lt. Williams rushed down to get the men up and out of the house.

Taylor went back down the hall again and watched the tank as it crept from the backyard to the side of the home. German soldiers moved out to cover the sides of the house. Taylor moved from the hallway and kneeled down in the doorway just inside a rear bedroom. A German soldier began to climb into the shattered window of the room. Taylor shot the man from only a few feet away, and staying low, moved back into the hallway. Gunfire erupted from the front door of the home. Wood chips rained down on Taylor as the doorframe beside his head exploded from the fire.

Taylor glanced toward the front door and saw two German soldiers, the source of the firing. A submachine gun fired off, the two men screamed and threw their hands up. Then the duo fell dead to the floor in a heap. Using his 'Thompson', Lt. Williams had mowed the two men down from the stairs of the cellar as they fired at Taylor down the hall. The men came up from the cellar and decided it was time to vacate the home.

John Taylor and William Oakley ran out the back door of the home firing their weapons from the hip. Taylor did a flip over a barbed wire fence and ended up behind the church in Foy. Others ran from the front of the home.

TOM ALLEY ● *It was a moonlit night and I rushed out the front of the home to see two tanks in the front yard. I ran right into one of the tanks in the street. I was so close to it that I ran right under its turret barrel, and kept on running until I got into a field across the street from the house.*

A column of German soldiers moving down the street were cut down by several rapid mortar rounds lobbed into their ranks by Luke Atkins. The men began to reassemble in small groups and tried to set up operations in another home.

Lt. Cooke was found lying wounded in the snow with a terrible leg wound. He was quickly treated and evacuated from town. Confusion still reigned in Foy as squads were split from their platoons, and platoons were cut off from the Company Command post.

JOHN HIMELRICK ● *I was on a two-man outpost north/northeast of town in a foxhole. It was covered with a wood sled, covered with dirt in a long and narrow slit trench. There was barely enough room for two people. We were there for several hours from midnight to 0400. The Germans then attacked Foy with tanks and infantry. There was a lot of tracer fire. Tanks fired into buildings. A runner came up and told us to head back to town. My foxhole roommate refused to get out of the hole. I had to physically pull him out. He was suffering from 'Combat Fatigue'.*

JOHN TAYLOR ● *We moved from house to house and finally about daylight, word came down for us to pull back in the high ground outside of Foy. We started sending the men up the hill and I know that I started crawling in a ditch to get up the hill. I had gone about one hundred fifty yards up this ditch when I heard the distinctive sound of an approaching tank. It was German and was coming pretty fast up the main road in the village.*

Taylor was stunned when a deafening blast went off right over his head. An American Tank Destroyer (TD) was camouflaged in the nearby tree line, and had fired at the approaching German tank. The German tank exploded and one crewman was observed to flee as the tank caught fire. The exhausted and hungry men of Fox Company took refuge in the tree line above town, and waited for support.

506TH AFTER-ACTION REPORT, 14 JANUARY 1945
The enemy attacking with 6 or 7 tanks with accompanying infantry at 0415hrs, our front under continuous pressure, withdrew to old MLR at 0600 to reorganize.

JOHN HIMELRICK ● *We were in a building, possibly the church and were trying to make contact. Lt. Stapelfeld, Pfc. Julian Sullivan with a radio and I, left to make contact with another Company. We made contact with the other Company. It got light out and we took a different route back. Along the way we passed a US armored column.*
A GI stepped out and called the password. I gave the counter sign but he

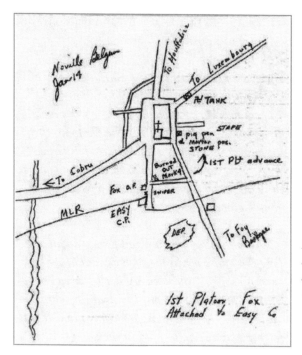

Lieutenant Stapelfeld drew a map of the action in his diary on January 14.

still fired, and hit me in the right arm and hip, through and through. Between my three to four layers of clothes I later found a bullet. It did not knock me down and the lieutenant asked me if I was ok. I told him I was hit, I had been shot with a forty five. The kid that shot me was crying, and I was taken off to the aid station.

I really did not want to leave Foy and the unit. But I did feel sorry for the lieutenant and Sullivan for having to return to the war. I knew I would be out a while.

JOHN TAYLOR • *A little later that morning, sure enough, the 11th Armored Division moved in and lined up 8 or 10 tanks on that hill. They brought up a couple of companies of men with them. The tanks opened up on the Germans with the big stuff. Fifty-caliber machine guns, now this was the way I was taught to fight a war. The fight went on all day, but without the use of small arms. The Germans fired some 'Screaming Meemies' at us, but missed.*

Once the village was finally secured, Lt. Robinson and I decided we'd go back into Foy and get all the stuff we had left in the cellar. We got back to that house, we found a dead German in one room, two at the door, and some in the yard. We got our stuff and went back to the top of the hill. Later that afternoon, around three, we got word to move to our left and make a flanking movement. We were going to attack at Noville.

Fox and Dog Companies moved out through heavy snow through the small villages of Recogne and Cobru. They left behind the village of Foy, with its battered and burned out buildings, debris filled streets, and piles of rubble. The smell of smoke, dead bodies, and rotting livestock swirled around in the bitter cold air. With temperatures near zero, they set up for the night in a draw just outside the town of Noville. No food made it out to them, and the men of Company F went hungry, again.

JOHN TAYLOR • *The ground was frozen solid so we could not dig in for protection against the Germans or the cold. I remember that night I got so damned mad at Hogenmiller and Joe Gillespie because they had rolled up in an old piece of parachute, laid down beside a log and gone to sleep. Jack Borden and I, on the other hand, were just walking up and down, trying to stay warm, and of course, got no sleep. It was just freezing.*
As we were walking, every so often one of the guards would go by and we had to give him the password, which I remember that night was 'Wiz & Wiper'. At one point the guards changed and a new guy wasn't going to take any chances. Jack gave him the word 'wiz' and the kid got excited and answered 'windshield wiper, windshield wiper, windshield wiper, windshield wiper!"

Clear skies met the frozen troops the next morning outside of Noville. Several men from the Second Platoon crossed the draw and enemy fire to get a hot breakfast with another unit. They were treated to oatmeal mixed with pineapple, and a ration can for each man containing eggs with bacon, as well as a hot cup of coffee. After eating, the men brought back hot chow for the remainder of the Company.

Forty-three men came off the line that morning and were evacuated with injuries and illnesses due to the freezing cold conditions. The Company now had seventy-eight men left out of the one hundred and forty that had gone into Bastogne. Attrition was chipping away at their effective fighting strength. The men suspected they could not last much longer at the rate they were going, and suspected everyone would eventually come off the line, wounded, sick, or dead.

The men moved out for the attack at 1030, supported by tanks, artillery, and air cover. They quickly moved into the town from the south, with the First Platoon attached to Easy Company for the attack. When a German tank rolled into town from the northeast, Dude Stone dropped a mortar round on its turret and forced it back into the open ground and the crosshairs of American fighter-bombers. The town was secured at 1145.

CHAPTER 22

ON THE RIVER

J anuary 20th the men moved out of the Bastogne area on large trac-
tor trucks with flatbed trailers. Wood panels on the side rails of the
trucks offered the only protection from the elements. Standing up, and
packed like sardines, the men miserably endured icy rain showers for over
twenty four hours as they traveled down muddy roads to the southeast.
Their only entertainment, aside from peering over the rails at the battered
countryside, was when Sgt. Bill Green sang country songs. Green's cowboy
ballads and mournful songs of good love gone bad entertained the men and
helped distract them from the rain and cold. Those who knew the words
sang along.

They arrived near the German border, at Waldhambach, France, and
spent several days trying to dry out in a reserve status off the front lines.
Everyone in the Company seemed to be battling a cold or the flu, and the
few days of rest helped strengthen the battered men. By January 30th they
were back on the line, this time on the Moder River at Grassendorf, France.
Aggressive patrolling from the town began almost immediately.

In the early morning hours of February 4th, almost two-dozen men assembled for a patrol across the Moder River into the German controlled territory surrounding Bitschhoffen, France. Cpl. Bob Noody went to wake up
Sgt. Bill Green who had volunteered for the patrol. Green had just returned
from the hospital and was not required to be a part of the patrol, though
he decided to tag along. After some difficulty, Noody woke Green, and the
two met up with Lt. Stapelfeld who would be in charge of the patrol.

The men headed out in a single column from Grassendorf and moved
through the woods north from the edge of Ringeldorf. They proceeded

down a ridge to the Moder River and waited to move north toward Bit-schhoffen. The patrol was to make a counterclockwise circle and end back in Pfaffenhoffen. The battalion executive officer, Capt. Richard Winters, saw the men off and waited for their return.

A heavy mist cloaked the men as they crossed the river and made their way north through the darkness toward the town of Bitschoffen. The patrol crept along without incident around the north side of Bitschoffen, and began their route back near the main road toward Pfaffenhoffen and the safety of the American lines.

WILLIAM MURPHY ● *We were crossing a roadway when a mortar dropped into the middle of our column. The flash from the explosion was so bright it appeared as though it was daylight for what seemed like several seconds. Bill Green was right in front of me and the mortar went off between the two of us. Everyone went down after the explosion.*

The Germans had been waiting for a patrol and had sprung an ambush on the men. As soon as the mortar dropped into the patrol lines, machine gun fire opened up and stitched back and forth along the patrol lines. Seven men were hit by the mortar blast. Sgt. Bill Green was knocked unconscious and had a leg severed below the knee.

Pfc. Tom Brayton, who had just returned to the unit from a prior wounding in action, was struck with shrapnel. Both Brayton and Company rigger, Pvt. Robert Bolchalk, were immobilized by their wounds. It took the entire patrol, several of whom were wounded, all their effort to drag and pull those more severely wounded from the line of fire. There was no one to drag Bill Green, and the decision was made to leave him and return for him with men who were not injured.

The group carried their wounded down to Pfaffenhoffen and the American lines. On their arrival Cpl. Bob Noody spoke with Capt. Winters about going back.

BOB NOODY ● *We asked permission to go back for Bill Green. Winters refused to let us go. We were so upset and near the point of tears, begging to go back for him. Winters said he was sorry, but to send us back would just get more of us killed or wounded. We knew Green had probably died from his wounds, but wanted to go get him anyhow. At the time we were angry*

STICK 81 *(L to R)* Len Hicks, Andrew Jellesed, James Swafford, Pat Casey, Don Emelander, Harvey Morehead, Carl MacDowell, Bill Green, Walter Pusker, Clyde Jeffers, Willard Sharp, Bill Olanie, Frank Griffin, and Robert Noody's hand and bazooka.

STICK 81 *(L to R)* Bill Olanie, Frank Griffin, Bob Noody, and Les Hegland.

STICK 81 *(L to R)* Emelander, Morehead, MacDowell, and Green.

Left: STICK 78 *(L to R)*
Bob Janes and George Martin.

Bottom left: STICK 76 *(L to R)*
Wilson, Right, Patruno, Yochum,
Roth, Peluso, Cortese, Replogle,
AAFx2, Crawford, Rasmussen, True,
Flick, Jackson, Stone, Houck, Mulvey.

Right: STICK 76 *(L to R)* Alvin
Wilson, Robert Stone, Julius Houck.

Bottom right: STICK 77 *(L to R)*
Grodowski, Robbins, Hogenmiller,
Watkins, Trimble, Cauvin, Borden,
AAF, Taylor, Moore, Gillespie, Tom,
Ochoa, Passino.

Left: STICK 77 *(L to R)* Gillespie, Tom, Ochoa, Passino, Waters, Haney, AAFx4, Grodowski, Robbins, Hogenmiller, Watkins.

Bottom left: STICK 78 *Left front:* Orel Lev; *right front:* Ken Hull

Below: STICK 78: Orel Lev and Dick Knudsen.

STICK 78: Dick Knudsen.

Left to right: Peterson, McNeese, Knudsen, Sharp, and Borden, England 1944.

Carl Pein and an anonymous British kid, Aldbourne, England.

Carl Pein on patrol in Holland, September 19, 1944

Merlin Shennum and Rody Byrnes on patrol, September 19, 1944

Roy Zerbe on patrol, September 1944

Byrnes, Pein, and Shennum on patrol, September 19th 1944

Prior to Operation Market Garden, a jumpmaster checks his men as they
climb aboard a waiting C-47.

Bill True and Johnny Jackson—London, July 1944

Injured paratroopers receive emergency treatment in an improvised aid station in Bastogne.

Bill True and Robert Stone—March 1945

Senior NCO's
Borden, Porter,
Morris, and
Replogle

John Taylor, 1945

Roy Zerbe, hospitalized following his injuries in Holland.

Zerbe's skin graft.

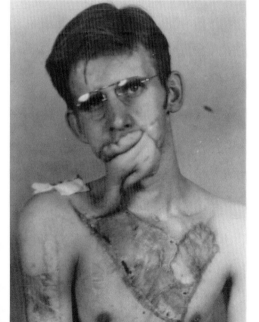

Roy Zerbe, recovered.

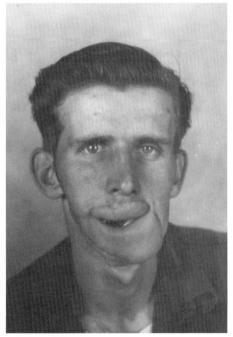

The 22-Man Patrol survivors, November 3rd, 1944.

Fox Company funeral service for 1st Lt. Andy Tuck.

we could not go back for him. But looking back on it later I am sure he [Winters] saved more lives by refusing to let us go.

Sgt. William Green's body was not recovered by the Americans after he was killed in action. His body was removed from the battlefield by local citizens and buried nearby. His remains were recovered after the war, identified by his jump boots, dental charts, and class ring. He is now forever at rest, at the Lorraine American Cemetery in St. Avold, France.

On arrival back to the Fox company position in Grassendorf, the men were advised to prepare to move out again. This time they would be traveling down the Moder River to the southeast, to the town of Haguenau. They boarded trucks the following afternoon, arriving in Haguenau several hours later. That evening they relieved the 313th Infantry Regiment of the 79th Infantry Division from their positions along the river.

As the men of Company F moved into their positions in town, Len Hicks managed to obtain a huge supply of mortar rounds from a sergeant in the 313th. The sergeant told Hicks there was no enemy action at location and he could have all the ammunition he wanted. Since Hicks knew they would use all they could get their hands on, he quickly took up the sergeants offer and stockpiled as much ammunition as possible.

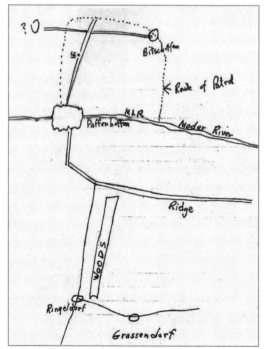

Drawing from Lieutenant Stapelfeld's diary, dated 4 February 1945.

The men of Company F settled into the homes along the Moder River where it twisted through the center of town. Many pockmarked buildings were missing their rooftops, and the streets matched the sky in a dull gray. Houses had collapsed from blasts of artillery and fire, and debris filled streets where walls once stood. But they were protected from the weather, and the conditions in Haguenau seemed like luxury living compared to the frozen foxholes where they had spent their last Christmas and month prior.

The Moder River in Haguenau for most of the year was nothing more than a glorified canal, with steep, vegetation-choked banks that was home to local waterfowl. However, in the winter the banks became swollen with floodwaters, and what was before a lazy river of less than twenty feet across was now transformed into a churning waterway of over a hundred feet wide.

An observation post was located in an abandoned ink pen factory along the river. For the next few days the men in the OP watched for movement from across the Moder on the German held side of the river. On the night of the 10th, First Platoon's Pfc. E. B Wallace called back on a field phone to report lights in a farmhouse across the river. An artillery fire mission was called in, and just before midnight 48 rounds of artillery fire rained into the farmhouse. The lights went out in the farmhouse, and the structure burned long into the next day.

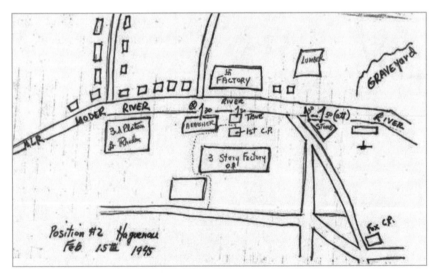

Lieutenant Stapelfeld sketched the company's Haguenau positions in his diary on 15 February.

Cpl. Bob Noody took his turn in the OP a few nights later. While scrounging around in the top floor office of the building, Noody came across brass horn. Being a bugler himself, Noody decided to give the horn a try and belted out a few notes. The Germans on the north side of the Moder River were not amused by the music, and responded with several artillery rounds of their own on the OP building. No one was injured. Noody stopped his band practice.

It was dangerous in Haguenau both in the buildings and out on the street. One afternoon Supply Sgt. Len Hicks and SSgt. Hugh Borden were having a conversation while standing behind a building, out of the German line of sight. A soft rifle shot snapped off and a bullet crackled past their heads. After a quick check of the surroundings, the two men figured where the shot had come from. They ran over to a home nearby.

The residence was rather ornate in comparison to other row houses along the block. This home had a large iron gated archway, and a driveway leading to the front of the home. Borden and Hicks squeezed over the gate and entered the home. In an upstairs bedroom looking down on their previous position, a bolt action, single shot .22-caliber rifle was located, along with a good supply of ammunition. The two men could not locate the sniper in the home, so the rifle was taken, along with the ammunition and a table top radio. The items were loaded into a Citroën car found in the home's garage. Hicks kept the car for shuttling supplies and the .22 rifle as a souvenir.

On February 15th the men moved to a new location in town. Floodwaters separated houses and factories that butted up to the river. Only a hundred yards of swift, murky water separated the two fighting forces. It did not take long for the Germans to welcome the men of Fox Company to their new home.

Along with the new move came a change in command. 1st Sgt. Charlie Malley was fed up, as most of the men were, with the lack of leadership under their commanding officer, Captain James Nye. Malley complained about Nye in a letter, written outside the chain of command and directly to their regimental commander Colonel Robert Sink. Sink took the complaint seriously and called in all the Company officers and senior NCOs from Fox to the Regimental Headquarters.

Colonel Sink questioned each man about Captain Nye, and asked that they speak freely and honestly about his leadership. One by one the men explained how they did not like Nye's form of leadership, or lack thereof. John Taylor and Tom Alley were the last two sergeants to speak with Colonel Sink. On their arrival back to the Fox Company position, Nye, with his bedroll under his arm, was being driven by jeep from their Command Post. 1st Lt. Ed Thomas returned to help out as the executive officer, and 1st Lt. Andy Tuck took over as commanding officer of Fox Company.

On February 16th, T-4 Harry 'Dutch' Ostrander and T-5 Ed Bishop pulled up outside the Company CP in Len Hicks misappropriated Citroën 'supply' car. An artillery shell dropped into a building in front of the car, the blast peppering the vehicle with shrapnel. Both men were wounded and slid out of the vehicle and onto the roadway. The car caught fire from the impact of the shrapnel and began to billow smoke and flames.

As men rushed to get the two wounded men from out of the street, Hicks radioed for a tank to come to their aid. One was quickly dispatched to the scene and was directed to push the now fully engulfed vehicle down the street and away from the Command Post. They did not want the smoke to draw any more artillery fire into the area. The tank crew understood the request and quickly pushed the flaming car away, and when the fire died out, so did Hicks dream of having a Citroën 'supply' car.

An artillery piece was brought up just behind the front lines. The gun crew inquired within the Fox Company CP to see if anyone could help them find a home for their pack howitzer. The men had found a residence nearby with an arched gateway facing the river. The men wanted to have the large wooden gate removed from the property to allow them to wheel out the gun, fire it over the homes and river into the German lines, and then wheel it back inside the safety of the residence.

BOB NOODY ● *I went over with a box of explosives and the guys showed me the gate they wanted knocked down. I really did not know how much explosive to pack on the gate, so I placed it around the entire edge of the arch. When I set it off, it blew the gate off its mounts. The gate flipped through the air across the street and landed on the cannon setting there. Those guys were pretty angry, but jeez, I got the gate off for them!*

The first few nights at the new location were interrupted by a German machine gunner from the north bank. During the evening around midnight he would spray the houses that were occupied by Fox Company with a string of rapid fire. The men called him "Bed Check Charlie" and decided they had to put a stop to his nightly actions.

John Taylor was selected to lead a patrol across the river to capture or kill 'Bed Check Charlie'. The patrol planned to cross the river, travel through a graveyard, and check around the nearby housing. They were given some rubber boats to cross the swollen river. The men practiced in the boats in a pond behind the lines and came to the quick realization that due to their lack of boat experience, crossing would be harder than expected. 1st Sgt. Charlie Malley decided he would help the men out.

SSgt. John Taylor, Cpl. Bob Noody, Pfc. Calvin Wright, Pvt. Lewis Segal, and SSgt. Jack Borden assembled for the patrol. Three others would meet them at the rivers edge with two rubber boats. Noody borrowed an M-3 'Grease Gun' for the patrol. Noody hoped the submachine gun would be helpful in the suspected close quarter actions they expected to encounter. Segal and Wright would be manning a Browning Automatic Rifle.

Charlie Malley met the men near the river's edge and stripped down to his wool long underwear. It was an inky black night and the rain was relentless. Malley tied a rope off on a tree and disappeared into the water, swimming under the surface to the other side. Malley then planted himself in the mud on the north bank and pulled the rope taut. The patrol then entered the water and used the rope to pull them across the icy water. Once on the other side, Malley tied off the rope on the north bank, and slipped back into the rain dotted water for a return swim to the American side of the Moder.

JOHN TAYLOR • *It was raining. I sent Segal and Wright a little to the left of the graveyard and told them to just stay there. They had a Browning Automatic Rifle (BAR) in case we got in a fight. That would protect us on that flank if we got into trouble. Meantime, we had a couple of machine guns back on our side of the river that were set to open up on this particular German machine gun nest in case they found us.*

Well, you can plan and you can scheme, and think you got everything covered, and we thought we had. But we were wrong. We climbed over a wall and eased down into the graveyard and started crawling up through the tombstones. Immediately when we got into the graveyard, I knew we had not considered one thing. The walkways in the graveyard were gravel and we were making noise, much more than we wanted to make.

So we kept easing, easing, easing along in total darkness and Borden or somebody pulled my leg and whispered 'your watch, your watch!' I looked down and my watch was an illuminated dial shining like a star. I jerked it off and put it in my pocket. We moved down to a wall and we would stop and listen, stop and listen. We could hear the Germans apparently just moving in their positions for the night down to our left.

We crept around a wall which enclosed a house and listened. We heard quite a bit of movement and decided that we definitely should avoid getting into a firefight over there. We stayed and looked around for some time and figured we had done our job.

The men fell back to the riverbank and retrieved the BAR men along the way. Four men crossed using the rope to the south bank. Then Taylor and three others untied their stake and used the rope to send them downstream and over to the south bank as well. No flares were shot off in the crossing, no enemy fire, and no casualties were taken. The patrol was considered a success as they all made it back in one piece.

BOB NOODY • *I had borrowed a grease gun for the patrol. At one point when we were across the river, Taylor had me covering a door to a building in case anyone was flushed outside. No one ever came out and I did not have to fire. It was a good thing too. Once I got back to our side I decided to test fire the grease gun. It would not work. I was so angry. My life had depended on a weapon that could not even fire. I never again carried one of those grease guns, and I never borrowed another weapon.*

Thirty-one replacements arrived at the Company Command post in mid-February. Most notably was a Colorado native and machine gunner who was quickly dispatched to the First Platoon. Private William 'Bill' Hisamoto, an American of Japanese descent, volunteered for the paratroops to not only serve his country, but to be in the best unit possible. Being from a mountain state, he had been free from the internment tragedy that fell on the Japanese Americans on the west coast of the United States. Quiet, but confident and very skilled, Hisamoto quickly blended into the First Platoon.

Over in the Second Platoon a new replacement received a painful learning experience from a seasoned combat veteran who had just returned to the unit from the hospital.

BOB JANES • *I was down on the river one night with a field phone. I was hidden near the supports of a bridge that had been destroyed between our position and the cemetery across the river. I called back into the phone to give a status report and got no response. I tried again and got nothing. I figured a German patrol may have cut the lines between me and the platoon, so I made a wide circle back to our Command Post. I wanted to avoid any ambush the Germans may have set up at the break in the wire.*

When I got back to the other end of the line there was this kid there, a replacement. He had his feet propped up on the desk next to the phone, and was asleep in a chair. The line had not been cut at all. This guy had just been dozing the whole time, and with me out on the other end of the wire. So, I kicked the chair out from under him and knocked the hell out of the guy. I told him if he ever fell asleep at his post again I would kill him. I'm sure he never did it again.

By the end of February the men of Fox 506th, as well as the rest of the regiment, were finally pulled off the line in Haguenau. They traveled by both truck, then train, back to Mourmelon for a much-needed rest and restocking of supplies and replacements. Lt. Robertson allowed a few of the men to bring back with them a supply of goods that had been hoarded back in Haguenau—a shop full of carpentry tools, a large stock of jam and jelly, and a case of abandoned USGI mess kits. Instead of being housed in the old barracks and stalls they called home before Bastogne, the men now were dropped off several miles away at a tent city.

CHAPTER 23

TENT CITY

The olive drab housing that greeted the men on their arrival back to Mourmelon seemed like paradise compared to the chilly bombed out buildings of a rain soaked Haguenau. The tents had canvas cots to sleep on, stocked with wool blankets. A stove propped in the middle of the tent supplied much needed heat, and if properly stoked, could keep the interior and its occupants quite comfortable through the night.

The Company's electrical expert, T-4 Doug Roth, quickly got to work and in short order had wiring running a single light bulb and plug into each tent that housed the men of the Company. Men who had time in the Company were informed they would be given furloughs by raffle, with destinations such as Nice, on the French Riviera, London England, and Brussels, Belgium.

The men waited for the results of their furlough drawings by playing softball, having boxing matches, and drilling with the replacements. One afternoon a stove went out in a tent used by the Second Platoon. Some wood was gathered and a gas can was obtained to soak the wood, expediting the fire and heating process. Unknown to the men at the time was that the gas can leaked. Fuel accidentally trickled down the company street and into the tent, then onto the stove.

When the fuel soaked wood in the stove was lit with a match, it flashed over and a line of fire raced out of the tent and down the street. The tent was instantly engulfed in flames and men scrambled out under the sides to avoid the smoke and fire. Only those near the tent door had time to grab their belongings and flee. The rest lost their spare uniforms and clothing to the fire, which destroyed the entire tent.

When the furloughs were handed out, several men in the Second Platoon were without their Class 'A' dress uniforms, lost in the fire. Sgt. Bob Janes loaned SSgt. Marion Grodowski his uniform, essentially giving him a demotion by letting him wear his uniform with one less chevron on his tunic. Grodowski did not mind a bit, and headed off for a drunken stay at the French Riviera.

Janes decided to wear his wools with a combat jacket during his furlough into Brussels, Belgium. He also carried a holstered .45 automatic on his belt when he was dropped off at the Hotel des Colonies on Rue de Croisades, along with several other sergeants from the 506th.

BOB JANES • *We walked around a bit and could not find a single bar to get into. All these troopers were packed inside and out the doors of these bars. And most of them were not even combat troops. Well after a while I got tired of all that. I stood just outside the door of one bar and I pulled out my forty-five. I started shooting it off into the air, right over the door. Guys spilled out of the bar. They could not get out of there fast enough.*

Once the bar cleared out, us paratroopers walked inside. We acted surprised as if we did not know what was going on and asked the bartender what had happened. He explained someone had been shooting outside. We acted shocked, but then walked up to the bar, sat down, and ordered some drinks.

John Taylor, Charlie Malley, Vic Tamkun, and Dog Company's Jack Sandridge headed off to London. They passed through the French port of Le Havre and took a ferry to Southampton, England. French Francs were quickly cashed in for English Pounds.

JOHN TAYLOR • *They stamped our furlough passes and we took the train to London where we rented an apartment and drank forty-two bottles of God awful Red Label scotch for seven days. We spent all our money. We came back to Southampton and got on a boat. We chatted up the captain who was in charge of returning us to camp, and conned him into going back by way of Paris. Our only problem was that we were totally broke.*

Fortunately, Charlie Malley came up with an inspiring scheme to get us some cash for Paris. We scouted around and discovered where they kept the coffee on the ship. When we went down to chow that afternoon, I carried a blanket. As we passed this cage where they had the coffee, Malley stepped in

*that door real quick and pulled out a couple of packages. I wrapped them in
a blanket.*

On arrival back to Le Havre the men quickly divided up their coffee,
about five pounds, into one-pound sacks. As they entered Paris they quickly
sold off the coffee into the hands of locals. The sale resulted in five thousand
francs ($100) and four bottles of cognac. The last night of the furlough was
spent in Paris, in style.

The men on furlough arrived back to the tent city at Mourmelon and
joined back into the ranks of the Company. In the tents and latrines stories
were swapped between those who went on pass to nearby Rheims, and those
who obtained lottery furloughs out of the area. It was decided that regardless
of where they went, it was much needed and deserved.

Physical training began to increase with the men, as well as drill, bayonet drill, and time on the rifle range. Night marches and field problems
filled their agenda as well, as the veterans rushed to teach the replacements
the skills they would need to survive in combat. One field problem involved
the Company taking the nearby town of Louvercy in a mock assault. They
spent almost a week at the location practicing their skill at clearing the town,
seizing the town's bridges, and defending its choke points. For the combat
veterans it was all too easy, but was important for the development of the
replacements.

Promotions were given on March 14th, and many of the veterans of
the unit moved up in rank. Sgt. Alan Summers, Sgt. Tom Alley, Sgt. Charlie
Jacobs, Cpl. Bob Noody, Cpl. Marion Grodowski, Cpl. Merlin Shennum,
T-4 Doug Roth, Sgt. Ray Aebischer, and Sgt. Bob Vogel all were promoted
to staff sergeant. Cpl. Norman Trimble, Cpl. Rody Byrne, T-5 Joe Hogenmiller, Cpl. Warren Bell, Pfc. Bill True, and Pfc. Troy Gilley all made promotions to 'buck' sergeant.

On March 15th the men of the Company assembled and paraded for
General Eisenhower at Mourmelon. Gen. Eisenhower awarded the entire
division the Presidential Unit Citation for their actions in holding Bastogne.
It was a second Presidential Unit Citation for Fox 506th. General Eisenhower's speech to the 101st:

It is a great personal honor for me to be here today to take part in
a ceremony that is unique in American history. Never before has a

full Division been cited by the War Department in the name of the President, for gallantry in action. This day marks the beginning of a new tradition in the American Army. With that tradition, therefore, will always be associated the name of the 101st Airborne Division and of Bastogne.

Yet you men, because you are soldiers of proved valor and of experience, would be the last to claim that you are the bravest and the best. All the way from where the Marines are fighting on Iwo Jima, through the Philippines and Southeast Asia, on through the Mediterranean and along this great front, and on the Russian frontiers, are going forward day by day those battles sustained by the valor of you and the other Allied units that are beating this enemy to his knees. They are proving once and for all that dictatorship cannot produce better soldiers than can aroused democracy. In many of those actions are units that have performed with unexcelled brilliance.

So far as I know, there may be many among you that would not rate Bastogne as your bitterest battle. Yet it is entirely fitting and appropriate that you should be cited for that particular battle. It happened to be one of those occasions when the position itself was of the utmost importance to the Allied forces.

You, in reserve, were hurried forward and told to hold that position. All the elements of drama, of battle drama, were there. You were cut off, you were surrounded. Only valor, complete self confidence in yourselves and in your leaders, a knowledge that you were well trained, only the determination to win sustain soldiers under those conditions. You were given a marvelous opportunity, and you met every test.

Therefore, you become a fitting symbol on which the United Nations, all the citizens of the United Nations, can say to their soldiers today, "We are proud of you," as it is my great privilege to say to you here today, to the 101th Division and all its attached units, "I am awfully proud of you."

With this great honor goes also a certain responsibility. Just as you are the beginning of a new tradition, you must realize, each of you, that from now on, the spotlight will beat on you with particular brilliance. Whenever you say you are a soldier of the 101th Division, everybody, whether it's on the street or in the front line, will expect unusual conduct of you. I know that you will meet every test of the future like you met in Bastogne.

Good luck and God be with each of you.

With the parade and awards ceremony with General Eisenhower over, the men returned to their tent city. Sgt. Bob Janes ended up in a fight almost immediately on their return.

MARION GRODOWSKI • *We had some new guy we called Eight Ball, because he was a screw up. He decided to challenge Janes to a fight. Immediately after it started Janes was on him. But the guy started to bite Janes. I was going to break it up, but Janes ended up winning. I told Bob to pull his eye out. He did and the fight was over. Eight ball ended up ok.*

BOB JANES • *Some new guy challenged me to a fight out in the Company street and I agreed. He said he would be back and left for about five minutes. When he returned, he had his shirt off and was covered with grease. I thought we were going to have a fair fight. Well the fight started and I got a good hold of him. He bit down on my fingers, on my wedding band finger, almost to the bone. I yelled that the guy was biting me and Grodowski told me to pull out his eye. So, I reached in his eye socket and popped out his eyeball. He stopped fighting, screamed and ran down the Street holding his eye. The medics put his eye back in, and my wedding band had to be cut off. I guess it all worked out.*

The men were alerted to move out at the end of March, and spent the last few days in Mourmelon drawing equipment, cleaning weapons, and stocking up on supplies. Early April they once again loaded up on flatbed paneled tractor-trailers and headed off to war.

CHAPTER 24

THE RHINE

The men were trucked up to the south side of the Rhine River, just south of the city of Dusseldorf Germany. They immediately set up the Company from the town of Sturzelberg, through the fortress town of Zons facing a bow in the river, and down to Dormagen. The Fox Company Command Post was set up in Sturzelberg. The Germans were right across the river around the town of Benrath.

The Company dug in as usual out on the line and placed two observation posts down by the river. Just as in Haguenau, boats were obtained for small patrols across the river. Aggressive patrolling was conducted along the American side of the river as well. But not all contact along the river was with the German Army.

Pfc. Ted Ulrich and Sgt. Merlin Shennum took one such patrol along the Rhine. Shennum had acquired the nickname of 'Goat'. The most famous railroad at the time in Montana was the Great Northern Railroad Company, and their company logo was a silhouette of a mountain goat. Since Shennum was a Montana native, and members of the Third Platoon were familiar with the railroad, Shennum was nicknamed 'Goat'.

TED ULRICH • *One spring day Goat and I were on patrol on the west side of the Rhine, the far side being loosely held by the Germans. We approached a deserted farmhouse on a dike by the river. Deserted that is, except for a giant white gander. The gander took issue with Goat's approach. Goat took issue with the gander's loud noise and menacing actions. The two crashed in arm-to-arm, or arm-to-wing combat, dust arising along with feathers. A helmet rolled out of the dust cloud. The gander's head started*

253

unwinding clockwise owing to the several twists its neck had been given. The body slowly headed in the opposite direction on large, flat webbed feet.

Patrols were frequent as the Company lines were thin, spread out over an area almost four miles long. The only way to ensure security to the positions was to send men out, just as when they were on the dike in Holland, to keep the Germans from moving into the Company lines. There was one benefit to the dangerous patrolling—eggs. Along the bank of the Rhine there were small cottages, farmhouses, and a boathouse. The residents of these structures had long since evacuated, leaving behind a small stock of wandering chickens. The population of the abandoned fowl had boomed and the chickens seemed to be everywhere. Along with the chickens came nests of daily fresh eggs.

Each morning patrols were sent out along the Rhine with two objectives. Keep the Germans on the other side of the Rhine, and recover as many eggs as possible. In one abandoned farmhouse a stock of hanging sausages and hams was located. The daily supplement of smoked pork and fresh eggs became a welcome change to the usual canned ration diet for the men of the Company.

A new item was issued to the Company on a temporary basis while on the Rhine, a sniper rifle. The Second Battalion Headquarters issued out a new scoped Springfield bolt-action sniper rifle to the Company. It was to be on loan for short periods of time, and rotated back to the Battalion HQ for reissue to the other sister Companies. Although it had to be sighted in by the user, it was an interesting addition to the Company arsenal.

On April 12th Lieutenants Perdue and Stapelfeld conducted a morning patrol from their First Platoon CP out to the edge of the Rhine River. As they moved up to the boathouse in front of the platoon's position, Lt. Perdue walked into a trip wire. An instant later the German trap sprung and an explosion peppered Lt. Perdue's backside and right hand with shrapnel. The two men walked back to their CP and a jeep ran the bloodied Lieutenant Perdue off for treatment at a field hospital. His injuries were such that he would not return to the unit: his war was over.

During the early morning hours of the 13th, as darkness soaked into their positions, a small boat was observed drifting down the river past the location of the dug in First Platoon, just west of Zons. With no information of any friendly units in the area, they opened fire on the boat and its occupants. Machine gun and rifle fire skipped across the water and stitched up the small craft, which quickly sank. The boat debris and bodies drifted west down the Rhine and out of view of the First Platoon. A suspected German patrol destroyed.

A short time later word traveled into the Fox Company position that Major William Leach, the Regimental S-2, and several enlisted men had taken a boat into the river in an attempt to cross over and patrol the far embankment. No one had been told of the patrol. Major Leach, as well as Pfc. Frank Pellechia, Pfc. Robert Watts, Pfc. Michael Koval were killed. Several days later their bullet-riddled bodies were pulled from the banks of the river on the Company's left flank at Sturzelberg.

Word soon traveled along the Company lines that President Franklin Roosevelt had died. The entire Company was shocked and felt a tremendous loss. President Roosevelt had been the only leader of the United States that most had even known. The men had listened to Roosevelt with admiration through the tough times of the depression, and were motivated by his speeches of encouragement as they went to war. Many wondered if there could be anyone to really replace him.

Over the next few days the Germans shelled Fox Company's First Platoon in Zons. Over a dozen artillery shells landed or exploded in bursts over the American positions each day. There were no American casualties. The bulk of the injuries sustained were to the local population, with one elderly lady, one baby, and one young girl killed. Several other civilians were wounded as well. The men of Fox Company did not fire back.

MERLIN SHENNUM • *We could look across the river using field glasses, and see the trenches along the bank were filled with young boys, about grade school age. They were wearing these oversized German uniforms and helmets, and playing games in the trenches. The Germans put these little kids on the line to make us think their trenches were all occupied. Although we were getting fired on from behind their position, we did not shoot back. All we would have accomplished would have been to kill a bunch of small boys. And we were not about to do that.*

The weekend of the 14th, morale was boosted with the issuing of a pair of new wool socks to each man in the Company. Additionally, they were each given three bottles of Coca-Cola and two bottles of beer. It was a late but much appreciated Easter gift. After another week of patrolling along the river, the men prepared to pull off the line on the 22nd of April, 1945.

With mail delivery into the Company, SSgt John Taylor found out that a letter had been published that he had written to the editor of his hometown paper in Lufkin, Texas. The newspaper column was titled "I Could Be Wrong" and was printed back in February:

Today's column has a guest editor, Staff Sergeant John H. Taylor, who writes a most interesting letter from somewhere on the 'Western Front':

Dear Sir:
Today (Feb 1) I had the good fortune of receiving several copies of the Daily News. Receiving the hometown paper is always a morale booster to me, and something I always look forward to. While reading the Oct. 15 copy, I could not help but notice the column "Letter to the Editor." The letter from Sid Robinson, Jr., was very good, and expresses my opinion of German prisoners.

I would just like to add or say a few things regarding this matter that the general public does not know or just hasn't thought about. We all know that the German prisoners in the States are treated swell— much better than our own soldiers on the battlefronts.

It is true that when many German soldiers are captured they are ready to put forth their hand and say, "I am sorry." Not sorry that they started the war, but sorry that they are losing it. The people of the Allied Nations cannot take that hand and clasp it and say "all is forgiven." Some people will say why not? I think I can tell them why.

That is the hand that leaps skyward, like a bunch of trained puppets, every time someone yells "Hitler"! That is the same hand that murdered the people, burned and looted the villages and towns of Russia, Poland, Greece, Belgium, Holland, and France. That's the hand that has taken the lives, legs, arms, and eyes of thousands of American soldiers. That is the hand of a Nazi.

I have met the German soldier in the hedgerows of Normandy, on the flat lowlands and dykes of Holland, and in the frozen woods at Bastogne in Belgium. He is the same everywhere, a shrewd and cunning killer. He will stay out there with his 'burp' gun, or at the breech of an 88 and give you hell. An hour later when he has no other choice he will come out with his hands on his head. That soldier hasn't changed from a Nazi to a peace loving PW in an hour. He is still a Nazi and always will be.

I don't mean to take everything from the German people when the great day arrives. Give them their property rights, civil rights, and freedom of religion, but by all means keep a firm hold on that hand. Keep it down, down so it will never rise to harass the peaceful nations of the world again.

I think it is the duty of all newspapers whether daily, weekly, or semi-monthly, to convince the American public that we cannot extend our hand and say "All is forgiven."

I'll close by saying I hope I receive another "Daily News" in tomorrow's mail.

Respectfully yours, S-Sgt. John H. Taylor

The Company moved out from their positions on the Rhine and loaded onto a train around noon on Sunday the 22nd of April. Each man was given an armload of K rations, and then along with their gear, climbed into small railroad cars. Nothing more than a drafty box on wheels, they were vintage 40 and 8's, supposedly able to accommodate forty men or eight horses. They were cramped, cold, and uncomfortable, but at least the men were out of their foxholes along the river.

The train slowly lumbered away from the Rhine and by late evening had rolled southwest into Maastricht, Holland. As the train continued on to the south, the men took turns sitting on the roofs and hanging in the open doors, admiring the scenery into Luxembourg, then passing east into Germany through Ludwigshafen, Mannheim, and finally halting two days later in the small town of Widdern.

Moving from train to truck the men continued southeast around Stuttgart down toward Munich, stopping in the small town of Buchloe, west of Landsberg. Dismounted and waiting on gasoline, the men were assigned different tasks. The First Platoon cleared the town of all weapons and ammunition, finding a husband and wife hanging inside a home at #2 Adolf Hitler Plaza, an apparent suicide.

Second Platoon swept through the woods to the south of town, expecting to round up members of the German Waffen SS. Ordinary German Army soldiers that were located or surrendered were disarmed and sent to

Division POW enclosures. German soldiers began to surrender en masse to the 506th. The war in Europe was winding down.

During this time some members of Fox Company headed east toward Landsberg and made a grim discovery. They came upon one of the satellite work camps from the Dachau concentration camp system, liberated the day before by members of the 12th Armored Division. Kaufering IV was one of eleven camps in the area. It was located between the towns of Kaufering and Hurlach, and was a pooling place for the diseased and those dying of starvation. The camp's prisoner barracks had been hastily burned as German guards retreated from the area, and those who tried to flee were shot. Piles of emaciated and disease-ridden bodies covered the grounds. Those on scene from Fox Company tried to help the camp survivors.

E. B. WALLACE • *1st Squad from First Platoon went to the camp. We had orders not to let any prisoners outside the camp wire. I went around the camp and it was the most awful sight. There were dead bodies everywhere. There was a long shed there with white stuff in it. I think it was lime the Germans used to pile onto all the dead bodies. In a boxcar out on the railroad tracks I found a rail car filled with wheels of cheese. I decided to take some of the cheese to the prisoners. A doctor stopped me, a Major, and he told me not to do it. He told me food was coming, and to give them the cheese would kill them.*

Lieutenant Tuck was there with us. A German officer was located hiding in a hole near the camp. We brought him back to the lieutenant. He made the mistake, for some reason, of slapping Jesse Orosco. The German Officer ended up getting a real beating from Orosco for that, he ended up really quite battered.

Moving out away from the camps and Buckloe, the men boarded DUKW's and went out onto the highway. DUKW's, also known as "ducks," were large boats built on truck frames, able to not only drive in the water, but on roadways and light terrain as well. A squad was piled into each amphibious DUKW truck, and Lt. Tuck along with the men of Fox Company convoyed toward the Alps.

CHAPTER 25

THE ALPS

E arly May 1945 saw the men and their "ducks" convoy slowly rolling into the snowcapped Alps. The destination of the 506th was
Hitler's mountain retreat in the Bavarian town of Berchtesgaden, Germany.
Along the way they took refuge for the evening in roadside homes, kicking
out the local occupants for a night of comfort and relative warmth. During
the day the men threw candy to the occasional groups of children that lined
the road along the convoy route.

The company passed columns of surrendering Germans soldiers and
abandoned German vehicles. During one stop for refueling, the company
stumbled on a squadron of gray and green camouflaged German fighter
planes tucked off the roadway in a nearby lush tree line.

TOM ALLEY ● *We found quite a few planes in the forest along the highway. They could not be seen from the air, but could be moved quickly out to
the highway which could substitute as a runway. There was no one around so
we decided to start dropping grenades into the cockpits of the aircraft. I know
I dropped grenades into six different planes, destroying each one. I think that
made me the first and only Ace in the 101st Airborne.*

On May 5th the company moved without resistance into Berchtesgaden
just after noontime. Their transportation parked on the side of the street
near the Hotel Berchtesgaden and the men dismounted. They were immediately assigned security details to the Hotel, Hermann Goring's residence,
a nearby railroad tunnel, rail cars, and an ammunition dump. The troopers
witnessed revenge being dealt out by other Allied troops, already in the town.

TOM ALLEY ● *As we came into Berchtesgaden some of the French military were stopped on the road behind us. They were lining up German soldiers along a wall on our right, near some cliffs. The French opened up and killed dozens of soldiers that were standing there with their hands up.*

The men tried their best at souvenir hunting while posted at their assigned details. German military items and booze topped the list of the prized possessions. Bob Janes and Len Hicks discovered a closet full of cameras inside Hermann Goring's residence. Inside they found a case of tiny Minox spy cameras, each not much larger than a pack of chewing gum. They were quickly pocketed and distributed out to the men of the Second Platoon. Jackets, children's clothing, flags, and uniforms were snatched up and stuffed into packs. Most of the larger cameras had to be left behind, as only men like Hicks in supply, and company officers, had the ability to get larger items shipped home.

Marion Grodowski waited on guard outside Goring's home and made small talk with German Army Major General Kastner, who was currently a guest, occupying a room in his home.

MARION GRODOWSKI ● *I was talking to this general who was staying in Goring's place when we came into Berchtesgaden. He and I talked a bit. It was about the day, the weather, nothing too interesting. He spoke very good English. After our conversation ended he went back inside to his room. A short time later we heard a gunshot. We went inside and found this general had shot himself in the head, committed suicide.*

Well I took the general's pistol. I figured he would no longer need it. So I pocketed it. And no one initially came to get him. So, each morning as we passed his room we would greet the body. We would say 'Morning Fritz' as we headed off for chow, or assigned duties. It took several days before someone finally came and removed the body.

Just three days after their arrival into Berchtesgaden, the war in Europe ended. Victory in Europe Day, or V-E Day was May 8th, and was celebrated by the men of Fox Company at their hotel. Most of the men had obtained at least a case of assorted alcoholic beverages from Hermann Goring's wine cellar. It had contained approximately ten thousand bottles of the world finest alcohol, until the 506th arrived.

WILLIAM MURPHY • *Bill True and I had a room in the Hotel Bercht-esgaden on V-E Day. We celebrated the surrender of Germany with several cases of alcohol. We would take the cork or top off of a bottle, take the biggest gulp we could, and then toss the bottle out the window. Well, we were on the second floor and the bottles were smashing into the pavement below. After a while the locals began to assemble below our window, and tried to catch the bottles that we threw out. We kept it up until we could not drink anymore.*

JOHN TAYLOR • *Although there was no formal celebration, we did mark the occasion by downing quite a few bottles of champagne that we had gotten out of the Luftwaffe barracks there in town. Now that was prime stuff. It was hard to celebrate too much however, because the war with Japan was still going full force. As a paratrooper, I was certain I would be sent over there, and that thought hung over my head for a long time.*

Due to problems of debauchery, the men were quickly removed from their alcoholic beverages by the leadership of the battalion. All the alcohol was boxed up and put on guard in the carport of the hotel. Once the routine of the guards was established, men were still able to sneak by to steal a bottle, but the mass drunkenness had ended.

May 10th saw the company off by truck, jeep, and stolen cars to the state of Salzburg, Austria. They twisted through mountains to the small town of Kaprun, at the base of a glacier in the Zell am See district. The men were stunned by the beauty of their new home. Picturesque houses, like gingerbread homes in a storybook, were huddled at the bottom of a lush green valley. A bubbling stream was winding in through town from the snow-dusted mountains that surrounded them. It was simply amazing.

The men of the company were again assigned details—searching the mountains for hiding German SS soldiers, dealing with refugees, and transporting German Army prisoners of war. One German soldier had been with the unit for several weeks as an interpreter, and Tom Alley decided to get him to his home in Munich, avoiding the POW roundup.

TOM ALLEY • *We told Lt. Tuck that we wanted to take this German home and he agreed to let us go. Conrad Ours obtained a German kubelwagen [jeep], and the three of us took off for Munich. This German*

*had not seen or heard from his family in over a year. We got to the first
US Army checkpoint and the MP asked us for our papers. We did not have
any. The MP let us go on, but told us we would not get far without
paperwork for the trip.*

*We pulled up to the next house we found and went inside. We located a
typewriter and some paper and I made up fictitious paperwork for our trip,
complete with a signature for an airborne officer who never existed. We went
out and painted a star on the vehicle, complete with hood numbers that
matched our paperwork. The paintjob was sloppy but worked.*

Alley, Ours, and the German soldier continued on. Alley would pull
out the forged paperwork as they approached each MP checkpoint, and to
their amazement they were waved on through without further investigation.
The ruse worked every time.

The trio raced down the highway to Munich. Ours was driving and
was considered a lead foot as a jeep driver. As fast as the kubelwagen would
go was as fast as Conrad would drive it. His two passengers held on for dear
life, and tried to take in the scenery to avoid focusing on their dangerous
speed. As they pulled into the ruined buildings of Munich, a rear wheel flew
off their vehicle and continued on down the rubble filled streets without
them. The vehicle spun to a stop and the men got out, heading out on foot.

The German soldier was able to lead them through the damaged neighborhood to his home. No one was found inside, but the residence was not
vacant, so the men waited. Later that evening the German family returned
and there was a joyous homecoming. A small but hearty meal was made for
all three men, and they were up late celebrating. The following morning
Alley and Ours left the German family behind and hitched a ride in an
American supply truck back to Kaprun.

The men were constantly being assigned details on the platoon level,
and often would be gone on assignments for several days. One such detail
was dropped in the lap of the men in the Second Platoon.

JOHN TAYLOR • *A few days after we arrived in Kaprun, my platoon
was called out in the middle of the night to go by trucks about fifty miles
up in the mountains. The road stopped at the entrance to a railway tunnel
carved five miles straight through the solid rock of the mountains. On the
other side of the tunnel was Italy. Our initial orders were to try to stop the*

war refugees and the other displaced persons from coming into the country through this tunnel.

In the first place, once the refugees made it through the five miles of tunnel, it opened up in an isolated area fifty miles up in the mountains. There was no food, clothing, or medicines for these people. In the second place, even if they did make it out of the mountains on their own, Austria had no capacity to take care of these people since the Austrians themselves were also low on food and other rations. Finally, the military had no way to take care of the refugees at this time.

My orders as platoon sergeant of the Second Platoon were to go through the tunnel by train to the other side and contact the British Command in charge there about restricting the entrance to the tunnel from their side. We put a flat car up front of the train with a machine gun and a bazooka to protect us in case we ran into any trouble. Through interpreters we told the train conductor to take us to the other side of the tunnel, slowly.

The tunnel was well equipped with lights. We got out on the other side and saw hundreds of misplaced persons and a few English soldiers. We had carried a German Volkswagen on one of the flat cars on the train and drove that about ten miles down the road to the British Command Post. We explained the situation to them and then stayed in the mountains in this little Italian village for three or four days until we received orders to return to Kaprun.

When the men returned to Kaprun, and were not on work details, they were allowed to roam the hillsides hunting, write and receive mail, or travel up the nearby ski slopes for some brief, powdery recreation. Sgt. Bob Janes penned a letter home at this time:

Somewhere in Austria 1945

Dearest Mom & Dad

Sure haven't had much time to write this week. I inherited about six details right in a row and including a day and night that I was on a ski trip, that didn't leave much time to write letters. I was Sergeant of the guard for 24 hours and had come off that one evening at 5 o'clock, came back the next evening and went right on C.Q. [Charge of Quarters]. I was C.Q. all night and got relieved the next morning, had breakfast and then went home and hit the sack until yesterday evening in time for supper. I was really on the ball last night though, I pressed three pairs of pants, one shirt, and a blouse. Then I boxed up a few things for Nadene, [wife] had a shower and hit the sack again.

Well folks this is just about the diary of a victorious paratrooper. You can see I am not having it too rugged. Most of our training is over it seems for the present. All I have is Athletics and a few inspections. The weather is beautiful and the Country is about the most beautiful I have ever seen since leaving the wild and wooly West. In fact, as long as there is snow in these mountains to ski on, this soldier is almost happy in the service. I would much rather be right here when that war in the Pacific ends as to be down there in it. That doesn't worry me much though as I believe that all combat troops will be coming home before ever going to the Pacific. The only thought that keeps me going is that I will be coming home to all you folks again before too long.

Oh well all I can do is sweat it out and wait for the next move. In the mean time please don't worry about me and take care of yourselves for me because as far as fighting in this theater, I have had it. Well folks I have to quit now and get the guys on the ball for the inspection this morning. I will finish this letter after we are through . . .

Gosh I started this letter last Sat– and here it is Monday morning and I still haven't finished it. I went skiing Saturday evening and came back Sunday evening. Sure had a swell time too. There were just two of us and my good friend the Check. We rode up to the end of the cable lift and then went up to Salsburger to the first cabin and stayed there the first night. We had plenty of chow and maybe you don't think I didn't take on a load of it after the climb up from the ski lift. The next morning we climbed on to the Hotel about a mile up, about 1500 meters above. We stayed up there all day skiing and lying around in the sun. We waited until about five in the evening after the sun went down so the snow would be better for the ride back down. Boy what a ride too, about two miles of snow fields. They are too damn steep to come down straight so you had to twist and turn all the way down.

Gosh folks I wished you could see this Country down here. We are stationed here in a little town right in the middle of the Austrian Alps. The name of the place is Kaprun. I just came back from having a physical exam a few minutes ago. I seem to be okay but of course I tried to play up that piece of scrap iron that is in my knee, yet not to great success I don't believe. Never was good at such things.

Bob

In the middle of May the company took on almost two dozen new replacements in the enlisted ranks. T/Sgt, Hugh Borden was promoted to 2nd lieutenant, following in the earlier footsteps of Huber Porter and Don Replogle. As he went out of the company with his newly deserved rank, a new company commander arrived. Captain Philip Dean joined the unit on the 31st of May from a stateside assignment. Dean would be the last company commander of Fox 506th. He was initially reserved around the enlisted men, but he was quickly found to be a very capable leader, and warmed up to the men within a few weeks, and they to him.

MARION GRODOWSKI • *Captain Dean had the men assembled and looked us over. He introduced himself to us. We learned we had to follow the rules with him. But he was very fair. If you asked something of him, or to him, he would give it some thought. And then you would get an answer. He was very reasonable with us, and we gained a lot of respect for him.*

Not everyone was pleased with the new arrival. Lieutentant Tuck was assigned back to his duty as company executive officer, and although he had been with the unit since its founding, Captain Dean, fresh from the states, replaced him as company commander. Lt. Tuck wrote about the shift in a letter home:

Saalfelden, Austria / June 3, 1945

My Dear Father—

Tonight my letter to you must reflect my most heartfelt blow. A few days ago I was relieved as commander of Fox Company. I can't pretend that I am not deeply hurt, although I'm ashamed of this feeling. My record is spotless, my rating in leadership and military technique in field & garrison is from excellent to superior— so I say to myself, "why."

A Captain from Fort Benning, Ga, has taken over. He seems like a fine man and as his executive officer I will support him to the utmost, of course. But—I can't do my best. This is my fourth bad break. "Relieved without prejudice" due to existing overage in T-O. To "Soldier" is one thing—to bleed to death in your heart is another. I can't say it all—it's just something else that I want to talk to you about. A word to another man would show weakness. To leave my outfit will damn near kill me & to stay will too.

Are your mumps clearing up? You know, you must admit you're a big boy to be having that sort of thing. Not enough "Junket," I guess. Take good care of yourself. We have so much to make up for don't we.

Lovingly, Ed

A system was announced to the company in June concerning the rotation of men from the unit back to be discharged from the service in the United States. It was a points system established for time in service, rank, campaigns, awards, and decorations received. Each man had his own tally of points based on the criteria given, and a minimum of eighty-five points was needed for rotation home. Those without enough points would either be delayed on returning home, or shipped off to the Pacific to continue in the war. When the program started, only one man was found to have enough points, newly appointed 2nd Lieutenant Hugh Borden.

The men scrambled to tally up every ribbon, wound, and service time in an effort to bolster their point score. Eventually, combat jumps were added to the point system, and senior men in the company began to close in on their required eighty-five points. However, Army life in Austria continued. SSgt. Bob Janes related in a letter home:

Kaprun, Austria / June 14, 1945

Dearest Mother & Father,

Please excuse me for not writing more than I have been because there is nothing to write about, and I hope that you folks haven't been worrying about me, as now that the war is over I am in no danger. I haven't heard from you folks now for a couple weeks but I know everything is alright and you are waiting for me, just like I am waiting to come home. Sure I don't know anything about that either. All there is are a bunch of rumors flying around here and nothing for sure. I don't see how there could be much more for us to do around here.

We have only made one move since we hit this little town of Kaprun and that was to another place up the valley by the name of Saalfelden, about ten miles from here. We were there two days and they sent me out on a detail with a convoy of kraut prisoners. I was out for two days and when I came back the outfit had moved back here and another company had taken over our places in Saalfelden. Damn, we had a big beautiful set up in that place too. The whole squad had a big house to ourselves with a shower in almost every room, and also a private bar that I had rigged up in a spare room. I lost my good camera in the deal too. I had a room all to myself and when the outfit moved out one of the fellows packed my stuff and evidently he missed one of the drawers in the dresser because my camera came up missing, and several other things.

Well I went back there to get it and some big assed Officer had taken over my room. I asked him about it and he said he found everything but my camera and gave them to me, but wouldn't admit finding the camera. I know damn well he had the camera, but the son of a bitch laid there and lied to me. This American Army has some of the biggest pricks as Officers that the world knows.

There were four Sergeants and an Officer that were on this convoy detail. We were way up by Munich. I had a big kraut driving a motorcycle for me and we had about one hundred and fifty truck loads of krauts to herd along. Maybe you don't think that wasn't a job. They have some of the worst damn wrecks that they call trucks and they were always breaking down. Instead of our Officer letting the big shot of the krauts take us to where he had orders to travel, our Officer thought he would be a big hero and went where he wanted to go. Well we ended up about as far from the right place the first day as we were when we started, so we had to wait till morning and it took another day to get back to our destination. After two days of riding on the back of a motorcycle I was pooped out.

I did get to see some beautiful Country. After we left Austria and the Alps we dropped down into Germany. The land tapered down into low rolling hills and valleys dotted with small villages and lakes. Most of the terrain was covered with green fields and yellow wheat. This part of the Country was hardly touched by the war.

It has been raining here quite a bit lately. In fact it is raining here this morning so hard we haven't even fallen out for the usual run and exercises. I hope it rains all day. I will just lay around and sleep. I couldn't do too much on this chow we are getting. I have never seen such short rations since being in this outfit. Even PX rations are something extinct around here. We only have cigarettes half the time. That is the reason I haven't been going skiing lately because I can't get any chow to take with me, and when a guy climbs those damn mountains he has to eat.

I have been getting lots of mail from Nadene. She seems fairly happy with her job. She is a private secretary to some big shot there at the place she has been working at all this time. I guess she will be plenty happy though when I get home and she won't have to work anymore. Thinking of home and my wife is the hardest thing about lying around like this. A guy has too much time to think. Outside of that I am feeling fine and just waiting. I hope it isn't much longer either.

Well folks I hope this letter finds all of you feeling fine and having nice weather. Maybe it won't be too much longer now before we are all together again. Please take care of yourself and write. Tell everyone hello.

Your Son Bob

Lt. Hugh Borden was shipped off to the 501st at the end of the June, along with transferring Lieutenants Holland Oswald, and Edward Thomas. They would be the first in the process for being shipped home. Lt Thomas would be going home with a considerable amount of money as well. Both he and 1st Sgt. Charlie Malley had taken a two-and-a-half ton truck into Paris filled with alcohol from Hermann Goring's collection. They sold the booze, and then the truck. Business on the black market was good.

1st Lieutenant Andy Tuck again wrote home after receiving a motivational letter from his parents. His spirits had changed after his assignment back to executive officer:

Austria

My dearest Mom & Dad—

I can't say how wonderful it was to receive your letter "softening the blow." Many a man receives much greater ones [blows]— infinitely more men, without the aid of such consolation. I'm a soldier Dad— and soldier I will, come what may. No need, then—to worry about the support & loyalty I shall render. Duty is governed from above by command, from the troops by demand, and in ones heart by pride. Take first my belongings, then my sustenance, then life—then my command— but you can only covet my pride.

And Mother how can a man be bitter while in a shower of your love & understanding. If I appeared at all hard or forgetful of your gentle ways—it was never meant. And if I choose to further serve, it will be for your world of thoughtfulness, generosity & love of mankind. The world that was & will be 'cause God meant it to.

I'm not saying all I mean. But Mom & Dad need what isn't written. All my love to you both & to our wonderful girls.

Lovingly, Ed

While in Austria the men were tasked with obtaining all the firearms from the local town and area residents. The firearms had been turned in and dropped off at local hospitals. Lt. Tuck and E. B. Wallace took a jeep to recover the firearms.

E. B. WALLACE • *Tuck, a jeep driver, and I went to pick up these weapons. There were so many that we filled the back of the jeep, piled it really high. But there was no room for me on the return trip. So we found a German officer at the hospital who spoke crude English, and Tuck got him to find us a truck to borrow. It ran on a charcoal burner. We filled the back of the truck with firearms.*

On the way back down the mountain I found out that the truck had a problem. It had no brakes. I was flying down the mountain almost out of control. The roadway rolled out into a valley and I barely made the turn into the straight portion of the roadway. I flew right past the C.P. with Lieutenant Tuck outside, and began up another turn in the roadway. The truck could not make the turn and rolled into a ditch.

As I got out of the crashed truck Lt. Tuck was standing there slapping his leg laughing. I didn't think it was funny at all. I was so mad. I'm sure the krauts knew the truck had no brakes too.

July 4th was celebrated with the entire 506th on the lake in Zell am See. There was a victory parade, sports competitions, races on horseback, boat races, track and field events, music, local dance displays, a baseball game between the 101st Division Artillery and the 506th, movies, and a parachute jump demonstration right into the lake. Every man in attendance was required to bring only one item, his own spoon!

Lt. Robertson spent the day riding around on a champion horse from the 1936 Olympics. Others took rowboats out on the lake to take in the scenery and relax. The event was well received by the men of the company, and a change from the usual 'secret' drinking and boring civil affairs work.

On July 7th, 1st Lt. Andy Tuck, jeep driver Sgt. Conrad Ours, and replacement Elmer Novak headed out by jeep for a trip just over the border into Czechoslovakia. They were making a repeat trip to the home of a doctor who threw lavish parties, surrounded by a visually stunning group of female partygoers. A sergeant in the Company Headquarters had made the trip in the past with Lt. Tuck, but this time declined, and Private Novak took his place.

Clad in their dress uniforms, the men left towing a trailer behind their jeep, with the intent of picking up a supply of sporting equipment on their return to the unit. It would be a win-win for everyone. Late that evening news began to trickle in to the company, rumors of an accident, brakes failing, and men being injured or killed.

Just in view of the town of Bad Ischl, Austria, the jeep had rolled on the freeway and all three men had been ejected. Jeep driver Conrad Ours received minor scrapes and bruises, having been thrown to the roadside grass. Help was quickly summoned and the three men were taken to the nearby 16th Field Hospital for treatment. Lieutenant Tuck, who had been with the unit since its founding in Toccoa, was dead. He had been killed instantly when he was thrown into a roadside mile marker, and was DOA at the field hospital. Elmer Novak was treated for several hours for a skull fracture. Novak died of his injuries at 2150.

The company was in shock. Two jeeps left from Kaprun, one with Lt. Frary and Lt. Stapelfeld, the other with Pfc. Nick Cortese, and headed northeast to Bad Ischl. Once at the field hospital, the officers were given the task of identifying the two deceased men. Nick Cortese then had the unpleasant task of driving his friends' bodies to the cemetery.

Class A uniforms were pressed, boots were shined, and brass buttons were polished. The men of F/506th held a memorial ceremony for Lieutenant Tuck. Although in appearance the men looked sharp and lacked emotion, the veterans of the unit were deeply saddened by the loss of 'Little Andy' Tuck. He was remembered as "A good officer who took an interest in the men." His leadership and friendship left a lifetime of fond memories with the men of Company F.

After the ceremony the men went back to their civil affairs duties in

Austria. Five men transferred home on July 10th: SSgt. Ted Justice, Pfc. Ray Ballew, Pfc. Marvin Crawford, Pfc. Matthew Carlino, and the fearless Sergeant Ed Peniak. Forty-five other enlisted men were transferred off to the 513th Parachute Infantry, a part of the 17th Airborne. They were preparing to head off to Japan, as the war still raged in the Pacific.

The problems with food and supplies continued to plague the paratroopers. Boxed rations remained the typical meals rationed out to the men. Wanting a step up in cuisine, the troopers began to resort to their old combat ways by stealing local farm animals and hunting down livestock. No longer able to claim animals had been injured by "shrapnel damage," most of the thievery occurred during the hours of darkness.

One such incident involved Sgt. Merlin Shennum, frustrated over the ration situation. Being a proud Montana native and self-sufficient paratrooper, Shennum set out one dark evening for some beef. When he located a suitable cow he drew his .45 automatic and pointed it at the forehead of the potential meal staring back at him. Shennum squeezed the trigger and the gunshot seemed like a cannon blast in the quiet of the evening. Shennum was furious when he discovered the bullet had ricocheted off the forehead of the cow and off into the darkness.

The cow stared back at Shennum, seemingly oblivious to the entire incident. So Shennum returned to his billet and grabbed his M1 rifle. He returned to the scene and the process played out again. A visual standoff, a gunshot shattering the darkness, but this time the cow dropped where it had stood. Shennum quickly butchered off their needs and headed back to his squad. Others soon headed out into the night to take their cuts for a supplement to their rations. The cattle rustlers of Company F had struck once again!

CHAPTER 26

MOVING BACK

The veterans of Fox Company began to cycle home as their points jumped with changes to the scoring system and the awarding of additional medals by the division. On 16 July Sgt. Bill True, Pfc. Tom Brayton, and Sgt. Conrad Ours shipped off to the 501st. Operations sergeant Tom Alley was able to transfer out with the same men as well. The bulk of the Toccoa men were fading away fast with their transfers home.

Sgt. Bob Noody was tasked with taking out some new replacements on 21 July for some training, which had been recommended by the battalion HQ. However, his platoon leader advised him to skip the training and just take the men off and kill some time. So Noody did as he was told.

BOB NOODY ● *Major Winters showed up with my platoon leader and asked me what I thought I was doing. I made up some story about what we were doing, but Major Winters was not buying it. My lieutenant never stepped in and explained that he had told us what to do, and I kept lying. The more I told, the more I could tell that Major Winters was getting disappointed in me. He busted me to the rank of private right on the spot.*

Looking back on it I realize it was the best thing for me to lose my stripes. I was sure unhappy about it, but I had it coming! It really taught me a lesson about being honest. I would never do it again. Major Winters gave me my stripes back a month later.

By the end of July the company had moved out of the Alps to a tent city in Joigny, France. The bulk of the combat-experienced men were now in the process of going home, the others heading off to occupation duty in Germany. Unknown to the company at the time, their three captured troopers from Holland were on their way home as well. Sgt. Eldridge Gaston, Cpl. Otto MacKay, and Pvt. William Sievers were liberated from POW camps back in May. They had been prisoners since their capture on the dike eight months earlier.

The month of August saw the end of the war, and many of the men went off on leave to various locations around Europe. Sergeants Bob Janes and Marion Grodowski headed off to Paris and John Taylor to the French Riviera. While Taylor caught up with his brother in southern France, Janes and Grodowski ended up narrowly avoiding a military prison in the French capital.

BOB JANES • *Grodowski and I were drinking in a bar and got kicked out. On the way out, Grodowski punched his hand through the glass entry doors, shattering them in the process and getting cut as well. I ended up with blood on my uniform from Grodowski. We staggered along a row of trees and decided they needed to be watered. We must have been loud while doing so, and unknown to us we were right outside the window of some US Army general's quarters. He told us to be quiet. We told him what we thought of that. We ended up arrested.*

The MPs saw the blood on our uniforms and quickly accused us of rape and murder. They really gave it to us. Unknown to us, some GIs had raped and killed some French woman the night before. The MPs called our HQ and were able to confirm that we had been in our own barracks the night before on bed check. So we were released. Lucky! If someone had not done their bed check roster, we could have ended up hanged!

On 20 September the men made their final jumps for the 506th, outside Joigny.

JOHN TAYLOR • *The end of the war in the Pacific in mid-August 1945 assured that I would not be jumping over Japan, as I once had feared. In September orders were issued that if we wanted to continue drawing the extra fifty dollars a month jump pay of a paratrooper, we had to make another jump. If you didn't want to jump, you didn't have to, but then the extra pay was discontinued. Most everybody chose to make the jump.*

We all went out one afternoon on three planes. Our regimental commander had been good enough to have our landing field plowed beforehand so it would be a soft touchdown.

We went up to twelve hundred feet and jumped out. We had no guns or equipment, just our parachutes. I knew then that this was going to be my last jump, and it was a thrill. I think that was the sweetest ride down, apart from my first jump, that I ever had. It was the end of an important chapter in my life.

Others moved up in rank to fill the gaps in the company. One man was chosen by T.Sgt. John Taylor to fill his boots in the Second Platoon.

JOHN TAYLOR • *After we had first arrived in Joigny, we got a few new men in F Company. One that I chose for our Second Platoon was a tech sergeant named George Dunaway. When I left for home he took my place as first sergeant for F Company. In the late 1960s he became division sergeant major.*

He later on ended up being sergeant major of the United States Army, the highest rank an enlisted man can hold in the service. There is only one of those at a time.

In the fall of 1945, the final groups of paratroopers shipped home. For one paratrooper, remembering the moment was bittersweet.

MARION GRODOWSKI • *I sat on the back of a truck as we prepared to pull away to head off away from the boys. I said my goodbyes. I really wanted to go home to my family in Chicago. But in some ways I felt as though I was leaving my family here as well. We had all done so much together—the training, the parachute jumps, the fighting. We were like family. I really had to hold back the tears and got a little choked up saying goodbye.*

There were two types of people who served in the war: those of us who did the killing and those who liked to dress up and play soldier. I would never want to go through it again, but I am proud of who we were and what we accomplished.

JOHN TAYLOR • *We were no better or no worse than any other unit in the 506th. We all had our good days, and we all had our bad days. But the men who were in Company F were a damn fine bunch of soldiers. I was proud to be one of them.*

On 30 November 1945, after 544 days of distinguished service in the European theater, including key roles in the Normandy invasion, Operation Market Garden, and the Battle of the Bulge, Company F of the 506th Parachute Infantry Regiment was deactivated.

TWO MEN WHO FOUGHT

BY TERRY POYSER

While conducting the interviews and follow-up interviews for the research on this book, I used a detailed list of questions for the members of Fox 506th. They covered enlistment, training, parachute school, maneuvers, life overseas, combat, and an extensive roster of members of the company. I always asked, "Who was your foxhole buddy or pal?" And I asked, "Who was the best soldier in the company?" Every answer to the second question was the same: Sgt. John Taylor.

The Texas native was respected by the members of not only his platoon but his entire company. In garrison life Taylor was the first in formation each morning—not a speck of dust on his glossy jump boots, his uniform in textbook form. He looked like someone who would be used for a recruiting poster for the paratroops.

In combat he used common sense and an intense understanding of his training and tactics to survive, and to keep his men alive as well. Without his outstanding leadership ability, men of the company suspected that the unit casualties would have been much higher. According to the men, his award of the Silver Star was much deserved.

When I asked what qualities were displayed by Taylor to make such an impression on the members of his company, a unique list of comments were noted:

"Self-confident but not cocky"   "Best soldier in the unit"
"The best"   "Very caring"

"A soldier's soldier"	"Smart"
"Sharp"	"Led the way"
"Up front"	"Was an example to follow"
"Brave"	"Could do anything"

I asked Taylor himself what were the qualities and expectations of a good NCO. He told me that to be a leader, you have to keep aware of what is going on and relay that information to your men. You should never say anything negative to your men—just be an example to them. You have to be a good reader of maps and compasses. You have to know each trooper's strengths and weaknesses, and use the strengths to benefit the unit. You have to watch for personal problems and resolve them. You have to be the one up front in all the action, leading from the very front. And you have to feel you are a part of something in order to produce something in everyone else.

When John Taylor passed on in 2007, his wife received a card from his former battalion executive officer, Maj. Richard Winters. Winters wrote: "John was one of the best men we had! John was outstanding in Normandy. John was with me on the dike in Holland. I'll always remember him as we charged Noville, at Bastogne. Hang Tough, Dick Winters."

John Taylor had the admiration of not only the members of his company but his battalion command staff as well. His leadership, integrity, and dedication to his duty were an example to everyone in the 506th.

While interviewing the members of Fox 506th, I also always asked at the end of my interview, "Who was the toughest man in the unit?" The answer was always "Roy Zerbe."

Roy, or "Josh" as he was known to his friends, grew up in Schuylkill County, Pennsylvania. His childhood hunting and fishing grounds were rolling farm country with a checkerboard of dense, colorful forests butting up against the nearby rugged mountains mined for coal. He was very active in sports and well respected in the community. A member of the conservative Schuylkill Church of the Brethren, his family life was centered on a devotion to Christianity. Although his church practiced nonviolence, its members were not pacifists.

When the war broke out, Zerbe's cousin joined the paratroops, and Zerbe quickly followed in his footsteps. Both members of the family ended up in the 101st Airborne, with his cousin Ralph in Company B of the

502nd Parachute Infantry Regiment. Due to his excellence in sports and his active outdoor lifestyle, Zerbe had little difficulty adapting to Army life and the demands of physical training. He was only eighteen at the time of his enlistment and was considered the baby of the Third Platoon.

Zerbe was considered an excellent soldier by his peers. He was wounded three times in combat—once in Normandy and twice in Holland. Once, in a ditch outside Eindhoven, Zerbe stopped to speak in Dutch to several wounded German POWs. When ordered by his platoon leader to shoot the prisoners, Zerbe refused, based on principle. Threatened with a court-martial for failing to obey the order, Zerbe held his ground and saved the men's lives. No charges were ever brought up.

The night Zerbe was wounded on the dike in Holland, his life changed forever. For most men their lives would have ended—but not Roy Zerbe! He suffered without complaint, despite having his entire jaw blown off as well as a portion of his upper mouth. In the hospital he was bunked next to a soldier from B Company of the 502nd, who told him that Ralph had been killed in action. He was saddened, but was still determined to fight on.

Once in a regular hospital, Zerbe wanted to see the extent of his facial injuries, curious about how severe his wounds really were. He went into a bathroom and removed his bandages. From the shock of seeing the lower portion of his face missing, Zerbe passed out. A nurse who heard him hit the floor got him back into bed and redressed his injuries.

Zerbe was fortunate enough to be injured at a time when the British were making rapid developments in reconstructive surgery through skin grafts. Treated by a British medical staff, he went through a battery of procedures and operations. Skin was grafted from his right shoulder to make an upper lip. His chest was cut in a circular pattern daily, just a fraction of an inch in depth, until a large portion of thick skin could be pulled up to make a covering for his lower jaw. His lower jawbone was made from rib bones and hip bone. To feed him, nurses blended meat and potatoes and forced them down Zerbe's throat with a large syringe and plastic tube.

The five-foot-ten-inch Zerbe weighed 128 pounds when he arrived in Toccoa in 1942. Army life and good eating put on plenty of muscle, and by the time he was in combat he weighed 165. But after several years of hospitalization, Zerbe's weight dropped to a stunning 98 pounds. Never one to stay down too long, Zerbe was transferred to a US Army hospital in the States where he defied the doctors and staff by routinely sneaking out of his bed to join in basketball games or go deer hunting in the nearby woods. Even having his appendix removed could not keep him in bed. To his doctor's amazement (and anger), he was always on the move.

Zerb eventually had over sixty surgeries, primitive by modern standards, to reconstruct his face. And despite his unique appearance, Zerbe moved on with his life. He married, had four children, and lived a comfortable life as a rural mail carrier back in Schuylkill County. Still a regular at church, he allowed his faith and trust in God to guide him through his blessed life.

Members of his company said they could never have gone through what Zerbe went through to survive. All admitted that they would have quit at some point, most likely during the first cold night up on the dike in Holland. And the surgeries would just have been too much to bear. I have to agree with them.

Meeting and interviewing this man was one of the most moving and empowering moments for me during my research. He was forced to wear a permanent reminder of his sacrifice for his county, and we all owe him a debt we can never repay. But Roy Zerbe asked for nothing but a smile, a handshake, and a good laugh. He was a testament to all that is good about the United States and our troops.

COMPANY ROSTERS

OFFICERS

Brierre, Eugene
Brooks, William
Colt, Freeling†
Eggie, Herbert
Hall, Russell†
Hill, Andrew
Havorka, Keith
Hudelson, William
Macdowell, Carll†
Mcfadden, Frank
Nye, James
Mulvey, Thomas
Perdue, Robert
Rhodes, Thomas
Schmitz, Raymond†
Semon, Charles†
Staplefield, Ben
Thomas, Edward
Tuck, Andrew†
Dean, Philip
Brewer, Robert

Mcfadden, Norman
Moore, James
Pisanchin, John
Oswald, Holland
Thompson, John
Edward, Thomas
Cowing, Robert
Richey, Ralph
Williams, John
Cooke, Bob
Robertson, William
Frary, Donald
O'Shaughnessy, John
Ritter, Louis
Jaye, Leonard
Witkin, J. C.
Camdus, John
Tyson, Breck
Brussart, Robert
Ritter, Louis
† Killed in action.

NCOs and ENLISTED MEN

Aebischer, Raymond
Alley, Thomas
Apodaca, Demetrio
Ballew, Raymond
Barnson, Macrae
Beauchamp, Armand†
Beck, Henry
Bell, Warren
Bettelyoun, Waldron
Bishop, Edgar
Brennan, Edward
Brayton, Thomas
Brown, Linus
Bright, Sylvester
Borden, Hugh
Bruscato, Joseph
Buchter, Richard†
Burton, Louis
Byrne, Rody
Carlino, Matthew
Casey, Patrick
Cauvin, Ray
Cedeno, Marcus
Ceniceros, Salvadore†
Chappelle, Joseph
Cioni, Louis
Clark, Chelan
Clemens, William
Cortese, Nicholas
Crawford, Marvin
Darah, Nicholas
Davenport, Robert
Davis, Donald†
Dickerson, Jack
Dickey, Lyman†

Edwards, David
Emelander, Donald
Farley, Gerald
Fausnet, Bernard
Fitzgerald, Earl
Flick, Joseph
Foley, Richard
Fuller, Calvin
Gaston, Eldridge
Gentile, Rudolph
Gillespie, John
Gilley, Trody
Goodridge, George
Gray, Howard
Green, William†
Griffin, Frank
Grodowski, Marion
Hale, William†
Haney, Manning†
Harms, Donald†
Henry, Donald
Heglund, Lester
Henderson, Charles
Hicks, Leonard
Himelrick, John
Hogenmiller, Joseph
Holcomb, Billy
Hopkins, Oliver
Hosey, Leonard
Houck, Julius†
Hull, Kenneth†
Hult, Walter†
Jacobs, Charles
Hurst, William
Jackson, John

Jacques, Edward
Janes, Robert
Jellesed, Andrew
Jeffers, Clyde
Johnson, James
Jones, Daniel
Joy, Willaim
Kelley, Courtney
Kee, William
Kermode, Ray†
Kiesnowski, Vincent
Kuntz, Wendelin
Knudsen, Richard
Largoss, Harold
Lee, Wilson
Letendre, Albert
Lev, Orel†
Lovell, George†
Mcneese, William
Mackey, James
Mackay, Otto
Madruga, Edmund
Maletich, Christ
Malley, Charles
Manley, Jack
Mann, Robert
Martin, George
Mather, Gordon†
Mercier, Kenneth
Metropolis, John
Mika, Nicholas
Moontz, Millard
Morehead, Harvey
Morris, Willie†
Mottern, Kenneth

Murphy, William
Nakelski, Chester†
Napier, Carl
Napieralski, Chester
Navarro, Paul
Nocera, Frank
Nestler, Martin
Newhouse, Delmar
Noonan, David
Noody, Robert
Neubert, William
Oakley, James
Occipinti, Vince
Ochoa, Raul
Odegaard, Iver
Ohara, James
Olanie, William
Ostrander, Harry
Ott, Ray
Ours, Conrad
Orosco, Jesse
Passino, Raymond
Payne, Floyd
Pearce, Robert
Peniak, Edward
Patruno, Mario
Pein, Carl†
Peterson, Arthur
Peterson, Paul
Peluso, Angelo
Porter, Huber
Provenzano, Ralph
Psar, Thomas†
Puskar, Walter
Pustola, Steve
Rasmussen, Loy
Rhodes, Martin

Replogle, Donald
Rice, Farris
Riddick, Robert
Rivenbark, Charles
Robbins, Ralph
Rockwell, Harold
Roller, George
Romano, Walter
Roth, Doug
Reese, Charles
Scheurich, Charles
Schwenk, Russell
Senko, Andy
Shaffer, Charles
Sharp, Willard
Shears, James†
Sheffield, Arnold
Shemik, Frank
Shennum, Merlin
Sherwood, Robert
Shropshire, Robert
Sievers, William
Simioni, Dino
Simms, George
Skaggs, Eugene
Skelton, Eugene
Shrout, Clarence†
Slusser, William
Segal, Lewis
Smith, Homer†
Smith, Hubert
Steinke, Kenneth
Stewart, Kenneth
Stokes, Roy
Stone, Robert
Sullivan, Julian
Summers, Alan

Supko, John†
Swafford, James
Tamkin, Victor
Taylor, John
Temko, James
Tom, Bernard†
Trimble, Norman
True, William
Trpelka, Joseph†
Tindall, Leslie
Ulrich, Theodore
Vallieres, Clifford
Van Cott, George
Vick, Horace
Vogel, Robert
Wallace, Ernest
Warnbok, Harold
Waters, James†
Watkins, Joseph†
Webster, David
Westman, Kenneth
Williams, John
Wilson, Daniel
Wilson, Alvin
Wolford, Thomas†
Wood, Don
Wright, Calvin
Yochum, George
Zelesnik, Edward
Zerbe, Roy
May, Otto
Meeker, Harry
Duncan, Thomas
Knight, James
Burkey, Rafael
Roush, Harry
Setzer, Carl

Riley, Paul
Wright, Leroy
Reed, Thomas
Pillen, Leland
Mcguire, Donald
Maestas, Jose
Potter, Wallace
Kelly, Donald
Hosier, Robert
Harmon, Walter
Holden, Clifton
Lane, Robert
Kelly, Sam
Jones, James
Jepsen, Espar
Hernandez, Mois
Harshman, Howard
Foltz, Wilbur
Gould, William
Allie, Ambrose
Yurick, Jack
Seifer, Frederick
Miller, George
Mox, Clifford
Petran, Joseph
Medenwaldt, Eldon
Kruppa, Joseph
Hume El, Roy
Hayes, John
Hendricks, Glyndon
Lewis, Ervin
Kusel, Glen
Kirschbaum, Don
Johnson, Axel
Horn, Arthur
Hiler, William
Hahn, Joseph

Gibbons, Morton
Guzman, Yseidro
Adams, Harold
Justice, Theodore
Nickerson, Nathaniel
Shuster, Joseph
Letendre, Albert
Rinehart, Donald
Zelik, Maurice
Bridges, Carl
Burger, Charles
Caldwell, Charles
Eckenrode, Robert
Glover, George
Jones, Glenn
Kerlin, Arthur
Mc Robbie, William
Martley, Michael
Morelock, William
Murray, Charles
Olgetree, Bert
Pederson, Cyral
Pena, Faustina
Rankin, John
Rhodes, Martin
Rodiger, Robert
Romero, Robert
Schultz, Lloyd
Toomey, Stanley
Westmoreland, Ewell
Whiteley, Gordon
Wilking, Harry
Wooley, Durward
Armstrong, Harvey
Barnoski, Adam
Bolchalk, Robert
Bumgardner, Frank

Campos, Theodore
Cassingham, Donald
Christensen, Robert
Elmerson, Roy
Hager, William
Hesse, Tracy
Hewitt, George
Hisamoto, William
Holis, Marshall
Maas, Waldimar
Massey, Ralph
Mongeau, William
Noonan, David
Philpot, Clyde
Stude, Vernon
Sumpter, Richard
Wagner, George
Watters, Robert
Williams, Richard
Wilson, Daniel
Wittaker, Loyal
Young, George
Anderson, Wilford
Long, Dallas
Robertson, Clifford
Roller, George
Boduck, Stanley
Gates, Robert
Henson, Donald
Kiesel, Walter
Ott, Ray
Tucker, William
Goodman, Chester
Hestler, Martin
Nosera, Frank
Selmarts, Harry
Stanford, Clarence

Villa, Jose
Finkelstein, Morris
Werts, William
Rutkoski, Frank
Weekley, Charles
Fitshenry, Joseph
Bailey, William
Elliott, George
Birmingham, Peter
Egolf, Virgil
Hamlin, Milec
Adams, Orval
Brooks, Paul
Curry, Henry
Hanson, Arthur
Luts, Robert
Morrissey, Philip
Snedden, Donald
Uplinger, George
Botesheller, Gus

Strunk, Alfred
Baker, Thomas
Lucero, Alfred
Baird, William
Droogan, Joseph
Thompson, Phillip
Moore, Millard
Pepper, Charles
Dusich, Mark
Novak, Elmer†
Martinson, Lloyd
Rankin, John
Rytell, John
Rasmus, Edward
Morelock, William
Selby, Howard
Stude, Vernon
King, Raymond
Bright, Sylvester
Mather, Maurice

Picha, Richard
Scully, Francis
Seedman, Butler
Veinson, Duell
Belin, Paul
Cantrell, Alfred
Colley, Lee
Gonzalez, Jose
Jones, Glenn
Kelly, Sam
Kordon, Werner
Massey, Raplh
Pillen, Leland
Toomey, Stanley
Weinerman, Harold
Prostman, Thomas
Richmond, James
Abrahamian, Armen
Madrid, Ben
† Killed in action.

D-DAY STICKS

STICK 74	STICK 75	STICK 76	STICK 77
TUCK	RHODES	MULVEY	SEMON
DAVIS	AEBISCHER	WILSON	HANEY
BUCHTER	BROWN	HOUCK	WATERS
HALE	CLEMENS	WRIGHT	GRODOWSKI
HULT	SULLIVAN	STONE	PASSINO
WALLACE	EDWARDS	PATRUNO	ROBBINS
KERMODE	STEINKE	JACKSON	PROVENZANO
SUPCO	GILLEY	YOCHUM	HOGENMILLER
NAVARRO	TEMCO	FLICK	OCHOA
OROSCO	OURS	TRUE	WATKINS
NAPIERALSKI	OSTRANDER	RASMUSSEN	TOM
LOVELL	DROOGAN	CORTESE	TRIMBLE
MACKEY	MAY	CRAWFORD	GILLESPIE
ODEGAARD	OCCIPINTI	REPLOGLE	CAUVIN
VOGEL	BRENNAN	PELUSO	MOORE
MATHER	ALLEY	BURTON	TAYLOR
MORRIS	TAMKUN	ROTH	BORDEN

STICK 78	STICK 79	STICK 80	STICK 81
HALL	COLT	BROOKS	MACDOWELL
KNUDSEN	PETERSON	JONES	HICKS
MCNEESE	RICE	BECK	HEGLAND
HULL	ZERBE	NEWHOUSE	NOODY
JACOBS	SCHWENK	DAVENPORT	GRIFFIN
LEV	SUMMERS	GASTON	SWAFFORD
NAKELSKI	SHENNUM	BALLEW	OLANIE
JANES	OHARA	KELLEY	CASEY
BELL	BYRNE	MACKAY	SHARP
DARAH	OAKLEY	DICKERSON	EMELANDER
TRPELKA	VICK	MIKA	JEFFERS
DICKEY	HURST	CLARK	PUSKAR
CARLINO	PENIAK	REESE	GREEN
MARTIN	BAIRD	MALATICH	JELLESED
KEE	BEAUCHAMP	PAYNE	PEIN
NEUBERT	RIVENBARK	CHAPPELLE	MOREHEAD
VANCOTT	WOLFORD	PORTER	BETTELYOUN
		RIDDICK	

OREL LEV'S DISTINGUISHED
SERVICE CROSS CITATION

HEADQUARTERS XVIII CORPS (AIRBORNE)
APO 109, UNITED STATES ARMY

GENERAL ORDER 11   9 DECEMBER 1944

AWARD OF THE DISTINGUISHED SERVICE CROSS,
POSTHUMOUS

1. AWARD OF DISTINGUISHED SERVICE CROSS, POSTHUMOUS

Under the provisions of AR 600-45, 22 September 1943, as amended, and pursuant to authority contained in paragraph 3 c, section 1, circular number 32, Headquarters, European Theater of Operations, United States Army, 20 March 1944, as amended the Distinguished Service Cross is awarded Posthumously to the following enlisted men;

OREL H. LEV, 39252131, Private First Class, Infantry, United States Army, distinguished himself by extraordinary heroism in action. On 23 September 1944, his company was in action against the enemy in the vicinity of Veghel, Holland. His platoon was protecting the left flank of the defense when the enemy attacked that flank with three half tracks, one mark IV tank, and infantry troops. The platoon was forced to withdraw, after suffering heavy casualties, but Private First Class LEV elected to remain and cover the withdrawal of the platoon. Although exposed to heavy enemy fire, he fired his rocket launcher at the leading half track and killed four of the enemy. At this time, the fire from the tank became a very serious threat to the withdrawing platoon, since its fire was being directed by the commander from an open turret. Realizing this Private First Class LEV killed the tank Commander and halted the advance of the tank. He then returned and gave invaluable information to friendly artillery whose effective fire disrupted the enemy attack. In a later action, while moving his machine gun to a better position in order to deliver effective fire on the enemy, he was mortally wounded. His actions were in accordance with the highest standards of the military service. Entered military service from South Gate, California.

By Command of Major General RIDGWAY;

RALPH P. EATON
Colonel, GSC
Chief of Staff

OFFICIAL;
A/Herbert L. Nelson
T/Herbert L. Nelson
Lt. Col. A.G.D.

MANNING HANEY'S DISTINGUISHED SERVICE CROSS CITATION

GENERAL ORDER
NO. 21

HQ FIRST ALLIED AIRBORNE ARMY
APO 740, U.S. ARMY
13 MARCH 1945

AWARD OF DISTINGUISHED SERVICE CROSS (POSTHUMOUS)

Auth; Under the provisions of Executive Order 9419, 4 Feb 44, (Sec 21, Bull 3, WD 1944) and pursuant to authority contained in AR 600-45, and Cir 32, Hq European TO US Army, dated 20 Mar 44, as amended by Cir 66, Hq European TO US Army, dated 27 May 44, the following enlisted man is awarded the medal indicated (posthumously).

By direction of the President, a DISTINGUISHED SERVICE CROSS is awarded posthumously to CORPORAL MANNING G. HANEY, 19123417, 506th Parachute Infantry.

CORPORAL MANNING G. HANEY, 19123417, Parachute Infantry, while serving with the army of the United States, distinguished himself by extraordinary heroism in action. On 7 October 1944 his squad was in a defensive position on a dike in the vicinity of Randwijk, Holland. Finding an unused .50-caliber machine gun, he moved it into position on the dike in order to supplement the rest of his weapons. When an enemy force of approximately sixty men attempted to penetrate the platoon area, CORPORAL HANEY manned the gun under heavy enemy small arms and mortar fire, and returned such effective fire that the enemy was forced to withdraw. On the following evening he again set up the machine gun on the dike.

When the enemy launched another attack on the position, CORPORAL HANEY opened fire but found that the gun was not properly adjusted. He re-adjusted the gun while under heavy enemy fire. He again opened fire with such accuracy that the enemy concentrated all its fire on his position. CORPORAL HANEY realized that the enemy was too strong for him to stop single-handed but with complete disregard for his own safety, he manned his gun until an enemy mortar shell blasted him off the dike, killing him instantly. His actions were instrumental in repelling the enemy attack and preventing a penetration of the platoon area. Next of Kin: Mrs. Florence Haney (Mother); 305 Park Avenue, Fulton, Kentucky.

By command of Lieutenant General BRERETON;

F. L. PARKS
Brigadier General, GSC
Chief of Staff,

OFFICIAL;
W. F. SMITH
  Lt. Col, AGD,
  Adjutant General

SELECTED BIBLIOGRAPHY

BOOKS

Bando, Mark. *Avenging Eagles: Forbidden Tales of the 101st Airborne Division in WW2.* Detroit: Bando Publications, 2006.

———. *Breakout at Normandy.* Osceola, WI: MBI, 1999.

———. *The 101st Airborne at Normandy.* Osceola, WI: Motorbooks, 1994

———. *The 101st Airborne: From Holland to Hitler's Eagle's Nest.* Osceola, WI: Motorbooks, 1995.

———. *101st Airborne: The Screaming Eagles in World War II.* St. Paul, MN: Zenith, 2007.

Koskimaki, George E. *The Battling Bastards of Bastogne: A Chronicle of the Defense of Bastogne (December 19, 1944–January 17, 1945).* Sweetwater, TN: 101st Airborne Division Association, 1994.

———. *D-Day with the Screaming Eagles.* Madelia, MN: House of Print, 1970.

———. *Hell's Highway: Chronicle of the 101st Airborne Division in the Holland Campaign, September–November, 1944.* Sweetwater, TN: 101st Airborne Division Association, 1989.

Mitchell, Harris. T. *The Story of the First Airborne Battalion.* Rockville, MD: Twinbrook Communications.

Nordyke, Phil. *All American, All the Way: The Combat History of the 82nd Airborne Division in World War II.* St. Paul, MN: Zenith, 2005.

Norwood, Leonard, and Arthur J. Rapport Jr. *Rendezvous with Destiny: History of the 101st Airborne.* Konecky & Konecky, 1948.

True, Bill. *The Cow Spoke French: A Paratrooper's Story of World War II.* Merriam Press, 2002.

Winters, Dick. *Beyond Band of Brothers: The War Memoirs of Major Dick Winters.*

Winters, Harold et al. *Battling the Elements: Weather and Terrain in the Conduct of War.* Baltimore: Johns Hopkins University Press, 1998.

DIARIES AND MEMOIRS
Lt. Ben Stapelfeld
Lt. Robert Perdue
Cpl. Len Hicks
Sgt. Vince Occipinti
Sgt. John H. Taylor
Cpl. Joe Hogenmiller

LETTERS HOME
Cpl. David Edwards
Sgt. Robert Janes
Pvt. John Supco

UNIT NEWSPAPERS, 506TH PARCHUTE INFANTRY REGIMENT
Paradise Press (1943)
Paradise Poop (1945)

ARCHIVAL SOURCES
Cornelius Ryan Collection, Ohio University (Fox Company Questionnaires)
National Archives
After Action Report 506th PIR February 1945
After Action Report 506th April 1945
After Action Report 506th January 1945
After Action Report Jan–May 1945 101st Airborne Division
Air Invasion of Holland IX Troop Carrier Command, report on Operation Market
   (101st)
506th After Action Report Operation Market
506th S-1 Journal Sep–Nov 1944
First Allied Airborne Army Operations in Holland 1944
General Order #11 XVIII Corps (ABN) 09 DEC 1944 (LEV)
General Order #21 1st Allied Airborne Army 13 MAR 45 (HANEY)
German After Action 59th Infantry Division in the Netherlands
German After Action LXXXVIII Corps June–Dec 1944
G-3 Journal Jan 1945 101st Airborne Div.
G-3 Journal 101st Airborne December 1945
G-3 Journal Operation Market 101st Airborne Div.
G-3 Journal Operation Neptune 101st Airborne Div.
History of Fighting Fox Company by George Goodridge
History of the 101st Airborne in Holland, Operation Market
Overlay 31 Jan–5 Feb 45 506th PIR

Public Relations Report 101st Airborne Div.
Report of Operation Market 101st Airborne Div.
Report on those who failed to jump, Market Garden Battle Experiences
Unit Journal Operation Market 101st Airborne Div.

UNPUBLISHED MANUSCRIPT
Webster, David Kenyon. "Parachute Infantry."

INDEX